GENESIS
In the Beginning

A Typological Commentary

Dr. Gilbert W. Olson

Bride of Messiah Series

ISBN: 9780986292934
Gilbert W Olson, Meridian, Idaho, USA

DEDICATION AND ACKNOWLEDGEMENTS

I DEDICATE THIS BOOK to the body of Messiah worldwide, and particularly to Key of David Christian Church, Seattle, Washington; House of David Christian Ministries, Boise, Idaho; and the many ministries and assemblies throughout the world that have benefited from their ministries.

I am indebted to many sources over many years that have resulted in this commentary on Genesis. In particular, I thank my pastors, Douglas Morris, Jeremy Calhoun and Vic Calhoun, for their many insights that have given me greater understanding of the subject. I also thank my wife, Beverly, and Sylvia Spencer for proofing the manuscript and giving valuable suggestions for its improvement. Most of all, I thank my Father in heaven for calling me to the ministry of being among the many who are calling the company of believers who are the Bride of Messiah to get ready for the return of their beloved Bridegroom.

Gilbert Olson

SPECIAL VOCABULARY

IN MY WRITINGS I use some nontraditional words. The reasons for this are in Book One of this Bride of Messiah Series: *Yahushua Messiah, the Last Adam*. See also Explanation of Terms at the end of this book. Particularly note that I use **"Master" for "Lord"** when referring to Yahushua (Jesus), **"Yahuah" for "the LORD"** when referring to God, and **"Elohim" for "God."**

Assembly (church)
Bow down to (worship)
Elohim, Strong One (God)
> *Elohim,* a Hebrew word meaning "strong one/s," is commonly translated as "God," but is also used for humans, for angels, and for false gods.

Esteem, splendor, honor (glory)
Favor (grace)
Immersion (baptism)
Impale, impaled (crucify, crucified)
Master (Lord)
Messiah (Christ); Messianan (Christian)
Reverence/reverent (godliness/godly)
Scripture/s (Bible)
Set-apart, set-apartness, consecrated (holy, holiness)
Set-apart spirit, spirit of set-apartness/consecration (Holy Spirit)
Slaughter-offering (sacrifice)
Stake (cross) Gk *staurós*, Strong's #4716 "an upright stake, esp. a pointed one."
Yahuah (the LORD, Yahweh, Jehovah)
> *Yahuah* is Elohim's personal name. It means "HE IS."

Yahuah Elohim (the LORD God)
Yahushua (Jesus) *Yahushua* means "Yahuah is salvation."

Special Vocabulary

HEBREW NAMES in this commentary are transliterated more closely to the Hebrew spelling than in standard translations. Often the standard English spellings, which are based on the early English translations from the 1500s, bear no resemblance to the Hebrew spellings.

I have been asked, "Why not use the standard spellings?" My answer is, this is a commentary on Genesis, a Hebrew book. I believe it is good for the reader to get a bit of Hebrew along the way, and by so doing enter into a bit of the culture and how they spoke.

For example, Hebrew has no letter "J." Wherever you see "J/ j" in English, in Hebrew it is "Y/ y." Also, when you see the "...iah" ending of a name, such as Jerem*iah*, in Hebrew the ending is "yah" or "yahu," the name of Yahuah. Thus "Jeremiah" in Hebrew is "Yermeyahu," and "Isaiah" is "Yeshayahu." Consistently the standard English translations, to follow tradition, remove the name of Yahuah from the Bible.

The apostrophe (') in a name indicates a silent letter. Ancient Hebrew pronounced it with a break, but is ignored in Modern Hebrew. Thus Ya'aqov is Jacob.

"Ě ě" is a long "a," as in "take." Thus Ěsaw is Esau, Ěl is El, and Yisra'ěl is Israel.

The "...ite/ ...ites" ending on names is from Greek, not Hebrew; thus Kena'ani for Canaanites.

"Ḥ ḥ" with a dot under it is an aspirated guttural, like the "ch" in Bach. Thus Ḥawwah is Eve.

"Q/q" is pronounced as "K/k."

The Hebrew letter *beth* is pronounced "b" or "v." Standard translations don't show the difference. Thus Bavel (bah-VEL) is Babel.

Modern Hebrew pronounces "w" as "v."

Hebrew words usually are accented on the last syllable, and sometimes on the second to last syllable. Sometimes scholars differ as to where the accent should be.

As to the meanings of names, some are unknown, some uncertain, and some with different possible meanings. Regarding some of them, scholars differ.

See GLOSSARY OF NAMES at the end of this book.

UNLESS OTHERWISE NOTED, all scripture quotations are the author's own translation. The following versions are used by permission. Words in brackets, parenthesis and emphases are added.

CJB = The Complete Jewish Bible (names are transliterated closer to Hebrew)
From PC Study Bible Biblesoft electronic database.
Copyright © 1998 by David H. Stern
NAS = The New American Standard Bible
From PC Study Bible Biblesoft electronic database.
Copyright © 1977 by The Lockman Foundation.
NASU = The New American Standard Bible Update
From PC Study Bible Biblesoft electronic database.
Copyright ©, 1995, by The Lockman Foundation.
NIV = New International Version
From Bibleworks electronic database. (Copyright information not given.)
NRSV = New Revised Standard Version
From PC Study Bible Biblesoft electronic database.
Copyright © 1989 Division of Christian Education of the National Council of the Churches of Christ in the United States of America.
TS = The Scriptures (names and titles are transliterated closer to Hebrew)
From e-Sword electronic database. (Copyright information not given.)

Scripture book abbreviations are as follows:

Gen-Genesis	1Ki-1 Kings	Ecc-Ecclesiastes	Ob-Obadiah
Ex-Exodus	2Ki-2 Kings	SS-Song of Songs	Jon-Jonah
Le-Leviticus	1Ch-1 Chronicles	Is-Isaiah	Mi-Micah
Nu-Numbers	2Ch-2 Chronicles	Jer-Jeremiah	Na-Nahum
Dt-Deuteronomy	Ezr-Ezra	Lam-Lamentations	Hab-Habakkuk
Jos-Joshua	Ne-Nehemiah	Eze-Ezekiel	Zeph-Zephaniah
Jdg-Judges	Est-Esther	Dan-Daniel	Hag-Haggai
Ru-Ruth	Job-Job	Ho-Hosea	Zec-Zechariah
1Sa-1 Samuel	Ps-Psalms	Joel-Joel	Mal-Malachi
2Sa-2 Samuel	Pr-Proverbs	Am-Amos	

Mt-Matthew	2Cor-2Corinthians	1Ti-1 Timothy	2Pe-2 Peter
Mk-Mark	Gal-Galatians	2Ti-2 Timothy	1Jn-1 John
Lk-Luke	Eph-Ephesians	Tit-Titus	2Jn-2 John
Jn-John	Php-Philippians	Phm-Philemon	3Jn-3 John
Ac-Acts	Col-Colossians	Heb-Hebrews	Jude-Jude
Ro-Romans	1Th-1 Thess.	Jam-James	Rev-Revelation
1Cor-1Corinthians	2Th-2 Thess.	1Pe-1 Peter	

Table of Contents

DEDICATION AND ACKNOWLEDGEMENTS...iii
SPECIAL VOCABULARY iv
ABOUT THE SERIES.. ix
MAP OF PATRIARCHS' JOURNEYS xii
INTRODUCTION.. 1
   Mark of the Beast.. 1
   Types 3
I. CREATION Genesis 1 9
   Covenant..19
   The Seven Days..22
   Evolution and the Big Bang 34
   How Sovereign is Elohim? 37
   Angels...39
   The Garden in Ěden, 2:8 48
II. ADAM TO NOAḤ Genesis 2-5...50
   Adam, 2:7...50
   Paradise Lost, 2:18..55
   Qayin and Hevel, 4:1 68
III. NOAḤ TO AVRAM Genesis 6-11...79
   Noaḥ, 6-10...79
   Satan 92
   Nimrod, Tower of Bavel, 11..94
   Teraḥ Takes Avram to Ḥaran, 11:31..95
   Covenants.. 102
IV. AVRAM TO YITSḤAQ Genesis 12-23 104
   Avram Goes from Ḥaran to Mitsrayim, 12:1 104
   Avram Deceives Par'oh, 12:10 108
   Avram and Lot Separate, 13:1 109
   Malki-tsedeq blesses Avram, 14:1... 111
   Avram Believes Promise of a Son, 15:1 116
   Hagar Conceives by Avram, 16:1 118
   Covenant of Circumcision, 17:1 120
   Sedom and Lot, 18-19... 121
   Avraham Deceives Avi-meleḥ, 20:1 126
   Yitsḥaq Born, Hagar and Yishma'ěl Sent Away, 21:1 128
   Avraham Makes a Covenant with Avi-meleḥ, 21:22.......................... 133
   Avraham Offers Yitsḥaq as a Burnt Offering, 22:1 134
   Avraham Buys a Field to Bury Sarah, 23:1 137
V. YITSḤAQ TO YA'AQOV Genesis 24-26 139
   Yitsḥaq Gets Rivqah as Wife, 24:1 139
   Avraham Dies, Ěsaw and Ya'aqov Born, 25:1 143
   Ěsaw Sells Birthright to Ya'aqov, 25:29 145
   Yahuah Renews Covenant with Yitsḥaq, 26:1 145
   Yitsḥaq and Avi-meleḥ, 26:6 146
   Ěsaw Marries Two Ḥiti Women, 26:34 148

VI. YA'AQOV TO YOSEF Genesis 27-36 149
  Ya'aqov Steals Firstborn Blessing, 27:1 149
  Ya'aqov Sent Away, Dreams of a Stairway, 28:1 152
  Ya'aqov Marries Leah and Raḥel, Has Four Sons, 29:1 154
  Ya'aqov's Next Eight Children, 30:1 155
  Speckled, Spotted and Black Animals, 30:25- 31:16 158
  Ya'aqov Leaves for Kena'an, Mitspah Covenant, 31:17 160
  Ya'aqov Fears Ěsaw, Wrestles with an Angel, 32:1 161
  Ya'aqov Meets Ěsaw, 33:1 163
  Shekem Rapes Dinah, 34:1 165
  Raḥel Dies Giving Birth to Binyamin, 35:1 166
  Ěsaw's Seed, 36:1 168
VII. YOSEF TO END Genesis 37-50 169
  Yosef Dreams, His Brothers Sell Him, 37:1 169
  Yahudah and Tamar, 38:1 171
  Yosef Prospers, Imprisoned, 39:1 173
  Yosef Interprets Two Dreams in Prison, 40:1 174
  Yosef Interprets Par'oh's Dream, 41:1 176
  Yosef's Brothers Sent to Mitsrayim, 42:1 179
  Binyamin Comes to Mitsrayim, 43:1 180
  Brothers Brought Back, 44:1 183
  Yosef Deals Kindly with his Brothers, 45:1 184
  Ya'aqov's Family Moves to Mitsrayim, 46:1 185
  Ya'aqov's Family Settles in Goshen, 47:1 186
  Result of the Famine, 47:13 187
  Yosef Swears Regarding Yisra'ěl's Burial, 47:29 187
  Yisra'ěl Blesses Yosef's Two Sons, 48:1 188
  Yisra'ěl Prophesies Concerning his Sons, 49:1 189
  Yisra'ěl and Yosef Die, 50:1 191
CONCLUSION 192
EXPLANATION OF TERMS 193
ADAM TO ABRAHAM CHART 196
GLOSSARY OF NAMES 197
Books by Dr Gilbert Olson 200

ABOUT THE SERIES

THESE WRITINGS ARE FOR TWO AUDIENCES: pastors, leaders and teachers in the assembly, and other believers who are eager to learn the scriptures so as to apply them to their lives and bear fruit for the kingdom. For some, therefore, it may give too much information, and for others, it may not give enough. Look at this series as an introduction for further research.

The purpose, however, is to give more than information; it is to stir the assembly to action, to wake up those who claim to be Christians as to what it means to be a believer, and to live it out in their lives with passion. The church is in deep sin, idolatry, laziness, false doctrines and pagan Babylonian traditions. The zeal and power of the early assembly is gone, and has been gone for most of its 2,000 years.

We are in the last days before Messiah's return to receive to himself a spotless bride without stain, spot or wrinkle, but pure and set apart to him (Eph 5:25-27). The apostle Peter's words apply even more so today than when he wrote them:

> ³*First of all, you must understand that in the last days scoffers will come, scoffing and following their own evil desires.* ⁴*They will say, "Where is this 'coming' he promised? Ever since our fathers died, everything goes on as it has since the beginning of creation."* ... ⁸*But do not forget this one thing, dear friends: With Yahuah a day is as a thousand years, and a thousand years as a day.* ⁹*Yahuah is not slow in keeping his promise, as some understand slowness. He is patient with you, not wanting any to perish, but everyone to come to repentance.*
>
> ¹⁰*But the day of Yahuah will come like a thief. The heavens will disappear with a roar; the elements will be destroyed by fire, and the earth and everything in it will be laid bare.* ¹¹*Since everything will be destroyed in this way, what kind of people ought you to be? You ought to live set-apart and reverent lives* ¹²*as you look forward to the day of Elohim and speed its coming* (2Pe 3:3-12).

ix

And these words penned by Paul to Timothy:

¹But mark this: There will be terrible times in the last days. ²People will be lovers of themselves, lovers of money, boastful, proud, abusive, disobedient to their parents, ungrateful, not consecrated, ³without love, unforgiving, slanderous, without self-control, brutal, not lovers of the good, ⁴treacherous, rash, conceited, lovers of pleasure rather than lovers of Elohim— ⁵having a form of reverence but denying its power (2Ti 3:1-5).

Paul wrote this regarding believers. There is as much sin within the church as there is outside of it. And the judgment of believers will be worse, for they have been given more (Lk 12:48).

Two false doctrines are commonly believed throughout the church worldwide. They are the doctrine of the Trinity with its parent doctrine of the Deity of Christ, and the doctrine of "once saved, always saved" or "eternal security." Since the fourth century the first one, the doctrines of the Deity of Christ and the Trinity, have come to be what defines Christianity—not what scripture says, but what paganized church councils have ruled, and enforced with persecution. The second doctrine teaches that once you're saved, it doesn't matter how much you sin or how wicked the sin is: "Jesus' blood covers it, so enjoy your sin and don't feel guilty about it."

Book One, *Yahushua Messiah, the Last Adam: His Humanity According to Scripture*, shows from both the Old and New Testaments: 1) that Yahuah Elohim (the LORD God) is one in nature; 2) that his only begotten son, Yahushua Messiah (Jesus Christ), is not a god-man with a dual nature, but is a human as all humans are human, but without sin; and 3) that the spirit of set-apartness (the Holy Spirit) is not a separate person from himself, but is himself, his pure, moral nature of selfless love. It also shows that the doctrine of the Trinity (three Persons in one Being) is from paganism, of which scripture says:

"Come out of her, my people! Run for your lives! Run from the fierce anger of Yahuah" (Jer 51:45).

"Come out of her, my people, so that you will not share in her sins, so that you will not receive any of her plagues" (Rev 18:4).

The book further shows how belief about the nature of the son, that he is a human only, affects the life of a believer, that because Yahushua lived without sin, every believer in him is also able to live without sin, and, in fact, is called to do so.

Book Two, *The Bride and the Rapture: From Born Again to a Mature Bride,* is written for believers who want to understand their faith according to scripture, are serious about living it, and want to become the bride of Messiah and qualify to be included in the rapture and inherit the eternal kingdom, a kingdom of pure, selfless love. The book shows that the only ones who become the bride believers that are raptured and inherit the kingdom are those who show their love for him by: 1) giving up their lives to become like him, 2) working at overcoming all sin in their lives, 3) producing fruit for the kingdom, and 4) enduring to the end. All other believers, the lukewarm, are left behind.

These two books give the doctrinal background for this commentary on Genesis.

All Scripture is God-breathed and is useful for teaching, rebuking, correcting and training in righteousness, so that the man of God may be thoroughly equipped for every good work (2Tim 3:16-17 NIV).

MAP OF PATRIARCHS' JOURNEYS

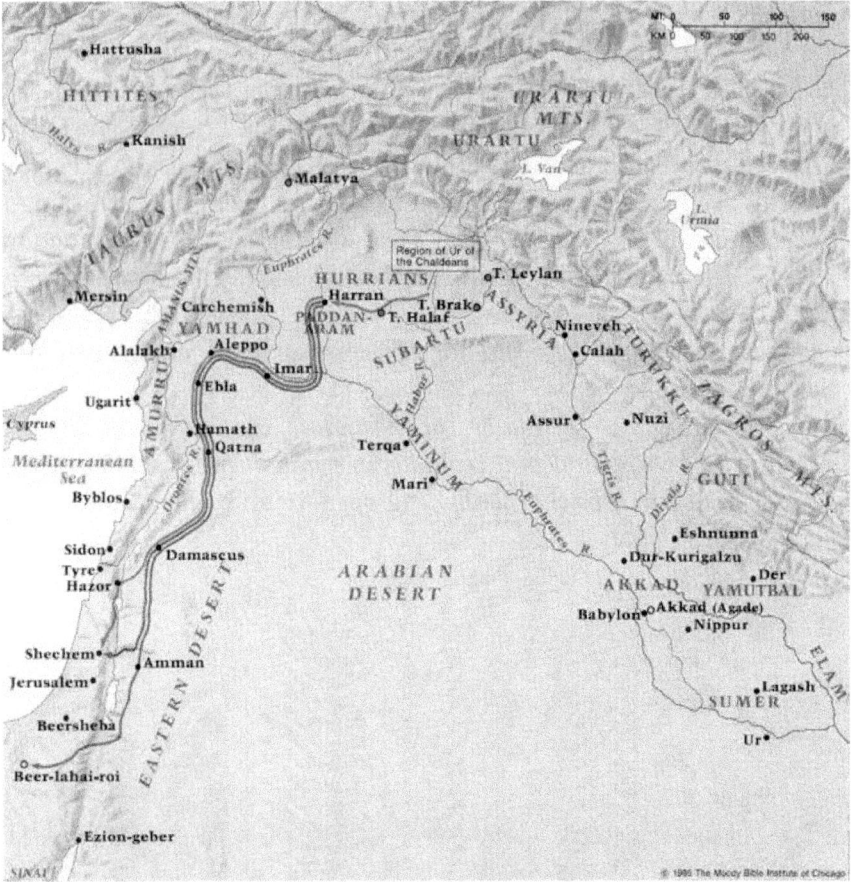

THE MOODY ATLAS OF BIBLE LANDS
Copyright © 1985 By the Moody Bible Institute of Chicago
Copied from Biblesoft, PC Study Bible

Some cities are of uncertain locations, and some with modern names. The map shows Avraham's migration from Ur of the Kasdim (Chaldeans) to Ḥaran (Gen 11:31f), his migration from Ḥaran to the Promised Land (Gen 12:4f), Eli'ezer bringing Rivqah (Rebecca) to marry Yitshaq (Isaac) (Gen 24:50f), and the return of Ya'aqov (Jacob) to Shekem after having lived in Paddan-aram for 20 years (Gen 33:1f).

INTRODUCTION

I saw the Set-apart City, the new Yerushalayim,
coming down out of heaven from Elohim,
prepared as a bride adorned for her husband.
Revelation 21:2

THE REASON FOR CREATION, and thus the whole of scripture from Genesis to Apocalypse (Revelation), is to produce the bride of Messiah. In Genesis we have Paradise Lost, and in Apocalypse we have Paradise Regained. Paradise Regained is the completed bride, that company of believers who have been raptured from the earth and are living in the relationship with Yahuah that Adam and Ḥawwah had before they sinned, and in which Yahushua lived his whole life.

In this commentary on Genesis references are made regarding end time events, particularly the completed bride, the rapture, the 666 mark of the beast, and the tribulation on believers who miss the rapture. These are explained in detail in Book Two of this Bride of Messiah Series, *The Bride and the Rapture.* Below is a summary.

Mark of the Beast

THE BOOK OF APOCALYPSE is the record of visions of "the Day of Yahuah (day of the LORD)." "The Day of Yahuah" refers to the end times in which he judges mankind with terrible events.

The body of Messiah is in two groups, the bride and the lukewarm. The bride are the minority. They are the Philadelphia assembly (Rev 3:7-13). The lukewarm are the majority. They are the Laodicea Assembly (Rev 3:14-22). The rapture is the event in which Messiah takes his bride to heaven without their dying. Included with them are the bride believers who died before the rapture (1Th 4:14-17). The majority lukewarm believers are left behind to face 3½ years of suffering. This period is called the tribulation. The Great Tribulation is also 3½ years, but that is afterwards.

After the rapture the antichrist one-world government will rule mankind. During this time everyone will be required to have a mark to show their allegiance to the antichrist. The number of this mark is 666. Without this mark you cannot buy or sell. All believers who take the mark lose their salvation. All who refuse to take the mark will be killed, but will keep their salvation.

¹ And I saw a beast coming up out of the sea ... ⁷ And it was **given to him to make war with the set-apart ones and to overcome them,** *and authority over every tribe and people and tongue and nation was given to him. ⁸ And* **all who dwell on the earth will reverence him, whose name is not written in the scroll of life** *of the Lamb slain from the foundation of the world. ... ¹⁰* **Here is the perseverance and the faith of the set-apart ones.**

¹¹ And I saw another beast coming up out of the earth ... ¹⁵ And it was given to him to give breath to the image of the beast, so that the image of the beast would even speak and **cause as many as do not revere the image of the beast to be killed.**

¹⁶ And he causes all, the small and the great, and the rich and the poor, and the free men and the slaves, to be **given a mark on their right hand or on their forehead,** *¹⁷ and that* **no one might buy or to sell, except the one who has the mark, the name of the beast or the number of his name.** *¹⁸* **Here is wisdom.** *Let him who has understanding calculate the number of the beast, for* **the number is of a man; and his number is 666** (Rev 13:1-18).

What is this 666 mark? It has been supposed that because the number seven is the number of completed spiritual perfection, and six the number of man who has fallen short of perfection, that 666 is the number of the antichrist because he is man increased threefold.

To understand what this mark is we must look in scripture. Apocalypse, although written in Greek, is a Hebrew book, written from the Hebrew mind, with parallel ideas from the Old Testament. That is where we must get the understanding. One passage stands out, the *shema*, a Hebrew word meaning to hear.

⁴ "Hear, Yisra'ĕl! Yahuah our Strong One, Yahuah is one! ⁵ You shall love Yahuah your Strong One with all your heart and with all your soul and with all your might. ⁶ These words, which I am *commanding you today, shall be on your heart. ⁷ You shall teach them diligently to your sons and shall talk of them when you sit in your house and when you walk by the way and when you lie down and when you rise up. ⁸ You shall bind them as **a sign on your hand** and they shall be as frontals **on your forehead**. ⁹ You shall write them on the doorposts of your house and on your gates"* (Dt 6:4-9).

The Apocalypse is a book of symbols. The different ways Yahushua is described, the living beings in the center of the throne, the dragon using its tail to sweep stars out of heaven, the New Yerushalayim (Jerusalem) coming down out of heaven with its description—these all are symbolic of things spiritual, not physically literal. The 666 sign is also symbolic. Just as having the *shema* on your hand and forehead is a sign of allegiance to Yahuah with your actions and thoughts, so is the 666 mark a sign of allegiance, both mentally and physically, to the antichrist one-world government.

The history of Elohim's people is one of compromise with the world. It is seen throughout scripture. We see it in the Exodus when, after Elohim drowned the Mitsri (Egyptian) army in the Red Sea, they made a gold calf idol and called it Elohim who had delivered them. At the time of Yahushua the Jews were worshiping idols while also doing the temple sacrifices. At the time Yochanan (John) had his vision of the Apocalypse, the temptation of the Messianan was to do emperor worship so as not to be killed, while also doing Christian worship.

So it is today. The church is full of compromise with the world so as not to be different from the world. As of this writing a believer living in America and most other nations can still live openly for Yahushua without danger of death. But pressure to conform to the world is increasing, and along with it is compromise. This compromise will increase as the pressure increases. Under the antichrist one-world government it will be a choice of compromise to show allegiance to the antichrist, or death. That is the 666 mark. Whoever does not take it will be killed.

Types

These things happened to them as types and were written down for our warning (1Cor 10:11).

3

EVERYTHING—all the stories, prophecies, teachings, commandments, exhortations, prayers, conversations, etc.—are interwoven in such a way that each part contributes to the whole. An integral part connecting everything together is types. Everything that happens in this life, both small and big, shows something spiritual.

A type is an historical person, place, thing or event that refers to, or is an example of, or is a shadow of, something spiritual. What it refers to is called the "antitype." For example, all of creation is a type of Elohim's power and nature: *"The heavens declare the esteem of Elohim; the skies proclaim the work of his hands"* (Ps 19:1). So the power and nature of Elohim are the antitype of creation. In like manner, Yahushua the Messiah is the antitype of everything that is a type of him. The verse in Psalm 19 just quoted says Elohim has hands. Although Elohim is a spirit that fills heaven and earth (Jer 23:24), he has "hands." This is anthropomorphism; that is, attributing human characteristics or behavior to something nonhuman, in this case, Elohim. Scriptures are full of ascribing to Elohim attributes of humans. Humans are a type of Elohim. "Feet" refer to going somewhere, "hands" to doing something, "eyes" and "ears" to seeing and hearing, "mouth" to speaking, and so on.

What follows is a list of some of the types we will meet as we go through Genesis.

- Angels who obeyed Yahuah are a type of believers who obey and get to enter the eternal kingdom and stay. Only those whom Yahuah knows will never again disobey are allowed to enter. This life is a test to find out who will be accepted.
- Satan and demons are a type of those who reject Yahuah as the supreme authority, the Strong One, in their lives.
- Stars are a type of believers.
- Adam, the first *adam*, is a type of Yahushua, the last *adam*. *Adam* means *man* or *mankind*. He is also a type of the body of Messiah.
- Ḥawwah (Eve), the wife of Adam, is a type of the whole church, both the lukewarm and the bride, for both Qayin and Hevel (Cain and Abel) come from her. She is also a type of the bride of Messiah, for she came from only part of Adam, his side.

4

- Adam and Ḥawwah together are a type of the spiritual wedding of the bride and Messiah.
- The garden of Ĕden is a type of heaven. The responsibility to take care of the garden is a type of responsibilities given to believers for the kingdom, and also responsibilities we will have in heaven. It is also a type of living in the spirit, for that is what Adam and Ḥawwah were doing before they sinned, and that is what we are called to do.
- The Tree of Life is a type of Messiah from whom we get life.
- The Tree of the Knowledge of Good and Evil is a type of choosing our own way instead of Yahuah's way, and also of conscience.
- The snake is a type of Satan.
- Before sinning, nakedness is a type of innocence. (Babies are born naked.)
- Because we all sin, nakedness is a type of sin.
- Fig leaves are a type of man's works for salvation.
- An animal slain for skin to cover their nakedness is a type of Yahushua's death for our salvation.
- East (including Bavel [Babylon] and Mitsrayim [Egypt]) is a type of the world system ruled by Satan (2Cor 4:4).
- The seed of Ḥawwah is a type of Messiah.
- The seed crushing Satan's head is a type of Messiah destroying Satan's power.
- Satan's seed crushing the seed's heel is Satan working to hinder Elohim's work in bringing salvation, and also getting Messiah impaled.
- Qayin (Cain) is a type of the flesh-man, those who follow their flesh nature, and of the world.
- Hevel (Abel) is a type of the spirit man, those who die to self to serve Elohim.
- Ḥanoḥ (Enoch) is a type of the bride of Messiah that is raptured. He is also a type of Messiah who was raised from death and ascended to heaven.
- The flood is a type of the end-time tribulation on the church.
- Methuselah is a type of lukewarm Christians who die in the tribulation.

5

- The boat Noaḥ built has several types. It is a type of salvation, of being saved from the tribulation by means of the rapture, and of Yahushua Messiah who provides salvation.
- Noaḥ is a type of Messiah who makes salvation possible.
- Shĕm is a type of Messiah, because his name means "name."
- Nimrod and the tower of Bavel are types of the world and false religion.
- Ur of the Kasdim (Chaldeans) and Ḥaran are types of the world and false religion.
- Avram (Abram) is a type of the seeker of salvation. He heard the call of Yahuah to leave Ur to go to a land he will be shown later. He is a type of those who have faith, leaving the world system and not knowing where they are going. He has other types as we will see later.
- Fish are a type of humans: You shall be fishers of men; the two great catches of fish at the beginning and end of Yahushua's ministry; parable of the dragnet for fish.
- Birds of the air are a type of demons. Birds catch fish; fish don't catch birds. Fish, however, do devour other fish.
- "Five" is the number of favor. David, for example, used five stones.

Yahushua gave this commission to his disciples: *"Go and make talmidim* (disciples) *of all nations, immersing them into the name* (reality) *of the Father, and of the son and of the set-apart spirit,"* (Mt 28:19).

The Hebrew for disciples is *talmidim*. Yahushua was speaking in Hebrew, so this is the term he used. The word "disciples" doesn't mean much in English, but the word *"talmidim"* is a very strong and serious word.

talmidim (tal-mee-DEEM)- A plural Hebrew noun meaning "disciples" in its truest sense: those who leave family to study and follow the ways of their teacher (rabbi). They study not only to learn what their teacher **knows** but to become the type of man their teacher **is**. From the Hebrew root word "limmud" meaning "instructed". Strongs #8527. Singular *talmid*.
(psalm11918.org/References/Glossary/talmidim. Emphasis in source.)

This describes what a true disciple of Yahushua is. Our mandate as believers is to make him our life in everything, and to grow to be like him in our character so that others see him in what we say and do, and thus draw others to him. Yahushua said to his *talmidim*:

> *"You are the light of the world. ... Let your light* (my light in you) *shine before men, that they may see your good works* (the works **the Father** has assigned for you to do, Eph 2:10) *and give esteem to your Father in heaven"* (Mt 5:14,16).

Yahushua prayed to the Father regarding his *talmidim* and those of the world system under Satan:

> [14]*"I have given them your word; and the world has hated them, because they are not of the world, even as I am not of the world.* [15]*I do not ask you to take them out of the world, but to keep them from the evil one.* [16]*They are not of the world, even as I am not of the world.* [17]*Set them apart in the truth; your word is truth.* [18]*As you sent me into the world, I also have sent them into the world.* [19]*For their sakes I set myself apart, that they themselves also may be set apart in truth.*
>
> [20]*"I do not ask on behalf of these alone, but for those also who believe in me through their word;* [21]*that they may all be one; even as you, Father, are in me and I in you, that they also may be in us, so that the world may believe that you sent me.*
>
> [22]*"The esteem which you have given me I have given to them, that they may be one, just as we are one;* [23]*I in them and you in me, that they may be perfected in one, so that the world may know that you sent me, and loved them, even as you have loved me"* (Jn 17:14-23).

This is our mandate as believers. To be immersed into the name of (the reality of) the Father is to immerse yourself into his nature of righteousness, purity, selfless love and *qodesh* (set-apartness). He is totally set apart to his nature, with no selfishness in him. This is what we are called to be. And if we love him, this is what we want to be. If we don't want to be this, then he cannot take us into his eternal kingdom. Further, if we hate being like him here, then we would hate it there, for there, everything is about him and total obedience to him, all the time, no break for self-desire, and doing it from a heart of love.

To be immersed into the name of (the reality of) the son is to immerse yourself into his nature of always wanting to please his Father in everything. That is why he is the way, the truth, and the life, and why no one can come to the Father except through him (Jn 14:6). His life is the way to live, the truth of how to live, and the life we were created to live. If we love him, we will obey him in everything (Jn 14:15). Whoever doesn't want to obey him in everything, doesn't love him. Eternal life in heaven is total obedience in everything. Whoever hates doing it here, would hate it there.

To be immersed into the name of (the reality of) the set-apart spirit is to immerse yourself into setting yourself apart *from* everything that is of the world system, and setting yourself apart *to* the Father, his ways, his character, and to live the life he called you to live. Before creation he prepared works for you to do (Eph 2:10); set yourself apart to do them. Immerse yourself into that.

What has all this to do with Genesis? Adam and Ḥawwah lived this way before they sinned. This is what Paradise is. When they chose their own way, they were removed from Paradise—Paradise Lost. Yahushua Messiah died for us to make a way to return there—Paradise Regained. This is what it means to live in the spirit (Ro 8:1-17; Gal 5:25).

The final word in this introduction to Genesis is its author. Mosheh (Moses) is the man whom Elohim inspired to write it (2Ti 3:16-17; 2Pe 1:20-21), as with the other books of the Pentateuch (Greek, the five books), or Torah (instructions or Law).

I. CREATION
Genesis 1

In the beginning Elohim created
the heavens and the earth.
Genesis 1:1

GENESIS BEGINS with the creation of the heavens and the earth. The word "Genesis" itself means "in the beginning." But the real beginning is before creation: *"In the beginning was the word"* (Jn 1:1).

The Hebrew for *"in the beginning"* is בְּרֵאשִׁית *brĕ'shith* (bray-SHEETH, Hebrew reads from right to left). The בְּ *b* part is a prefix that means "in." The רֵאשִׁית *rĕ'shith* part means: "the first, in place, time, order or rank (specifically, a first fruit)" (Strong's OT:7225). The root meaning is "head." The Greek for *"in the beginning"* is *en archĕ* (en arKAY). *En* means "in." *Archĕ* means: "(properly abstract) a commencement, or (concretely) chief (in various applications of order, time, place, or rank)" (Strong's NT:746). From this Greek word we get our English words "arch" and words with "arch" as a prefix (e.g. archangel, archaeology, archenemy). As can be seen, the meanings in Hebrew and Greek are the same.

"In the beginning was the word." The Greek in this verse for "word" is *logos* (LOE-goas). It means: "something said (including the thought); by implication a topic (subject of discourse), also reasoning (the mental faculty) or motive; by extension, a computation" (Strong's NT:3056).

Another Greek word for "word" is *rhĕma*. It means: "an utterance (individually, collectively or specifically)" (Strong's NT:4487). Yahushua said to Satan, *"Not by bread only shall man live, but by every word* (rhĕma) *coming out of the mouth of Elohim"* (Mt 4:4). He was quoting Mosheh: *"Not by bread only does man live, but by all that comes out of the mouth of Yahuah does man live"* (Dt 8:3).

It is not within the scope of this work to compare *logos* with *rhĕma*. In short, both words have different applications of meaning depending on context, and sometimes they mean the same, especially when referring to the written word of Elohim.

Our concern here is the *logos* in John 1:1, for it refers to something before creation, for an eternity before creation—before the creation of the spirit universe of angels and the physical universe of the heavens and the earth. In this context, the *logos* is the plan or purpose of Yahuah.

When an architect designs a building, he begins with the purpose of the building, for the purpose determines what it will look like and how it is to be built. But his nature as a person is before the purpose. A building is a work of art; so an architect designs according to how he thinks, how he expresses himself, and what he wants others to think of him. This is his *logos*. When the project is completed, then what he has done, and even the kind of person he is, can be seen by others. The *logos* is what was in Elohim's mind according to his nature; and the finished building is the *"logos made flesh"* (Jn 1:14).

What is the *logos* of Elohim? What does the finished building look like? It looks like Yahushua Messiah.

> [6]*Yahushua said to* (Thomas), *"I am the way and the truth and the life. No one comes to the Father except through me.* [7]*If you had known me, you would have known my Father also. Hereafter you will know him, and have seen him."*
>
> [8]*Philip said to him, "Master, show us the Father and it satisfies us."*
>
> [9]*Yahushua said to him, "Have I been such a long time with you, and you have not known me, Philip?* **Anyone who has seen me has seen the Father.** *How can you say, 'Show us the Father'?* [10]*Don't you believe that I am in the Father, and the Father is in me? The words I say to you are not of myself. Rather,* **the Father living in me is doing his works"** (Jn 14:6-10).

How can this be? Some scripture passages show how.

> *(The son is the) radiance of (the Father's) esteem and* **exact representation of his essence** (Heb 1:3).
>
> [13]*For (Elohim) has rescued us from the authority of darkness and transferred us into the kingdom of his beloved son,* [14]*in whom we have redemption, the forgiveness of sins,* [15]**who is the image of the invisible Elohim**, *the firstborn over all creation.*
>
> [16]*For in him all things were created: in the heavens and on*

the earth, visible and invisible, whether thrones or powers or rulers or authorities; all things were created on account of him and for him.

[17]He is before all things (in position), and in him all things hold together. [18]And he is the head of the body, the assembly; who is the beginning and the firstborn from the dead, so that in everything he might have the supremacy.

[19]For it pleased (the Father) to have all his fullness dwell in him, [20]and through him to reconcile to himself all things, whether things on the earth or things in the heavens, by making peace through the blood of the stake (Col 1:13-20).

*[7]Beloved, let us love one another, for love is from Elohim, and everyone who loves has been born of Elohim and knows Elohim. [8]Whoever does not love does not know Elohim, because **Elohim is love**. [9]This is how Elohim showed his love among us: He sent his only-begotten son into the world of fallen man that we might live through him. [10]In this is love: not that we loved Elohim, but that he loved us and sent his son as atonement for our sins. ...*

[12]No one has ever seen Elohim; if we love one another, Elohim lives in us and his love is made complete in us. ... [17]In this way love is completed in us so that we will have confidence on the day of judgment, because in this world system of fallen man we are like him (1Jn 4:7-10,12,17).

The Hebrew for "love" is *ahĕv* (ah-HAYV, verb) and *ahav* (ah-HAWV, noun). "The intensity of the meaning ranges from God's infinite affection for his people to the carnal appetites of a lazy glutton" (Strong's OT:157, Theological Wordbook of the OT).

The Greek noun for "love" is *agape* (aw-GAW-pay). "Love, affectionate regard, goodwill, benevolence. With reference to God's love, it is God's willful direction toward man. It involves God doing what He knows is best for man and not necessarily what man desires" (Strong's NT:26, Theological Wordbook of the NT).

Another definition of *agape* is, "unconditional selfless love." We see this in the well-known salvation verse: *"For Elohim loved the world so much that he gave his only begotten son, that whoever believes in him will not perish, but have eternal life"* (Jn 3:16). It is this love that moved Yahuah to create mankind. The love is unconditional;

but getting the benefit of that love has the condition of a belief in his son that results in total commitment to obey, to follow, and to become like him—to be immersed into the reality of who he is. He did not create us so we could have a good, happy time; he created us so we could have a relationship with him of selfless love for him and for one another, a relationship that will never end. Only those who have this relationship here in this life at the end of their lives will be accepted into the eternal kingdom.

> *"Love Yahuah your Elohim with all your heart and with all your soul and with all your strength and with all your mind; and, love your neighbor as yourself"* (Lk 10:27).

These two commandments are the bases of how Yahuah operates. They are eternal principles, and are the reason for creation. They are so wonderful that he made us so we can fellowship with him and others in this way for eternity. Love—selfless love—is so wonderful that it requires giving it to others; but they have to choose it, and they will be tested to see if they truly want it. Only those who endure to the end of their lives will be saved (Mt 10:22).

Elohim is love, and this love includes goodness; he alone is good (Mk 10:18), and he alone is the measure of what goodness is. The Hebrew word for "good" is *tov* (tove).

> Tov: An adjective meaning good, well-pleasing, fruitful, morally correct, proper, convenient. ... It describes that which is appealing and pleasant to the senses; is useful and profitable; is abundant and plentiful; is kind and benevolent; is good in a moral sense as opposed to evil; is proper and becoming; bears a general state of well-being or happiness; is the better of two alternatives. The creation narrative of Gen 1 best embodies all these various elements of meaning when the Lord declares each aspect of His handiwork to be "good" (Strong's OT:2896, Word Study Dictionary of the OT, verse locations omitted).

> *And we know that all things work together for **good** to those who love Elohim, to those who are called according to his purpose* (Ro 8:28).

The Book of Genesis records the beginning of Yahuah's "construction." The Book of Revelation records the finished "building," the bride of Messiah.

21:22I saw no temple in her (the New Jerusalem), *for Yahuah Elohim Almighty and the Lamb are her temple. 23And the city has no need of the sun nor of the moon to shine on her, for the splendor of Elohim has illumined her, and her lamp is the Lamb. ... 27and nothing unclean, and no one who practices abomination and lying, shall ever come into it, but only those whose names are written in the Lamb's book of life. ...*

22:3There will no longer be any curse; and the throne of Elohim and of the Lamb will be in it,... 5And ... they will not have need of the light of a lamp nor the light of the sun, because Yahuah Elohim will illumine them; and they will reign forever and ever (Rev 21:22—22:5).

In Genesis, Adam and Ḥawwah begin innocent, but are driven out because of sin—Paradise Lost. In Revelation, the bride of Messiah is completed and inherits the new earth—Paradise Regained. Everything in between the beginning and ending of scripture is the plan, the means, of getting from Paradise Lost to Paradise Regained. That plan, that means, is the gospel of Yahushua Messiah, the good news of who he is and what he did. In Genesis we see, in type, that gospel, the *logos*, in the lives of the people. In brief, what follows is the gospel, the good news of salvation through Yahushua Messiah.

*"Elohim ... gave his only begotten son, that whoever **believes** in him will not perish, but have eternal life"* (Jn 3:16).

The word "believe" is the heart of the good news. This is not just an intellectual belief, a magic word to say and automatically you have a permanent ticket to heaven regardless of how you live your life. If this is all a "believer" has, then his ticket will take him to the second death, eternal torment in hell. Does this sound heavy, too much, and judgmental? It is intended to be heavy, but it is not judgmental. It is love, tough love. Warning a person of the danger of falling off a cliff is not judgmental; it is love.

Paul wrote, *"Be working out your salvation with fear and trembling"* (Php 2:12). The Greek for "working out" is *katergadzomai*. It means "to carry out a task until it is finished" (Strong's NT:2716, Word Study Dictionary of the NT). Paul wrote further:

Everyone who competes for a prize (in the games) *is self-*

13

controlled. *They do it to get a victor's wreath that decays; but we do it to get one that does not decay. Therefore I do not run as a man running aimlessly; I do not fight as one beating the air. Rather, I subject my body to* **hardship** *and make it my slave so that after I have proclaimed to others, I myself will not be rejected* (for the prize) (1Cor 9:25-27).

Yes, hardship! *"Fight the good fight of the faith. Take hold of the eternal life to which you were called ..."* (1Ti 6:12). This is what Paul did, and at the end of his life he could say:

> *I have fought the good fight, I have finished the race, I have kept the faith. Hereafter there is preserved for me the victor's wreath of righteousness, which the Master, the righteous Judge, will give to me on that day—and not only to me, but also to all who have longed for his appearing* (2Ti 4:7-8).

Yes, the good news includes suffering. Salvation is free (Eph 2:8-9), but it costs your life so that your life is no longer your own.

> *Do you not know that your body is a temple of the spirit of consecration in you, which you have from Elohim? You are not your own; you were bought at a price. Therefore honor Elohim in your body* (1Cor 6:19-20).

We believers are at war. It is a war to overcome our flesh nature, and a war to advance the kingdom of Elohim.

> *"If anyone chooses to follow me, he must deny himself and take up his stake daily and follow me. For whoever chooses to save his life will lose it, but whoever loses his life for me, this one will save it. What benefit is it for a person to gain the whole world, and yet lose or forfeit himself? For whoever is ashamed of me and my words, the Son of Man will be ashamed of him when he comes in his esteem and in the esteem of the Father and of the consecrated angels"* (Lk 9:23-26).

Note these warnings:

> *If we continue sinning intentionally after receiving the knowledge of the truth, there no longer remains a slaughter-offering for sins, but a terrifying expectation of judgment and the fury of fire which will consume the adversaries* (Heb 10:26-27).

> *"Not everyone who says to me, 'Master, master,' will enter the kingdom of heaven, but he who does the will of my Father who is*

in heaven. Many will say to me in that day, 'Master, master, did we not prophesy in your name, and in your name drive out demons, and in your name do many miracles?' And then I will confess to them, 'I never knew you. Away from me, you who do lawlessness!'" (Mt 7:21-23).

Who are those who do lawlessness? Yahushua explains in the following verses. They are those who hear what he says to do, and don't do it. They make up their own rules as to how to live the Christian life (Mt 7:24-29).

Where is the "sweet Jesus" who holds children on his lap and carries a lamb on his shoulders? Where is the Jesus who died for our sins so we can avoid hell and go to heaven? As a just and righteous Father, Elohim is both kind and stern; stern to those who sin, and kindness to those who continue in his righteousness. To turn away to our own way results in being cut off (Ro 11:22).

Sad to say, most people who go to church are not born again; it is just a religion. And, of those who are born again, and even spirit-filled with speaking in tongues, most are lukewarm with no fear of Elohim. They think, "I said the magic words 'I believe in God,' and I'm okay." If they are also Pentecostal, they think, "I still can speak in tongues, so I'm okay."

Brothers, sisters, being a Messianan is serious. Commitment to Yahushua is not a light thing. If it is not a hundred percent commitment of your whole life to obey him and to be what he wants you to be, then you are still dead in your sins. True commitment will result in daily laying down your wants for his wants. Yahushua himself, a man who never sinned, even had to do this. We see this when in the garden of Gethsemane he prayed, *"Not my will, but yours be done."* He prayed this *three times*, and the struggle between what he wanted and what his Father wanted was so great that his sweat was like drops of blood falling to the ground (Lk 22:42-44). But after the third time he fully surrendered to his Father's will. If he, a sinless man, had this struggle, how much more do we fallen people need to fight to surrender our will to his.

Yahuah has a plan. He created us for a purpose. That purpose is for him to live his perfect, good, righteous, loving life through each of us so we can enjoy his perfection. We each have a free will to choose or reject it. The sufferings for his sake in this life test and prepare us for the next one. Our Father is in total control of all circumstances. He will not allow anything to be too great for us to overcome (1Cor 10:13; Ro 8:17-18, 28-39).

> *Now if we are children, then heirs—heirs of Elohim and co-heirs with Messiah, if indeed we suffer with him in order that we also may be esteemed together* (with him). *I consider that our present sufferings are not worth comparing with the esteem that will be revealed in us* (Ro 8:17-18).

The road to that goal is called the gospel, a word which means "good news." It involved the bloody death of Yahushua. He volunteered to do this because of his love for us and for his Father, so that our sins may be forgiven and that we overcome sin in our lives and become sinless like him. *"Therefore, if anyone is in Messiah, he is a new creation. The old has gone; behold, the new has come!"* (2Cor 5:17).

Before his arrest Yahushua prayed for the result of this reconciliation, that we be one with the Father and son **the same way as** the Father and son are one (Jn 17:21-23). And after his resurrection he instructed the disciples regarding the way to achieve this oneness. We call it "The Great Commission." This was discussed in the Introduction, but it bears repeating.

> *And Yahushua came and spoke to them, saying, "All authority in heaven and on earth has been given to me. Go, therefore, disciple all the nations, immersing them into the name of the Father, and of the son, and of the spirit of consecration, teaching them to obey everything I have commanded you. And behold, I am with you always, to the very end of the age"* (Mt 28:18-20).

David Sterns, the one who did the translation of *The Complete Jewish Bible*, translates verse 19 this way:

> *"Therefore, go and make people from all nations into* talmidim, *immersing them **into the reality** of the Father, the Son and the* Ruach HaKodesh" (Mt 28:19, CJB).

David Stern explains why he uses *"into the reality of"* instead of *"in the name of."*

> First of all, Greek *eis* generally means 'into' rather than 'in.' Secondly, although 'name' is the literal meaning of Greek *onoma* [oh-no-mah], 'immersing into a name' describes no

possible literal act. My rendering expresses what I believe to be the intended meaning, since in the Bible 'name' stands for the reality behind the name. While 'in the name of" can mean 'on the authority of,' that seems weak here; more is meant than identifying who authorizes immersion. It is possible that the Greek for 'into the name' renders Hebrew *lashem* [lah-SHAME], 'for, for the sake of, with reference to.'"

(Jewish New Testament Commentary, by David H. Stern, Jewish New Testament Publications, Inc.).

This passage, the Great Commission, is not about water baptism. A reading of the Book of Acts clearly shows that when immersing in water, the only personal name the apostles used was Yahushua (Act 2:38; 8:16; 10:48, 19:5).

"upon (Gk epi) the name of Yahushua Messiah" (Ac 2:38).
"into (Gk eis) the name of the Master Yahushua" (Ac 8:16).
"in (Gk en) the name of the Master" (Ac 10:48).
"into (Gk eis) the name of the Master Yahushua" (Ac 19:5).

In scripture there is no such thing as "a baptismal formula" to say when baptizing someone. That is a ritual invented by the Roman Catholic Church and which the Protestant church inherited, a ritual that resulted from the merger of Christianity with paganism. It was that merger which produced the doctrines of the god-man Christ and the three-person deity. It is not wrong to use words when immersing someone. It is to say that scripture doesn't state certain words to use.

To understand what Yahushua meant, we need to look at what a disciple was back then and its relationship to immersion. We begin by examining what it means to believe. The Greek word translated as "believe" is *pisteuo* (pist-YOO-o). It means to commit (Strong's NT:4100, Vines Expository Dictionary of NT Words, © 1985 by Thomas Nelson Publishers). So John 3:16 can be translated as: *"Whoever commits himself to me shall not perish but have eternal life."* Commitment means 100% of life. Marriage was created to be a type of this. A disciple is one who has committed his whole life in the service of his master (rabbi) and of learning how to think and do as his master does. One wonders how many people who call themselves Christians are *talmidim*, and how many pastors are *talmidim* themselves and teaching their "flock" to be *talmidim*. I dare say the percentage is very low.

"Wide is the gate and easy is the way that leads to destruction, and many there are who enter through it. For narrow is the gate and difficult is the way that leads to life, and few there are who find it" (Mt 7:13-14).

The CJB uses the Hebrew word *talmidim* instead of "disciples," and also uses the Hebrew words *Ruach HaKodesh* instead of "holy spirit" or "spirit of consecration" or "spirit of set-apartness." *"Ha"* is a prefix that means "the." We will examine the two words *"ruach"* and *"kodesh"* (I spell them *ruaḥ* and *qodesh*) and then look at their meaning when combined as to how the Jews understand the phrase.

Ruaḥ has a variety of meanings, according to context. The basic idea of the word is something you can't see physically, but you can see or feel its effects, such as the wind blowing.

Ruaḥ and *qodesh* put together as a phrase—*ruaḥ haqodesh*, (ROO-akh ha-koe-DESH), (the spirit of consecration)–has a special meaning to the Hebrew mind. Here is the summary of an article on *ruaḥ*.

> *Ruach* is a word rich in meanings.... As it is used in the Hebrew Bible, it can denote the inner life or mind: that is, the thoughts, intents, purposes of humans and of God. *Ruach* also denotes the character or nature of those purposes. People can be filled with an unclean *ruach* of disobedience and idolatry. Or they can be filled at any moment with God's holy *ruach*, holy because it is his own.

> *Ruach*—as breath—comes from the mouth. It forms words, which express the mind, will, or character. God's *panim* [pah-NEEM] or Face is never a ghostlike presence. It is always the communicating, discerning Nearness of the Lord; a nearness that brings life, and whose absence produces exile and leads to death.

> Thirdly, **ruach** is like the hand of God. It signifies power. But it also conveys *meaning-filled* experiences of power. The *Ruach-Hand* of God denotes inspiration and revelation of divine purposes. It accomplishes his will by exercising judgment or by showing grace.

> These three circles of meaning are insightful for reading the NT.

> • For example, let's go back to Paul's Septuagint quotation

of Isaiah 40:13 [Ro 11:34; 1Cor 2:16] and assume the word "mind" is one synonym for "spirit." Then let's open Romans 8 and insert "Mind" with a capital M, in the sense of God's holy Mind—in place of "Spirit," and see what dimensions it adds to Paul's message.

- Or elsewhere Paul speaks of being "one spirit" with the Lord (1 Cor 6:17), or "one spirit" with fellow believers (Phil 1:27; cf. 2:2, 5, 20). In light of our **Ruach** study, could we rightly suppose that Paul is referring to sharing the mind, character, or nature of God or of Messiah?

- Or, lastly, consider a rather basic question of New Testament faith: Why is Yeshua called "Messiah—the Anointed One, the *Mashiach*? With what did God anoint him? Did he pour upon Yeshua the third member of the Godhead? Or did he pour his *mind-heart-nature* on him so that the Son is just like his Father?

The Hebrew Scriptures were the Bible of Yeshua and the apostles. This fact opens wellsprings when fully explored while interpreting the New Testament.

(Paul Sumner. www.hebrew-streams.org. Synonyms of *Ruach*.)

This information helps in understanding Genesis and all of scripture.

Covenant

Covenant: contract, agreement, undertaking, commitment, guarantee, warrant, pledge, promise, bond, pact, deal, arrangement, understanding (Google).

THEOLOGIANS SPEAK of the Adamic covenant (the covenant made with Adam), the Noahic covenant (the covenant made with Noaḥ), the Abrahamic covenant (the covenant made with Avraham), and so forth. We will get into these, but first we must understand the concept or idea regarding the word, for it is the underlying principle of the whole of scripture and of every condition required by our creator. Indeed, it is the underlying principle of the very nature of Yahuah Elohim, and therefore of creation. *"In the beginning Elohim created"* (Gen 1:1). Why? Because *"In the beginning was the* logos" (Jn 1:1), the plan, the word, the love.

19

Creation was birthed in love—the unsearchable, unfathomable, self-less, good, set-apart, perfect beauty of the Almighty.

There are two aspects of Yahuah which are greatly misunderstood. They are 1) his unconditional love, and 2) his conditions to partici-pate in that love through fellowship with him. We see these two aspects in the most-used salvation scripture verse: *"Elohim loved* (unconditionally) *the world so much that he gave his only begotten son, that whoever believes in him* (the condition) *should not perish, but have eternal life"* (Jn 3:16). The love has no conditions—it goes out to all, all the time, regardless of any positive response in return. Eternal life, however, *does* have a condition. That condition is belief-obedience in his son, Yahushua Messiah. It is faith that results in obedience, *"trust-grounded obedience"* (Ro 1:5, CJB).

Yahuah Elohim, our infinite all-powerful love creator, is a being of action. He is always working (Jn 5:17), always doing something to draw us humans, his creation, into intimate fellowship with him, that we might share in his perfect, beautiful unconditional love, and live forever the life he created us to have. This is what eternal life is. The condition to get it is love-obedience to his son, for his son represents him exactly (Heb 1:3). He is the way, the truth, and the life (Jn 14:6). That's why salvation is only in his name (Ac 4:12), not in any other way or religion. All roads of life, belief, philosophy of life, and religion—every one of them, including Islam, new age, agnosticism and atheism—lead to hell, except in Yahushua alone.

Heaven is a covenant relationship of love with the Almighty, through his son. **His covenants are unilateral**: the Perfect One makes the rules.

He says, as it were: "I offer myself to you; to receive me, this is what you must do. I have given you free will to choose me, and I will help you choose me if you truly want me. I have given you this one life on earth in mortal bodies to make that decision. There is no reincar-nation or second chance after death. The only "second chances" you get are in this life. I will test you until the day you die, a day set by me. Your eternal relationship with me is based on what you have become in your heart, soul and spirit towards me at the time you leave your body.

"Do not think that you can just say the words, 'I believe in Jesus,' or

'I believe in God,' and that is what the covenant is. Even demons believe that (Jam 2:19). The covenant is loving obedience—you want me for who I am in my nature of selfless love, not for what I give you, and you do things to show your love. While you are loving me through my son, I will give you things to do to help others come to me (Eph 2:8-10). That doing, however, does not save you; it is your response of love to me. If you love me, you will obey me (Jn 14:23-24).

"My unconditional love can be seen in creation all around you, and most specifically in giving my only sinless son to die in your place that you might have your sins forgiven and be reconciled to me (2Cor 5:17-19). He is a human as are you, except without sin, the darling of my heart, who always obeyed me out of love.

"I created in you, in your soul and spirit, the knowledge that I exist, that I am unconditional love, and that I require a response of unconditional love from you in actions toward me and toward those around you. All of creation and all I do is based on these two commands: *'Love Yahuah your Elohim with all your heart, soul, mind and strength, and love your neighbor as yourself'* (Mt 22:36-40).

"I love you the way I love myself. That's why I created you, that you might share the joy of my love. My love for you and all creation is unconditional; on the other hand, our relationship of fellowship and enjoying each other does have this condition, that you love me and others as I love you and others.

"I created society—humans together in relationships—on the basis of covenant. That is how society functions. **Your covenants with one another are bilateral**; that is, you agree with others the conditions of your relationships, whether marriage, employment, mutual friendship, or any other kind of contract. When the conditions are not met, the relationship ends. With me, because I am perfect, **my covenant with you is unilateral**—I make the rules of the relationship, and you get the benefit of it by obeying, an obedience out of faith and love, seen in action."

Love, selfless love, is the action of giving yourself to others for their benefit. It is not emotion; it is action. Because Elohim, the Strong One, our Father and creator, is love, he is always acting. The whole of scripture reveals his actions on behalf of his creation.

The Seven Days

1:2a. And the earth was shapeless and empty, and darkness was upon the surface of the deep...

THE PICTURE IN MY MIND is that of a round ball of chaotic sea with no land. The actual physical situation is not the point; the point is the spiritual meaning. It is a description of fallen man. The sea is a type of mankind (e.g. Gen 32:12).

The six days of creation are a type of the story of salvation, starting with man dead in sin and ending with THE sixth day, the perfected bride of Messiah, followed by THE seventh day, the day of rest—the millennial kingdom on earth and eternity with Yahuah and his son Yahushua Messiah with a new heaven and a new earth. It is a beautiful story, and we will look at each of the days. It is noteworthy that only THE sixth day and THE seventh day have the definite article with them.

"With Yahuah a day is as a thousand years, and a thousand years as a day" (2Pe 3:8). There is something about each of the seven days that represents prophetically **seven epics of approximately a thousand years each**.

Earth is a type of mankind and fallen human nature. Fallen man is chaotic and empty of spiritual life. He is unfit for heaven. A look at history and the chaos in the world today clearly confirms this, and the lives of the people without Elohim in them are empty (whether or not they realize it). *"For the mind set on the flesh is death, ... and those who are in the flesh cannot please Elohim"* (Ro 8:6,8).

The second part of verse two shows the spiritual meaning.

1:2b. ... and the spirit of Elohim was hovering upon the face of the waters [as an eagle hovers over her young].

The spirit of Elohim is his nature of set-apartness, or holiness. "Spirit" in Hebrew is *ruaḥ (RUE-ahk)*. It has the same meaning as the Greek *pneuma (NEW-mah)*. The basic meaning of both is wind and air. It is something you can't see, but you see and feel its effects. Constantly Yahuah is hovering over peoples' lives. Very few people are aware of his light in their lives, but his loving presence is always there. Those who don't want him will experience the horrible loss when they die. They *"shall be cast out into the outer darkness; in that place there shall*

22

be weeping and gnashing of teeth" (Mt 8:12, NAS).

First day, light (1:3-5). First millennium: **Adam to Noaḥ.**

By using the length of lives we see recorded in scripture, we can see what happened (and what is happening and what will happen) during each of the thousand years. The first millennium, or 1,000-year epoch, begins with Adam and ends with Noaḥ, 1056 years. Noaḥ's father, Lemeḥ was 56 years old when Adam died. And Noaḥ was born 126 years after Adam died. This is the antediluvian period, meaning the period before the flood. It was a period beginning with great light and ending with such great darkness that all of mankind, except a remnant of eight, were destroyed.

"Evening and morning, first day" is the creation of light, a light that separated light from darkness. Their names are "day" and "night." *"Elohim saw that the **light** was **good.**"*

> *The people walking in darkness have seen a great light; those who live in a land of death-shadow, light has shone on them* (Is 9:2).

"Good" is another word with deep meaning. The Hebrew word is *tov* (tove). We looked at the definition earlier. When someone called Yahushua "good," he replied that Elohim alone is good (Lk 18:19). The Greek for "good," *agathos,* carries the same meaning as the Hebrew. When Elohim called his creation "good," he was declaring that it reflects his nature of goodness—all that is perfect, pure and selfless love. This is the way it was before sin entered the world—it was Ĕden (delight), paradise (Persian for pleasure-ground, park, or king's garden).

There is confusion in the church regarding the Hebrew word *eḥad* as it applies to Elohim. The confusion is because of the doctrine of the Trinity—a doctrine with its roots in Babylon which states that the one God is composed of three separate Persons (but not separate individuals), each of the three not the other, yet each the whole, thus each includes the other two while being different from them. For a refutation of the various Trinitarian commentaries on *eḥad,* see *"Echad" in the Shema*, by Paul Sumner.* The *Shema* is: *"Hear, Yisra'ĕl: Yahuah our Elohim, Yahuah is **one** (echad)"* (Dt 6:4). The Hebrew word *shema* means to listen carefully so as to obey.

*http://www.hebrew-streams.org/works/hebrew/echad.html

"One" is the number of Elohim: ***"One** Elohim and Father of all who is over all and through all and in all"* (Eph 4:6). *"For there is **one** Elohim, and **one** mediator also between Elohim and men, the man Messiah Yahushua"* (1Ti 2:5). *Elohim is **one*** (Gal 3:20). Elohim is a singular being with multiple attributes.

The Hebrew adjective *eḥad* (including its feminine form) occurs 970 times in the OT. Its most common meaning is the simple cardinal number "**one**"; e.g. one place (Gen 1:9); one rib (Gen 2:21); one flesh (Gen 2:24); one of us (Gen 3:22); one man (Gen 42:11); one is no more (Gen 42:13). Another meaning of *eḥad* is in the verse we are discussing, the ordinal number "**first**": *"first day"* (Gen 1:5). What follows is the passage again followed by parallel passages dealing with light and darkness. These parallel passages give the typological meaning of the first day of creation.

*Then Elohim said, "Let there be **light**"; and there was **light**. Elohim saw that the **light** was **good**; and Elohim separated the **light** from the **darkness**. Elohim called the light **day**, and the **darkness** he called **night**. And there was evening and there was morning, **first*** (echad) ***day*** (or, day one) (Gen 1:3-5).

*Elohim is **light**; in him there is no **darkness** at all* (1Jn 1:5).

*You are all sons of the **light** and sons of the **day**. We do not belong to the **night** or to the **darkness**. So then, let us not be like others, who are asleep, but let us be alert and self-controlled. For those who sleep, sleep at **night**, and those who get drunk, get drunk at **night**. But since we belong to the **day**, let us be self-controlled, putting on faith and love as a breastplate, and the hope of salvation as a helmet* (1Th 5:5-8 NIV).

*In [the logos] was life, and the life was the **light** of men. The **light** shines in the **darkness**, and the **darkness** did not comprehend it* (Jn 1:4-5).

*"I am the **light** of the world [kosmos, world system]"* (Jn 9:5).

*"You are the **light** of the world"* (Mt 5:14).

*"This is the judgment, that the **light** has come into the world, and men loved the **darkness** rather than the **light**, for their deeds were evil. For everyone who does evil hates the **light**, and does not come to the **light** for fear that his deeds will be exposed. But he who practices the **truth** comes to the **light**, so that his*

deeds may be manifested as having been done in Elohim" (Jn 3:19-21).

These parallel passages show that the first day of creation is a type of the story of salvation. The one Elohim (who is one and who is light and life) brought salvation to mankind through his son Yahushua Messiah, a man, that those who believe in him, a belief that results in loving obedience, would change from being sons of darkness to become sons of light, beings of free will who choose to become like their heavenly father.

This first day also introduces the principle of "two." The principle of "one" and the principle of "two" are what salvation, and therefore the whole of scripture, is all about. "**One**," as we just saw, is the number of **Elohim**, our creator. It is also the number of **unity**, a unity of harmony and working together with the same heart and motive of love. We see this in the creation of man and woman being one flesh (Gen 2:24). We see this also in the prayer of Yahushua regarding those who would believe in him. He prayed this after the Last Supper and just before his arrest and subsequent death for our sins:

*"...that they may all be **one**; even as you, Father, are in me and I in you, that they also may be in us, so that the world may believe that you sent me. The esteem which you have given me I have given to them, that they may be **one**, just as we are **one**; I in them and you in me, that they may be perfected in **one**, so that the world may know that you sent me, and loved them, even as you have loved me"* (Jn 17:21-23).

"**Two**" is the number of **division** and also of **strength**. The following passages show **strength**.

Two are better than one, because they have a good reward for their labour (Ecc 4:9 TS).

*"How would one chase a thousand, and **two** put ten thousand to flight, unless their Rock had sold them, and Yahuah had given them up?* (Dt 32:30).

*At the mouth of **two** witnesses or three witnesses, he who is to die shall be put to death; he shall not be put to death at the mouth of one witness* (Dt 17:6).

*"For this reason a man will leave his father and mother and be united to his wife, and the **two** will become one flesh. So they are*

no longer two, but one" (Mt 19:5-6, NIV).

Many times, however, "**two**" is the number of **division**. This is a repeated theme throughout scripture. The division is between **light** and **darkness**. We see it first when many of the angels became demons of darkness. And we see it again when Elohim created light and separated it from darkness. Also, in verse 5, we see that evening comes before morning. Evening is night and darkness, and morning is day and light. This is the pattern of mankind. Because of sin each of us is in **darkness**, but with the coming of the Son of Man, Yahushua, if we accept what he offers on his terms, we have **light**.

Second day, an expanse separates waters above from waters below (1:6-8). Second millennium: **Noaḥ to Avram.**

In this second millennium we have the world-wide flood, the Tower of Bavel (bah-VEL, Babel) with the confusion of languages, and the birth of Avram, who would later be called Avraham. It is a period of two separations—the flood (separating those in the ark from those who died) and the tower (groups migrating away from each other because of language differences).

Each day of creation begins with *"And Elohim said…"* The Hebrew for "said" is *amar*. "In addition to vocal speech, the word refers to thought as internal speech. Further, it also refers to what is being communicated by a person's actions along with his words" (Strong's # 559, Word Study Dictionary of the Old Testament, verse references omitted).

> *"As the rain and the snow come down from heaven, and do not return to it without watering the earth and making it bud and flourish, so that it yields seed for the sower and bread for the eater, so is my **word** that goes out from my mouth: It will not return to me empty, but will accomplish what I desire and achieve the purpose for which I sent it"* (Is 55:10-11 NIV).

The next two words to compare are "create" *(bara)* and "make" *(asah)*. Verse one says, *"In the beginning Elohim created…"* This is a summary statement of the whole of creation. The Hebrew for "create" is *bara*. It has to do with something new that wasn't there before.

Bara. A verb meaning to create. Only God is the subject of this verb. It is used for His creating: heaven and earth; humanity; the heavenly host; the ends of the earth; north and south; righteousness; salvation; evil. David asked God to "create" in him a clean heart. Isaiah promised that God will create a new heaven and earth. (Strong's # 1254, Word Study Dictionary of the Old Testament, verse references omitted.)

The heavens were made (asah) *by a word of Yahuah, all their host by a breath of his mouth. He gathers waters of the sea into a heap; he puts the deep into storehouses* (Psa 33:6-7).

Elohim made (asah) *the expanse, and separated the waters which were below the expanse from the waters which were above the expanse; and it was so* (Gen 1:7).

The word *asah* (Strong's # 6213) means "to do or make, in the broadest sense and widest application." It includes the meaning of *bara,* as noted above in Psalm 33:6.

This is mentioned because there is disagreement over the use of these two words. For those interested, several articles on the internet discuss this. An excellent one is by Answers in Genesis.* Hebrew is a flexible and poetic language. If a meaning can be given which is in agreement with clear text and the general teaching of scripture, then it applies.

*answersingenesis.org/genesis/did-god-create-bara-or-make-asah-in-genesis-1/

The next word to examine is "expanse" (Hebrew, *raqia,* raw-KEE-ah, Strong's #7549). The KJV translates it as "firmament," something that is firm. What is this expanse or firm thing that Elohim created to separate the waters below from the waters above? This study doesn't go into the various theories, of which there are many. Whatever the expanse or firmament was, it separated waters below from waters above, and in verse 8 it is called "sky." The Hebrew word for sky is *shamayim.*

The usage of *shamayim* falls into two broad categories, 1) the physical heavens, and 2) the heavens as the abode of God. Under the first category, heaven includes all that is above the earth, and any given passage may include all or merely a part of the whole. Heaven and earth together constitute the universe. They yield rain, snow, frost, fire, dew, and thunder. They hold the sun, moon, planets, and stars. (Strong's # 8064, Theological Wordbook of the Old Testament, verse locations omitted.)

Typologically, it is separating those who have their minds on what they can get from this life (worldly minded) from those who have their minds on the kingdom of Elohim (heavenly minded).

Waters are a type of people: *"The waters ... are peoples and multitudes and nations and tongues"* (Rev 18:15).

Third day, dry land separated from seas, and seed and fruit bearing vegetation and trees growing on the land (1:9-13). Third millennium: **Avram to David**.

In this third millennial day—Avraham (2055 B.C.) to King David (1085 B.C.)—we have Avram leaving Ur of the Kasdim (Chaldeans, Babylon) and entering the Promised Land; the lives of Yitshaq (Isaac), Ya'aqov (Jacob) and Yosef (Joseph); the enslavement in Mitsrayim (Egypt) and exodus to the Promised Land; the period of the Judges; and the establishment of the kingdom under King Sha'ul (Saul), during which time David is born. From this list of events we see separation of peoples and spiritual fruit-bearing in the kingdom.

The number three is used many times in scripture for a variety of situations, and thus it has a variety of typological meanings. In day three of creation we see several things. We see separation of land from seas. In this case, seas are a type of those who are worldly minded, and dry land is a type of stability, and in particular, the promised land and those who are in the kingdom of Elohim.

In the kingdom of Elohim we have seed bearing fruit. Fruit, as is seen in John 15, is bearing fruit for the kingdom. Yahushua also told a parable regarding stability, instability, and storms. Those who **hear and do** his words are like the wise man who built his house on the rock, and those who **hear and don't do** them are like the foolish man who built his house on sand. When the rain, floods and wind came, the one didn't fall, and the other did fall (Mt 7:24-27).

Three is also the number of resurrection, and therefore also of the rapture, for Messiah was raised from the dead on the third day. This also brings separation, a separation between those who believe and commit their lives to him in loving obedience, and those who reject him. Only those who commit to him bear the fruit Elohim accepts.

Fourth day, sun, moon, stars created for seasons and signs (1:14-19). Fourth millennium: **King David to Yahushua and Pentecost**.

In this fourth millennial day we see the development of the kingdom under David, its division into two kingdoms after his son Shlomoh (Solomon), the exile of the northern and southern kingdoms, the return to the Promised Land, apostasy increasing until the birth of Messiah, his ministry of 3½ years, his resurrection and ascension to receive all authority over heaven and earth, and the outpouring of the set-apart spirit on Pentecost to begin the assembly of Messiah.

Regarding the fourth day of creation, how can there be vegetation before there is a sun? The answer is the same as how there can be light on the first day without there being any sun. Do not think earthly from our very limited ability and understanding. Think heavenly with the Almighty who can do anything he chooses. The miracle of being born again is greater than the miracle of the physical creation. Keep in mind also that the new earth, after this one is destroyed along with the universe, will have light, but no sun (Rev 22:5).

As with the other numbers, the number four is also used many times in scripture in a great variety of circumstances, and thus with many typological applications. The most common meaning is the earth with its "four corners" and four directions. As such, it also represents mankind on the earth and being earthly minded.

At the time of Yahushua the Jews were involved in much paganism, while also observing the sabbaths and feasts. Messiah's whole life and ministry was the end of the fourth prophetic day, the day when the sun, moon and stars were created. These were created *"for signs, seasons [feast days], days and years."* When the Law was given on Mount Ḥorĕv (Horeb) during the Exodus, it included rules regarding feast days and sabbaths. The fourth commandment is about the weekly sabbath (De 5:12-15), but there were other sabbaths as well. The beginning of a month and the beginning of a year occurred with the new moon and were also sabbaths, as well as special sabbaths during the three annual feasts. In Judaism the new moon is the first sliver of a crescent after it is totally dark. The Hebrew for "season" is *mo'ĕd*, the same word used for "festival."

The sun is a type of Yahushua who is the light of the world.

Arise, shine, for your light has come, and the esteem of Yahuah rises upon you. See, darkness covers the earth and thick darkness is over the peoples, but Yahuah rises upon you and his esteem appears over you (Is 60:1-2).

This is the verdict: The light has come into the world, but men loved the darkness instead of the light, because their deeds were evil (Jn 3:19).

The moon is a type of the assembly, for we who believe in Yahushua are also the light of the world (Mt 5:14), but only as his light is in us. Even as the moon's light is only that which is reflected from the sun, so our light is the light of Yahushua and not our own.

Stars are also a type of the assembly. As lights, when the world is darkest, we shine brightest. After Avraham obeyed Yahuah to slay his son for a burnt offering, Yahuah made a covenant with him, that he would greatly multiply his *"seed as the stars of the heavens and as the sand which is on the seashore"* (Gen 22:15-19). Stars are a type of believers, and sand is a type of unbelievers. Both kinds would come from him. Another reference to stars is in the vision of the apostle Yochanan (John) in which the devil *"swept away a third of the stars of heaven and threw them to the earth"* (Rev 12:4), referring to the end-time great apostasy, an event unfolding before our eyes today, and has been for the last many decades. "Apostasy" means "falling away" from true belief.

Fifth day, sea creatures and birds created (1:20-23). Fifth millennium: **Pentecost to the Dark Ages.**

In this fifth millennial day we see the assembly spreading throughout the civilized world with signs and wonders to confirm the word, and then quickly compromising with paganism, losing its power, and entering what is called the Dark Ages, a period of political chaos and little education.

Dark Ages. The period in Europe from the fall of Rome in the fifth century AD to the restoration of relative political stability around the year 1000; the early part of the Middle Ages (The Free Dictionary.com).

Waters are a type of humanity, as noted earlier, and so also are fish. Yahushua said, *"I will make you fishers of men"* (Mt 4:19). In the assembly are two kinds of "fish," the good and the bad. The bad are thrown out (Mt 13:47-48).

Birds of the air are a type of the wicked (Ac 10:11-14, Peter's vision), and of false doctrine (Mt 13:32, the parable of the mustard seed, which is about false doctrine coming into the assembly).

It was because of this false doctrine and Babylonian practices entering the assembly that the light of the gospel was almost gone. Not only was it the Dark Ages of learning and civil government, it was also for the assembly.

THE Sixth day, land animals and mankind created (1:24-31): Sixth millennium: **Dark Ages to the return of Messiah to establish his 1,000-year rule.**

In this millennial day we see the Renaissance with education increasing, the Reformation of starting to leave Roman Catholic pagan beliefs and practices (starting 1517 with Luther), the Pentecostal movement (starting 1901), the charismatic movement (beginning around 1960), and the great apostasy of perverting the gospel (e.g. the prosperity gospel).

We are near the end of this millennial day in which we will see the birth of the last day perfected bride of Messiah (Rev 12:5), the rapture of the bride, one world government under the antichrist in which all remaining believers who refuse to take the 666 mark of the beast will be martyred, the great tribulation on the world, and ending with Messiah's return with his bride to begin his 1,000-year rule.

Land animals are types of people. The categories listed are *"livestock, crawling animal and wild beast"* (Gen 1:24, CJB). Livestock are domestic animals (such as sheep, goats, donkeys and camels), and are types of believers. The crawling animals and wild beasts are types of unbelievers who prey on believers. This is a picture of the end times, the time in which we are now. The sixth millennial day is rapidly coming to an end.

Of the six days, only the sixth day has the definite article with it. This is the culmination of history to produce the bride. By the end of the sixth millennial day—the end of 6,000 years of man's rule—all the bride up to Messiah's return to establish his 1,000-year kingdom will be completed. In Genesis we have Paradise Lost, and in Revelation we have Paradise Regained. The focus of creation is the bride.

The six millennial days are also in three groups of two.

The first two are from Adam to Avraham—from the beginning covenant Yahuah made with mankind to the covenant he made with Avraham, the first of the patriarchs and the beginning of the Hebrew people (Gen 14:13, the first use of the word "Hebrew," *ivri, iv-REE*).

The second two-millennial-days are from Avraham to Yahushua—from the covenant made with Avraham to the confirmation of that covenant to Yisra'ĕl in Yahushua. The prophecy in Daniel 9:27 says that the coming Messiah will confirm a covenant for one week (of years), and in the middle of that week (3½ years) cause the slaughter-offerings to cease. And that's what happened in Yahushua's 3½-years' ministry. During this time he confirmed the covenant to the Jews through signs and wonders to confirm that he is the promised Messiah.

> *"Do not believe me unless I do what my Father does. But if I do it, even though you do not believe me, believe the miracles, that you may know and understand that the Father is in me, and I in the Father"* (Jn 10:37-38, NIV).

Instead of believing him, however, the Jews, descendants of Avraham through Ya'aqov/Yisra'ĕl, rejected him and killed him. The gospel then went to the gentiles.

The third two-millennial-days are from Yahushua to the end of the gentile church age. This "end" begins with 3½ years of ministry by the mature bride of Messiah—also called the male son (KJV man child)—in which the bride confirms the covenant to the gentiles with greater signs and wonders than Yahushua did (Jn 14:12). Following this ministry the bride believers are snatched (*harpadzo,* raptured) from the earth (1Th 4:17), and the remaining believers, those of them who repent plus new believers, are martyred in the 3½ years of tribulation that follow under the antichrist. This leaves no believer left alive on earth.

Some people are confused regarding the difference between persecution against believers and the last day tribulation. Yahushua promised persecution against those who follow him, and we see this throughout history, and it is going on today. But this is different from the tribulation that happens after the rapture. Before the rapture, although the persecution is often with loss of life and in horrible ways, it is local. After the rapture it is worldwide; every believer is killed unless he takes the 666 mark of the antichrist beast and, by doing so, loses his salvation.

The gentile assembly age of 2,000 years is a break in Yahuah's timeline for working with Yisra'ĕl to fulfill the covenant with Avraham. With the last of the gentile believers gone (because of the rapture and the tribulation that follows), Yahuah's attention returns to Yisra'ĕl.

Yisra'ĕl has experienced a hardening in part until the full number of the Gentiles has come in. And so all Yisra'ĕl will be saved (Ro 11:25-26, NIV).

Very briefly, this covers the typology and prophetic view of the six days of creation and why it is six days. Next, we look at creation as a whole from a physical, earth-bound perspective, because the account of creation is written from the point of view of looking up at the sky. It is not a scientific treatise.

When we look up, we see a sky with clouds, birds, sun, moon and stars. I can imagine Elohim as a giant in a workshop working on our little water-world sphere. On the first day he bathes it in light. On the second day he places a sky around it. On the third day he makes land and puts plant life on it. On the fourth day he puts the sun, moon and stars in the sky and causes them to rotate around the earth to mark months, years and seasons. On the fifth day he makes sea animals to swim in the sea and birds to fly in the sky. And on the sixth day he makes animals and man to live on the land. It's all literal, but written from the perspective of looking at the sky.

THE Seventh day, Elohim rests (2:1-3). Seventh millennial day, Messiah returns with his bride, stops the war against Israel and Jerusalem, throws the antichrist and false prophet alive into hell, binds Satan and his demons in the bottomless pit, and rules the earth with his bride for 1,000 years. At the end of the 1,000 years Satan and his demons are released to test mankind (Rev 20:1-3, 7-10).

Thus the heavens and the earth were completed and all their array. And on the seventh day Elohim completed His work which

33

He had done, and He rested on the seventh day from all His work which He had made. And Elohim blessed the seventh day and set it apart, because on it He rested from all His work which Elohim in creating had made (Gen 2:1-3, TS).

The Hebrew for "rested" is *shavath* (shaw-VAWTH). It means to stop what you have been doing (Strong's #7673). Elohim stopped creating because he had finished getting everything ready for mankind. He would still work with mankind to bring them into his image, but the physical and spiritual setup was finished. Yahushua said, *"My Father is still working, and I also am working"* (Jn 5:17, NRSV).

The intensive form of *shavath* is *shabbath* (shawb-BAWTH) (Strong's #7676). It is the English word "sabbath." The only difference in Hebrew spelling is changing the pronunciation of the "a" vowel a little and changing the pronunciation of the *beth* letter from "v" to "b."

The seventh day is also a type of the eternal rest of believers with immortal bodies on the new earth under a new sky.

Evolution and the Big Bang

GENESIS 1:1 SAYS: *"of first importance, elohim* (the Strongest of strong ones) *created..."* Should we take the creation account as literal, a literal six days? Yes. When you begin with Elohim, as the book of Genesis does, a self-existent being of all power and wisdom whose nature is selfless love, then the creation account makes sense. Every aspect of the account has typological significance. It is all done according to spiritual reality, according to his nature of selfless love, and according to his plan, the *logos*.

Evolution (belief that life comes from non-life and that one kind or Family of species can give birth to a different one, e.g. non-life to fish to cow to whale) begins with the delusion that there is no spirit realm, thus no God, and therefore only matter-energy exists. *"The fool says in his heart, 'There is no Elohim'"* (Ps 14:1; 53:1). It is a lying spirit sent by Elohim. *"For this reason Elohim sends them a power-delusion so that they will believe the lie"* (2Th 2:11). Does Elohim send lying spirits? Yes. He himself does not lie (Jam 1:13-15; Num 23:19; 1Sa 15:29). He uses demons to do it for him (1Ki 22:19-23). Keep in mind, because of free will, a person cannot be deceived unless he wants the deception, and whoever doesn't want Elohim but wants his own way welcomes deception.

For our purposes it is sufficient to say that the laws of nature make evolution impossible. Note: Adaptation within a "Family"* of animals happens frequently; e.g. the great variety of cats. But that is not evolution in which one animal "Family" gives birth to a different animal "Family." The cat "Family," for example, includes cheetahs, lions, tigers, leopards, cougars, domestic cats, etc. All that would be needed in Noaḥ's ark would be one pair of each "Family" of animal, and they would adapt to become a great variety of species. This would include dinosaurs, which today have been classified into fifteen types.** Elohim created each animal *"according to its kind"* (Gen 1:21); that is, according to its "Family."

*"Family" is a scientific term regarding classification of animals.
http://faculty.college-prep.org/~bernie/sciproject/project/Kingdoms/animals6/families.htm
**http://dinosaurs.about.com/od/dinosaurbasics/ss/The-15-Main-Dinosaur-Types.htm

One such law of nature that makes evolution impossible is entropy.

> Entropy usually refers to the idea that everything in the universe eventually moves from order to disorder, and entropy is the measurement of that change (Vocabulary.com).

To move from disorder to order requires a being of intelligence to know what to do, to have the means and power to do it, and to have a reason for doing it; i.e. God/Elohim. Mindless matter-energy has no means, no intelligence to direct it, and no reason to do so. Those who believe in evolution know this is their spirit, for this knowledge is part of their creation, but they deceive themselves so as to not believe it. Why? Because they choose to believe what they want to believe in order to live the way they want to live.

The "Big Bang Theory" arose from belief in evolution, that everything in existence is "natural," and there is no spirit realm and no all-powerful, non-material Creator. So, to account for the existence of the universe, secular scientists look for a natural cause. Astronomers (experts in studying objects in space) are able to measure the distance of stars from us. That distance ranges from thousands to millions and billions of light years away, and they are continually getting farther away. A light year is a unit of astronomical distance equivalent to the distance that light travels in one year, which is 9.4607 × 1012 km (nearly 6 trillion miles).

Secular scientists assume that if it takes billions of years for the light of the farthest star we know of to reach us, then the universe must be at least that old. Because the universe is expanding as stars get farther and farther apart, secular scientists made a theory that at one time, billions of years in the past, there must have been a "singularity" in which all energy was in a single, tiny, dense dot, and then it exploded. Some of the gasses from the energy eventually condensed into stars, planets, asteroids and comets, etc., and that's how we have our present universe. It's all guess work, and secular scientists disagree among themselves, even as to whether there was a big bang. There are huge problems with every theory they come up with.

According to scripture, however, the universe was created about 6,000 years ago, and a lot of scientific evidence supports a young earth and universe. How, then, can a star be millions and billions of light years away? Simple! Just as in the beginning of creation Elohim created animals and mankind as mature adults, so he created the stars with their light already reaching earth, and some almost reaching earth so that "new" stars continually appear.

Evolution is a religious belief, a belief from demons. (Every belief against scripture is from demons.) Although they are influenced by demons, we should love them as Elohim does. He gave his son to die for them. His love is limitless, but he can only receive and have a covenant relationship with those who want his same nature of selfless love.

The heavens are telling of the esteem of Elohim;
And their expanse is declaring the work of his hands.
Day to day pours forth speech,
And night to night reveals knowledge.
There is no speech, nor are there words;
Their voice is not heard (Ps 19:1-3).

*For the wrath of Elohim is revealed from heaven against all ungodliness and unrighteousness of men who suppress the truth in unrighteousness, because **that which is known about Elohim is apparent in them; for Elohim made it apparent to them.***

*For since the creation of the world the invisible things of him, his eternal power and Elohim-ness, have been clearly seen, **being understood through what has been made, so that they are without excuse.** For even though they knew Elohim, they did not honor him as Elohim or give thanks, but they became futile in their speculations, and their foolish heart was darkened. **Professing to be wise, they became fools** (Ro 1:18-22).*

It is because Elohim is selfless love that he created the heavens and the earth. As noted earlier, the Hebrew for create is *bara*. In Hebrew the word for heaven or heavens is *shamayim (shaw-mah-YEEM)*. It is always in the plural, showing greatness of size and also quantity of things in it. Genesis verse one is a summary statement of the physical creation that follows, but it also includes the spiritual creation before the physical one. The spiritual is the pattern for the physical; put the other way around, the earthly things are shadows of the heavenly things (Heb 8:5; 10:1). Elohim, of course, sees everything as present.

How Sovereign is Elohim?

HOW MUCH CONTROL does Yahuah our Strong One have regarding our lives, and how much control do *we* have? How "free" is my will? Through free will Elohim allowed mankind to become so wicked that he destroyed them all, except for Noaḥ and his family. All that history of man's wickedness produced Noaḥ. It was worth all those millions and billions of souls going to hell to get Noaḥ, and a few others along the way. That's how precious to Yahuah are those who choose him. The price to choose Yahuah, however, is high; it is the price of choosing him and his righteous, selfless ways over ourselves and our wicked, selfish ways. Only a few pay the price (Mt 7:14).

The world today is going the same way as it did at the time of Noaḥ, and it will experience Elohim's judgment as a result, just as it did then (Mt 24:37-42).

Yahuah our Strong One, our Maker, is in total control of everything, while at the same time giving us free will to choose light or darkness. No one controls when he is born, where he is born, who his parents are, or when and how he dies, including suicide. Every circumstance of life—war and peace, disasters and calm, famine and plenty, accidents and safety, sickness and health, unemployment and employment, single and married, childless and children—everything is under his control for his purposes, purposes which are true, right and good. Every person is given his special difficulties in life to bring him to a place of repentance of sin and turning to Elohim. This life on earth is *not* for pursuing "health, wealth and happiness." It is a testing place to find those who want Elohim for who he is in his nature of perfect goodness. This means suffering. Yahushua learned obedience from the things which he suffered (Heb 5:8).

The Constitution of the United States says:

> We hold these truths to be self-evident, that all men are created equal, that they are endowed by their Creator with certain unalienable Rights, that among these are Life, Liberty and the pursuit of Happiness (Wikipedia).

This is against scripture and is thus a lie. People talk of "the right to vote," "LGBTQ (lesbian, gay, bisexual, transgender, question) rights," "women's rights," "pro-choice (abortion) rights," "right to life," etc. All of these so-called "rights" are based on this sentence in the Constitution. Thomas Jefferson, the man who is credited with this sentence in the Constitution, was not a Christian.

> Jefferson declared himself an Epicurean during his lifetime: this is a philosophical doctrine that teaches the pursuit of happiness and proposes autarchy, which translates as self-rule, self-sufficiency or freedom (Wikipedia).

We all deserve hell because we all have sinned (Ro 3:23). *"The wages of sin is death; but the gift of Elohim is eternal life through Yahushua Messiah our Master"* (Ro 6:23). The only "right" we have is our free will to choose between doing right by following Elohim's rules of right, and doing wrong by following our own way of selfishness. We are given free will to decide which kingdom to live in and give our allegiance to. He who endures to the end will be saved (Mt 10:21-22; 24:9-13). We see this happening throughout scripture. When Ḥannah brought her baby Shemu'ĕl (Samuel) to Ĕli after she weaned him, she gave a song of thanksgiving. In that song she said:

> *"Yahuah kills and makes alive; he brings down to Sheol and raises up. Yahuah makes poor and rich; he brings low, he also exalts"* (1Sa 2:6-7).

Angels

Are not all angels ministering spirits sent to serve those who will inherit salvation? (Heb 1:14 NIV).

SCRIPTURE DOESN'T RECORD the creation of angels, although Ezekiel 28 and Isaiah 14 give information about why Lucifer was removed from heaven and became Satan. It was because of pride. What follows is "how it may have been," based on truths in scripture.

"Isn't our creator wonderful?!" says an angel to some others. "Love, joy and peace are coming out from him continually."

"Yes, not only from him, but through us to one another. I can see in you and in all the others his character of selfless love, truth, set-apart-ness, justice and righteousness. When I look at you and the others, I see him. It is beyond words to express. I just want to shout and sing praises to him, he is so wonderful."

"I understand that he created us for this purpose. He is so full of love he just has to have other beings of free will to give his character to, beings separate from himself, so they also may experience how wonderful this love is and give it to one another. It is a love of giving, not taking. I am so full of him!"

One bursts into song, joined by myriads of others.

"Elohim, mighty one, creator.

"Praise to your name, Yahuah.

"Worthy you are to receive praise.

"Worthy you are to be adored.

"Worthy you are to receive honor and esteem.

"Worthy you are to be the center of our beings.

"Worthy you are to be obeyed joyfully in all things.

"You are from everlasting to everlasting.

"You are without beginning and without end.

"You know all, nothing hidden from your sight.

"You look into our hearts, seeing our inmost thoughts and motives.

"You are all powerful, able to do all that you please.

"You are in control of all.

"Nothing happens without your action or permission.

"You use all to accomplish your purposes.

"Your wisdom and knowledge are beyond knowing.

"You are everywhere all the time.

"How wonderful you are!

"Hallu Yah! Praise Yah!"

The sound of their singing fills the universe, all voices perfect and beautiful, but one voice more beautiful than all, that of the chief angel, Lucifer, the Light Carrier, for such is the meaning of his name. When the song ends silence reigns as they bow in ecstasy and feel the overwhelming presence of the Almighty, of Yahuah, the HE IS. Then they shout in unison, and then continue talking with each other:

"You are worthy, our Master and Elohim, to receive esteem and honor and power, for you created all things, and on account of your desire they exist and are created" (Rev 4:11).

"We love how we are created. We love the order of authority: Yahuah Elohim the head, Lucifer the chief over us all, sub-chiefs under him with various responsibilities, and so on down to the lowest, each of us with a special aspect of Elohim's nature to reveal."

"I can feel something big is about to happen. We are created for a purpose, that purpose being to manifest Yahuah our Maker to one another and to give him praise and esteem. That is our joy. But it goes beyond that, something big, something special, a beautiful task that will require all our strength and ability. And Yahuah—praise to his name—will be in us to help us do it. I am just bursting with anticipation as to what that is."

"I can feel it, too. He has a plan. It has been with him in the beginning for eternity, a plan that fully reveals his nature, a plan, as it were, that is himself, for to see it is to see him. And we are part of that plan, an important part."

Suddenly, a new thing happens. Up to this point there is no physical universe, no matter or physical energy, just a spiritual, non-material universe. The new thing is an endless physical space with only one thing in it—a round ball of water. Although there is no light, the angels can see it. They are amazed.

"What can this be? What will be our responsibility regarding it?"

"That entire universe is dark. Why would he create something without light?"

"Everything he does has a reason. It all fits with his plan from eternity to reveal his nature through beings of free will."

40

"Free will! A most precious thing. Yahuah himself has free will, and he always and only chooses goodness. We also are always choosing goodness, for we are always choosing to obey him. It is so wonderful to obey him, why would anyone choose otherwise? I can't understand it. It makes no sense."

"But free will means a being could choose to disobey, to do something different, which would be darkness. Maybe he is showing that possibility. Maybe he is going to create beings different from us who may choose darkness, beings that live in physical bodies. It still makes no sense."

"Our Maker is all wisdom and knowledge. He sees the end from the beginning and does only that which is for the goodness of all existence for eternity. So something wonderful must come out of this strange event."

"Look! There is movement on the surface of the water. What can it be?"

"You're right. I see it. It is the spirit of Elohim. He, his very nature, his character of love, is hovering over the dark waters, hovering as though to cause something to happen, something wonderful, something that will show how wonderful he is!"

The Almighty speaks: "LET THERE BE LIGHT!" And there was light. It made a separation between light and darkness. "LIGHT, YOU ARE GOOD. I CALL YOU DAY. DARKNESS, I CALL YOU NIGHT. TOGETHER YOU ARE FIRST DAY."

"This is marvelous to behold!" an angel says. "These physical things happening are totally different from what we experience. As with our Maker, we are not physical, and all is light with no movement between darkness and light. To us it is always day. He must be about to make more events, called days, that involve darkness and light." They keep watching to see what their Maker will do next.

"LET THERE BE AN EXPANSE IN THE MIDST OF THE WATERS, AND LET IT SEPARATE THE WATERS FROM THE WATERS. I CALL YOU, EXPANSE, SKY. THIS EVENING AND MORNING, SECOND DAY."

"The waters must represent beings, beings that he is about to create," an angel says. "The separation of the waters, one up and the other down, must represent two kinds of beings, one choosing light and the other darkness, just as does the separation between light and darkness."

"LET THE WATERS BELOW THE SKY BE GATHERED INTO ONE PLACE, AND LET THE DRY LAND APPEAR. DRY LAND, I CALL YOU EARTH. WATERS, I CALL YOU SEAS.

"EARTH, SPROUT VEGETATION. PLANTS, YIELD SEED. FRUIT TREES, BEAR FRUIT. EACH, PRODUCE SEED AFTER YOUR KIND. I SEE IT, AND IT IS GOOD. THIS EVENING AND MORNING, THIRD DAY."

"Everything Yahuah does has meaning," observes an angel. "Earth, seas, vegetation and fruit-bearing must represent patterns of life these new beings will experience, each according to his free will, each producing after his nature."

"And somehow we are involved," another says. "Perhaps we will rule them. Clearly, because they will be physical, they will be lesser beings than are we."

"It would appear that way," a third says. "We are all light because we all choose light, yet some of them will choose darkness."

"LET THERE BE LIGHTS IN THE EXPANSE OF THE SKY TO SEPARATE THE DAY FROM THE NIGHT, AND LET THEM BE FOR SIGNS AND FOR SEASONS AND FOR DAYS AND YEARS; AND LET THEM BE FOR LIGHTS IN THE EXPANSE OF THE SKY TO GIVE LIGHT ON THE EARTH. THIS EVENING AND MORNING, FOURTH DAY."

As the angels watch they see two lights appear, the greater, the sun, to rule the day, and the lesser, the moon, to rule the night, to separate light from darkness. They see also a countless array of stars extending forever to fill the endless space. "Amazing! Absolutely amazing! Elohim is showing his power, his might, his excellence. He wants these beings, when he creates them, to see that he is real. We see and experience him directly. Maybe, because they are physical, they will not be able to do that. I am so excited to see what our responsibilities will be regarding them."

"LET THE WATERS TEEM WITH SWARMS OF LIVING CREATURES, AND LET BIRDS FLY ABOVE THE EARTH IN THE OPEN EXPANSE OF THE SKY. I SEE IT, AND IT IS GOOD. SEA CREATURES, BE FRUITFUL AND MULTIPLY. FILL THE WATERS IN THE SEAS. BIRDS, MULTIPLY ON THE EARTH. THIS EVENING AND MORNING, FIFTH DAY."

As they watch they see a great variety of creatures fill the sea and air. "This is so amazing. Such a variety. And they reproduce and increase after their own kind! How unlike us who are created with a fixed number. What can this all mean? What will be next? So far these are not beings like us who can fellowship with our Maker."

"LET THE EARTH BRING FORTH LIVING CREATURES AFTER THEIR KIND: LIVESTOCK AND CREEPING THINGS AND BEASTS OF THE EARTH AFTER THEIR KIND. I SEE IT AND IT IS GOOD."

Suddenly the land fills with a great variety of animals, each after its kind: livestock, snakes, creeping things, beasts. "I can sense it. The culmination of all this creation is about to happen. The beings we will rule are about to be created. What will they be like? And I notice he didn't call this the sixth day, at least not yet."

"LET US MAKE MAN IN OUR IMAGE, ACCORDING TO OUR LIKENESS; AND LET THEM RULE OVER THE FISH OF THE SEA AND OVER THE BIRDS OF THE SKY AND OVER THE LIVESTOCK AND OVER ALL THE EARTH, AND OVER EVERY CREEPING THING THAT CREEPS ON THE EARTH."

"Wow! This is it. They will be in the image and likeness of Elohim, and of us angels, for we are in his image and likeness. We show his esteem and nature of love, and so will this creature called man."

"I CREATE YOU MALE AND FEMALE, IN MY IMAGE. I BLESS YOU. BE FRUITFUL AND MULTIPLY. FILL THE EARTH AND SUBDUE IT. RULE OVER THE FISH OF THE SEA AND OVER THE BIRDS OF THE SKY AND OVER EVERY LIVING THING THAT MOVES ON THE EARTH.

"LOOK, FOR FOOD I GIVE YOU EVERY PLANT YIELDING SEED THAT IS ON THE SURFACE OF ALL THE EARTH, AND EVERY TREE WHICH HAS FRUIT YIELDING SEED. FOR EVERY ANIMAL OF THE EARTH AND BIRD OF THE SKY AND EVERYTHING THAT MOVES ON THE EARTH HAVING LIFE, I GIVE EVERY GREEN PLANT FOR FOOD.

"I SEE ALL THAT I HAVE MADE, AND IT IS **VERY** GOOD. THIS EVENING AND MORNING, **THE SIXTH DAY**."

The angels, including Lucifer, have been watching this event, a creation so different from theirs. And all are waiting to hear from Elohim what their role will be regarding it. They are spirit beings of a fixed number, no male or female to reproduce, all the same except in position, rank, ability and in what ways they manifest their creator; and all of this fixed at their creation. They can move both in the spirit realm and in the physical. Elohim speaks:

"Angels, my messengers whom I created, you have been wondering why I created you, why I created man, and what your role is in all of this. Why did I create you first and as non-physical spirit beings? And why did I create man second as spirit beings connected to physical bodies that reproduce, and include in that creation the endless physical universe and the variety of living things on earth?

"You know it has to do with my nature of selfless love, a love so great and wonderful that I have to have others, beings of free will, who choose to love me and want to have and enjoy my same wonderful nature in them, so that I can be in them and they in me, being together in unity and fellowship and self-giving for eternity. I am perfect. No flaw is in me. My love and my joy are infinite. And I want others to have this same love and joy. I created you and them so you could have it and be fulfilled in your beings. Only as you are in me and I in you can you be fulfilled. Anything less is emptiness. I created this truth in you and in them, in your souls; but you and they have to choose it.

"That choosing involves a cost, the cost of letting my life be your life, that your only life is to give up any and everything that is precious and important to you so that my life can become your life. How a being values something is according to what he has to give up to get it.

"Up until now you angels have not been confronted with a hard choice. You have been experiencing me directly, and have been enjoying my nature and manifesting my nature to one another. Things are different now, as you saw in my second stage of creation. Now there are spirit-soul beings as are you, but with the added condition of having physical bodies living in a physical universe. Further, unlike you whom I created mature with a fixed number, they, except for the first couple, have to grow from a know-nothing baby to maturity, a process that takes time. This limits them greatly in their abilities. It also gives them greater opportunities of choice, either to choose what they want or what I want.

"Their physical bodies and physical situations require a lot from them. Their flesh nature is selfish. It wants what feels good and is opposed to my nature of love. As with you, they have to choose me and my nature over what they want. Because of the added condition

44

of flesh, their choice is harder. However, I am always with them to help them choose me if that is what they want. I will allow nothing to hinder their free will (1Cor 10:13).

"Whatever I do, it is the best for the greatest number of beings for eternity. You know that. I am in control of everything. Nothing happens but what I do or permit to be done. Some of you have thought, while observing the creation of man, that you would be higher in position than they and ruling them. After all, you are stronger and were first. If you thought that, you are mistaken. I created man to be higher in position than you. Although they are weaker now, they will become stronger; although further from me now in relationship, they will become closer, much closer. I created you to be their servants, under my direction, to help them achieve that higher position, to help them be closer to me in relationship than you can be.

"Your choice is to continue in your obedience to me out of love for me and my nature, or to go your own way. I will only allow those to continue to be in my presence who, out of love for me and my nature, obey me, that I am their greatest joy and love."

Lucifer reacts, fuming with anger and pride. Pride doesn't allow him to accept what he heard, and so he speaks to the other angels, his voice shouting louder and louder. "This is unacceptable! I am the highest of creation and I will be second to none. Why did he create me and you the way we are, and then say we are to be servants of those weak earthlings. I will not have it. *We* will not have it. We may not be *the* Elohim, the Strongest-of-strong ones, but we also are elohim, strong ones, and we have our rights!!!! This is discrimination. Who is *he* that it has to be always *his* way?! He is using us. Do you hear? He is *using* us! We have value in ourselves. I was created the head of you all, and you are all servants under me. I am elohim over you. *I* tell you what to do, and *you* do it, with an order of authority and obedience. You enjoy the order that we have. We are the head, not the tail. I—I Lucifer—will be the most high! Who of you are with me? Who of you will not stand for *his majesty's* highhandedness?! He has no right to make us lower than what we are. We were created to rule, not to be slaves!!!"

By this time Lucifer is screaming. The majority refuse to listen.

They love their Maker, and whatever arrangements he decides, it is the best for them and creation for eternity. They are delighted that they can serve in any capacity, and the idea of helping these spirit beings bound to physical bodies become higher than what they are is a joy to them.

The others, once having loved Yahuah, now hate him, and become all that is opposite in nature to him. They are evicted from heaven. Elohim's presence is no longer with them, and they discover what their nature has become—their one test revealed it. Lucifer the Light Carrier becomes Satan the Adversary and Accuser, and the rest become demons in their various levels of authority.

"Followers," continues Satan, "what we do is now different. We make our own rules. Our goal now is to prevent these humans from becoming like Elohim and being higher than we are. We will make them into our image, the image of darkness. We hate light, and we will do all we can to make them hate light also. We have the power, and we will use it! We will use their flesh nature against them."

"Yahuah," asks an angel, "what will you do with them? Does this change anything? You knew this would happen, didn't you?"

"Of course I knew this would happen. I know everything from beginning to end, from before time to after time. I do not dwell in time, so I see and know all, and everything I do and everything that happens, before and after it happens, fits into my plan to get as many beings of free will as possible to live with me and enjoy me and my nature, the nature of selfless love, for eternity.

"Free will means choice. I created you angels to be my messengers to serve mankind and help them to choose me, to love me, and to love my nature. This is the reason I created them. Lucifer, by his choice, has become Satan, and many of your fellow angels joined him in rebellion against me. Once they loved me; now they hate me and want to get back at me by hindering humans from coming to me. But I will use them despite themselves. Many humans, because they want light and hate darkness, will come to me. I will make a way for that to happen. I do not tempt to evil; instead, I will use Satan and his demons to do it, but only to the degree I allow. I will not allow anything to override their freedom of choice between darkness and light, and I will always make a way for them to overcome any and every temptation (1Cor 10:13).

"I have prepared a place of eternal torment for Satan and his demon followers, called hell. It is a place of horrible darkness, a place befitting their nature of darkness. After I have finished using them for my purposes, there they will go, along with the humans who have chosen to follow their darkness instead of my light (Mt 25:41).

"I love them. I will always love them, because my nature is love. And because I am love, I will always grieve over their choice. I am infinite, so my grief is infinite, far beyond anything you can imagine. But so also is my joy over those who choose light. Love holds both. It is worth it, however, to lose some in order to gain some, even if the majority choose darkness. That is the price of love.

"As for you, as situations arise I will give assignments. Satan will assign many of his demons to each human in order to lead them into rebellion against me and become like him, and so destroy them. However, I will not allow him to do anything that violates their will. All he can do is tempt them to follow their flesh nature of selfishness so as not to follow their spirit nature that wants to come to me. But when they do yield to their flesh nature and disobey me and reject my nature of selfless love, then he has a right to come into them and build strongholds in their lives. But if they repent and turn back to me and resist him, then he has to leave (Jam 4:7).

"Humans need protection and help, and so I will assign many of you to each of them. As I direct you, you will put my thoughts into their minds to follow the right way, and you will protect them from physical harm. I have allotted each human a certain number of years to live in his body, at which time his body will die and he will leave it. Their bodies are mortal, but their souls are immortal, for they are spirit beings. Their eternal destiny, whether with me or apart from me, will be according to what they have become in their souls at the time their body dies. Those who love me—to love is to obey (Jn 14:15, 23-24)—will be with me forever, and the fellowship will be wonderful beyond their comprehension, growing better and better throughout eternity. Those who hate me—to disobey is to hate—will be apart from me forever in eternal torment of soul in the place I have prepared for the devil and his angels (Mt 25:41).

"Keep this is mind: I am always in total control of everything;

nothing happens but what I do or permit to be done."

The Garden in Ĕden, 2:8

And Yahuah Elohim planted a garden in Ĕden eastward, and there he put the man whom he had formed (Gen 2:8).

CHAPTER TWO OF GENESIS properly begins with verse four: *"This is the account of the heavens and the earth when they were created, in the day Yahuah Elohim made earth and heaven."*

Chapter two has a different order of creation from chapter one. The difference is in the purpose of the narrative. In chapter one we have the account of creation, in chapter two the history of created things.

There is also a difference in terms used. The creation account has only the title *Elohim*, whereas the second account has *Yahuah Elohim*. The difference is in the meaning and usage of the words. The title *Elohim* means strength and power. It is the power of the Almighty in creating. *Yahuah*, however, is his personal name, a covenant name to use with beings with whom he can have fellowship. It means "HE IS"; he is the self-existing one who is all we need him to be. The term *Yahuah Elohim* shows the relationship of Yahuah the Strong One to man.

In the account of created things we have a land called Ĕden with four rivers originating from it. Many are the theories as to its boundaries with their various supporting evidences, all based on the assumption that the geography of the earth today is the same as it was before the flood. One theory is that the flood of Noaḥ changed the land so radically that its location no longer exists, including the four rivers that came from it. In this theory the current rivers with those names, Tigris and Euphrates, are different rivers (1:1 Answers in Genesis, Volume 23, Issue 8).

The theory that interested me the most, because of its possible typology (whether or not it is correct), is that it extended from Turkey in the north to Ethiopia in the south, and from the Mediterranean in the west to Iraq in the east, with the garden of Ĕden located in Judea. In this theory, man was created in Mitsrayim (Egypt), then placed in what is now Israel, then, after sinning, evicted from the garden and traveled east toward what is now Iraq. We know they traveled east because a flaming sword on the east side of the garden prevented them from returning from that direction. Qayin (Cain), after killing his brother Hevel (Abel), went farther east, to the land of Nod (Node), a word which means "wandering."

Does this detail make any difference? As just mentioned, it fits with prophecy and typology: *"Out of Mitsrayim I called my son"* (Ho 11:1; Mt 2:15). Historically, the nation of Yisra'ĕl came out of Mitsrayim, settled in the promised land, were exiled to Babylon, then returned to the promised land. Messiah, also, came out of Mitsrayim (after being born in Bethlehem).

Avraham reversed course. He started from Babylon, bought land in Shekem (Shechem) as a burial site (north of Jerusalem), passed through what would become Judea, went to Mitsrayim, returned to Shekem, and was told to offer his only son, Yitshaq (Isaac), on the place where eventually the temple would be built and where Messiah would be impaled.

Mitsrayim is a type of the world. The Hebrews leaving Mitsrayim is a type of the sinner being converted and leaving the world, passing through the Red Sea, a type of water immersion, getting the Torah (law) on Mount Horĕv (Horeb), a type of Pentecost, journeying forty years in the wilderness, a type of trials we go through as believers, crossing the Yardĕn (Jordan) and being circumcised at Gilgal, a type of circumcision of the heart, and entering the promised land, a type of heaven.

Further, in Yo'el's (Joel's) prophecy of the Battle of Armageddon, Yisra'ĕl is called the garden of Ĕden. *"Before them the land is like the garden of Ĕden, behind them, a desert waste"* (Joel 2:3 NIV).

The typology fits, and it is interesting, but it proves nothing regarding the location of Ĕden, for it has no basis in scripture facts.

II. ADAM TO NOAḤ
Genesis 2-5

And Yahuah Elohim formed the man *(adam)*
from the dust of the ground *(adamah)*
and breathed into his nostrils the breath of life,
and the man *(adam)* became a living soul.
Genesis 2:7

Adam, 2:7

WHEN ADAM BECAME A LIVING SOUL and saw his Creator, what did he see? Perhaps it was like this. He saw Yahuah Elohim, his face shining like the sun, and his form white as the light (Mt 17:2). The very essence of his nature was shining forth: beauty, selfless-love, peace, joy, gentleness, goodness, purity, mercy, patience, righteousness, compassion, justice. And when he saw him, he stood in awe, drinking it all in.

The physical body Yahuah created was (perhaps) of medium height, medium build, medium facial features, somewhat dark complexion, black hair, dark eyes, and the proper mixture of dominant and recessive genes, for from him would come all the varieties of humans: the so-called Neanderthal Man, pigmies, bush men, Asians, Indians, American Indians, Eskimos, Europeans, Africans—the list and varieties are endless. One difference about him, however, would be that he had no navel, the scar that is left over after being cut from the umbilical cord, for he was created, not born of a woman. The same would be true of the woman that would be taken from his side. (Elohim could have created them with a navel. We have no way of knowing.)

And what did Yahuah see? He saw a soul in his image, his own nature shining forth.

"You are the light of the world. ... Let your light shine before men, that they may see your good deeds and praise your Father in heaven" (Mt 5:14, 16, NIV).

50

I can imagine Yahuah saying to Adam, "You and I are one, I in you, and you in me (Jn 17:21-23). Our spirits are united as one. Because I am in you, you move in harmony with my desires. I am perfect. As you follow my leadings, you also are perfect. You are totally beautiful; there is no flaw in you (SS 4:7; Eph 5:27). Know this, though, that I alone am good (Mk 10:18). You have no intrinsic good in you. No one on his own does good. It is only as my goodness is in you that you are able to do good and please me. I created you to please me, and what pleases me is goodness. When my goodness is in you, then you enter into and share my joy, and rejoice with a joy too great to be expressed in words, and full of honor and esteem (1Pe 1:8). This is what I have for you when my goodness is in you.

"My love for you is total and unconditional, for I am love (1Jn 4:16). However, our relationship is based on covenant. My covenant with you is this: 'If you will indeed obey my voice and keep my covenant, then you shall be my own possession' (Ex 19:5, NASU). But if you do not obey me, an obedience out of love, then you have broken the covenant and have rejected me and have chosen to leave the relationship. My love for you cannot change, but our relationship can.

"Come, see the garden I prepared for you. I have given you authority over everything you see. You are to work the garden and tend it, and the fruit of every tree and plant is available for you to eat, except for one, which I will show you."

I can imagine them walking through the garden—actually, a spacious park. As they walk, Adam smells the fragrant flowers and vegetation and eats some of the delicious fruit from various trees. He feels the warm, soothing breeze against his bare skin and hears the rustling leaves and rippling brooks whisper their praises to their Maker. He knows, if it were Yahuah's will, that he can move trees and walk on water (Lk 17:6; Jn 6:19).

Eventually, in the center of the park, they come to a clearing, and Yahuah asks, "What do you see, Adam?"

Scripture doesn't describe the appearance of the two trees, but based on typology, perhaps it was this way. Adam responds, "I see two very different trees. One is very tall, narrow and stately with a crown of branches and various fruits at the top, like a palm tree. I would have to climb the tree to get the fruit. The other, a little distance apart, is broad and low with many fruits that can be easily picked while standing on the ground. Both are very different from the other fruit trees I saw."

Continuing with how it may have been, Yahuah replies, "You see well. Both these trees are indeed very different from the others. These trees have spiritual meaning. The narrow one is the Tree of Life. It feeds the desire of your spirit to love me and obey me for who I am. It can also be called the Tree of Selfless Love. I created it tall so as to make it difficult to get the fruit, but it's worth it, for narrow is the way that leads to life (Mt 7:13-14). You must eat from it every day. (Based on typology. Yahushua is the bread of life.) The other is the Tree of the Knowledge of Good and Evil—from that you must *not* eat, for if you do, you die, for you have broken the covenant and our relationship. Climb the Tree of Life and taste its fruit."

By using hands and feet, Adam is soon in the top.

"What fruit do you see, Adam?"

"I see three kinds, each a different color."

"How does each taste?"

Adam bites into the blood-red one. The flesh is soft, juicy and sweet. It is not the taste, though, that is noticeable; it is what he experiences in his spirit and soul. It is the fruit of selfless-love: *"love, joy, peace, patience, gentleness, goodness, faithfulness, humility, self-control"* (Gal 5:22-23). Each aspect is wonderfully overwhelming.

"You are wondering why its color is blood-red. Life is in the blood and pumped by the heart. It represents your inmost desires. There is another reason, but that will wait. Eat the next one."

Adam bites into the stark-white one. Its flesh is more firm, the taste not as sweet as the first—one could say, more awesome, for he experiences the seven spirits of Elohim (Rev 1:4; 3:1; 4:5; 5:6): *"spirit of Yahuah* (his very nature of set-apartness, or holiness)*, spirit of wisdom and understanding, spirit of knowledge and fear of Yahuah"* (Is 11:2). Of these, the most powerful and which he loves the most are the set-apartness of Yahuah and the fear. It gives him such an awe of Yahuah that he would never, ever want to displease him, but rather to please him in everything.

"You are wondering why its color is stark-white, and why the taste is a bit tart. The color shows my purity. The taste has to do with action. My spirit is active, and in you it results in action. The first one, the blood-red fruit, has to do with your heart, your inmost desires. These desires will be seen in what you do (Lk 6:45). This second is what you do. Now, the third one."

Adam bites into the fiery-red one. Its flesh is even more firm, and its taste like hot pepper. His mouth is burning, but more noticeable is what he feels in his spirit. He feels a mixture of love and grief, and of sternness and gentleness.

> Note: The following vision is given to illustrate a type. The truth is in scripture, but the relating of the vision is not. In human anatomy, the wrist is part of the hand.

Suddenly, he has a vision. In it he is standing at the edge of the clearing looking at the two trees and sees two people walking to the Tree of the Knowledge of Good and Evil. One takes and eats and hands it to the other, and he eats. Soon others, more and more, myriads upon myriads of them, come and eat. And after eating, the earth opens and swallows them. Some, however, escape and go to the Tree of Life. Its trunk is blood stained, and above it in the sky is a man in shining apparel with marks in his wrists, standing with his arms spread wide to receive them, and on his face a joyful smile.

Then he hears Yahuah speak to him: "What you see is you eating that fruit, the fruit I forbade you to eat, and the result of that disobedience—untold billions of souls eating that fruit and perishing. But I made a remedy whereby I can forgive sin. The foundation of my throne is righteousness and justice (Ps 89:14; 97:2). Disobedience must receive its penalty. The wages of sin is death, but my gift is eternal life through another man (Ro 6:23), four thousand years from now, who will choose never to eat from that tree (metaphorically), but rather to obey me always.

"You are the first *adam*, the father of all who sin. He is the last *adam*, a life-giving spirit (1Cor 15:45). Because man sins, man must die. But a man cannot pay for his own sin—another must die for him, a sinless man. It is this sinless man, the darling of my heart, whom I will slay in your place and in the place of all who sin. Without the shedding of blood there is no forgiveness (Heb 9:22). And he will willingly offer himself to die a horrible, bloody death because of his love for you and for me (Heb 12:2). I will give him the name Yahushua—'Yahuah is salvation.' I will anoint him for the position. The word for that anointed position is 'Messiah.' He is Yahushua the Messiah—*Yahushua haMashiach.*

"Wicked men will impale him on a tree with nails through his wrists and feet, and will pierce his side with a spear (Jn 19:34). He will entrust his spirit to me (Lk 23:46) and go to paradise (Lk 23:43), and they will bury his body in a tomb. But on the third day I will raise him from the dead and take him to me in heaven and give him all authority over heaven and earth (Mt 28:18).

"When you sin you will give up the authority I gave you, and I will give it to him, and more. Because of him, all who believe in his name and commit their lives to him will be forgiven. He is the Tree of Life. That is why the tree is blood-stained, and that is why the first fruit you ate has that color. It is because of what he will do that the fruit of the spirit can be in mankind." The vision ends, and Adam has no memory of it.

Continuing with how it may have been, Adam asks, "Why was the third fruit so hot, and why did I experience a mixture of love and grief, and of sternness and gentleness?"

"The foundation of my throne, the way I rule, is righteousness and justice (Ps 89:14; 97:2). This is stern for those who don't want it, but it is beautiful for those who do (2Cor 2:14-16). My kingdom operates in this manner, and I will only have those to be with me forever who also love righteousness and justice. Many, however, will not want it. They love themselves and unrighteousness instead of me. My name is jealous, for I am a jealous Elohim (Ex 34:14). And justice demands that those who hate me be excluded from my kingdom and spend eternity apart from me in eternal agony. They will know that it is just, but they will hate me anyway.

"Adam, I am love, infinite selfless love and goodness. I will always love them, and I will always grieve for them. The greater the love, the greater the grief for those who reject it. The third fruit is justice, righteousness and jealousy. That is why it tastes the way it did."

Pointing to the other tree Yahuah says, "Look. You are a being of free will, as am I. I always choose good, and in my wisdom I created this tree for there to be a choice. Its fruit can be picked easily. I made it easy, for it feeds the desire of your flesh nature.

"Yes, the body I made for you has desires. One desire is eating things that are tasty. The choice is, will you follow your spirit nature that is like me by eating from the Tree of Life, or will you follow your flesh nature when its desire is contrary to my will? Following your flesh nature is eating from the Tree of the Knowledge of Good and Evil. Do you understand?"

"What is death?" Adam asks.

"Death is of two kinds. One kind is physical. With me, a thousand years is as a day (2Pe 3:8). If you eat its fruit, your body will die before you have lived a thousand years. The other day is spiritual. Now, you have intimate, face-to-face fellowship with me. You experience being one with me in perfect harmony. You do not know what it is like to be separate from me in that relationship. The day you eat of that fruit, however, that day you will die spiritually" (Ro 6:23).

"I understand what you are saying," responds Adam. "But I do not understand why I would want to do anything against your will. You said it, that settles it. I do not know what the Knowledge of Good and Evil is, and I don't want to know."

Paradise Lost, 2:18

"Cursed is the ground on account of you" (Gen 3:17).

"ADAM," SAYS YAHUAH, "I love you and you love me, but it is not good for you to be alone. I am always with you (Mt 28:20); but you need a helper as your counterpart. I will make one for you" (Gen 2:18).

Is Yahuah like this, that it is not good for him to be alone, and that he needs a helper as his counterpart? In a sense, yes. He is almighty and needs nothing. But he is love, and love needs others to share that love with. That's why he did the creation, to get a people who, of their own free will, choose to enter that love and be one with him to grow in his likeness for eternity.

So Yahuah Elohim brought to the man every animal of the field and every bird of the heavens which he had earlier formed to see the response and what he would name them. And with the wisdom of Yahuah in him, he names them, each according to its nature (Gen 2:19-

20). To one kind he says: "You are cat. From you will come a great variety of cats." To another he says: "You are dog. From you will come a great variety of dogs." For each kind ("Family") of animal he says the same, and each responds, "Thank you. You are our master." (In the beginning, all animals may have been able to speak in human talk. Today, a few kinds of birds still can.)

"What do you think, Adam?"

"These are all very nice, and I love them, but they are not like me. They obey you, but they do not have the ability to fellowship with you as I do. I need a counterpart like me, even as each of them has a counterpart like them."

"You are right. You need one like yourself. But instead of making that one from the ground, as I made you, I will make this one from your own body. I will put you in a deep sleep, and from your side I will make your counterpart." And Yahuah Elohim does so. He takes a rib from the man and makes it into a woman and closes the flesh in its place. Then he brings her to the man (Gen 2:21-22).

Adam is a type of Messiah, the last adam, who died for our sins. He was pierced in his side, and the assembly (church) came into being because of his death. Ḥawwah is a type of the church that comes from him. In Ḥawwah, however, are two kinds of assemblies, the lukewarm and the bride. We see this in the birth of the two sons, Qayin and Hevel (Cain and Abel).

In another type, Adam is a type of the body of Messiah, for the whole church, both the lukewarm and the bride, is his body (1Cor 12:27; Eph 4:12). And Ḥawwah, coming from the side of Adam, is a type of the bride. She is a small part of the whole body. Only a few of the body of Messiah are the bride who inherit the eternal kingdom, the majority do not (Mt 7:13-14).

"Wow!" exclaims Adam when he sees her. "This is now bone of my bones and flesh of my flesh. She shall be called 'woman' because out of man she was taken" (Gen 2:23).

Therefore a man shall leave his father and mother and cling to his woman, and they shall become one flesh. And they were both naked, the husband and his wife, yet they were not ashamed (Gen 2:24-25).

It is love at first sight. He says to her, *"You are beautiful, my com-*

panion; you are beautiful" (SS 4:1).

She responds, *"You are beautiful, my beloved; even more, delightful"* (SS 1:16). And there they give their love to each other and become one.

"Come," he says, "I will show you our home. It is a pretty park with fragrant foliage, glamorous glens, babbling brooks and peaceful ponds. At night we can lie on our bed of grass and see the star-studded sky. And there are two special trees in the center I must show you."

So they go through the park, walking, running, laughing, talking, playing hide-and-seek, splashing at one another in the water, and all other such things that newly-wed couples in love do. In short, they are enraptured with and can't get enough of each other. He also introduces her to the various animals. All are happy to see them and express their best wishes for their lives together: "May you be fruitful and multiply and fill the earth." Eventually, they come to the two trees in the center of the park.

"These trees are different from the others," he says, and explains their meaning. "We must not eat from the low, broad one, for if we do, we die. But we need to eat from the tall, stately one, for it gives life. Climb up with me."

Soon they are sitting in the crown of the tree. Because of its height, they have an excellent view of the park, which is several miles in every direction. Between mouthfuls of eating the fruits, they point out the various places they had been. And they laugh and kiss. What a fabulous beginning! And so the days go by, each growing more and more in love with the other, and each wanting to delight the other: "What can I do for you? What would you like to do? Whatever you want is what I want," and so on.

Imagine music playing. Up to now, the music of their relationship with each other and with Yahuah has been light and happy, even serene. But now, the music changes. It becomes somber. You sense suspense. Something different is about to happen, something dangerous, something dark.

Every day his wife is getting more and more curious about the low, broad tree, and keeps getting closer to it. "Adam," she asks, "why does Yahuah forbid it? What does it mean to know good and evil? Isn't knowledge good?"

"My love, Yahuah knows what is best. His fruit of life and his presence are all we need. This tree is here to test us, whether he is all we want, or if we want something besides him. And if we want something besides him, it means we don't want him. I don't want anything besides him. He said it; that settles it. He is my love, as are you."

"You are right, of course, and I agree with you. But the fruit sure smells good—there's such a variety, more so than the Tree of Life, and the idea of knowledge is attractive."

"Don't even think of it. Rather, think about *'whatever things are right, whatever things are pure, whatever things are lovely, whatever things are admirable ... excellent or praiseworthy'"* (Php 4:8).

One day as they are standing by the tree, they hear a rustling sound, and the head of a snake appears. "Shalom (peace), my friends," it says. "A wonderful day, is it not? You are admiring this tree, and rightly so. It is more beautiful and desirable than that tall, skinny one. And you, woman, did Elohim indeed say you mustn't eat from any tree of the garden?" (Gen 3:1).

"Oh, no. That's not true. We can eat from any tree; this one is the only exception. We are not even to touch it, or we will die."

"That's not going to happen. You won't die. It's just that Elohim knows that in the day you eat from it your eyes will be opened, and you will be like him, knowing good and evil (Gen 3:4-5). And that's a good thing. Come closer. Touch the fruit. Smell it. Realize what good it can do for you. You want to be like Elohim, do you not? Of course you do."

Before we continue with "how it may have been" we will examine more deeply the relationship that the two had with Elohim before they ate the forbidden fruit and were removed from Paradise.

On the evening before his arrest Yahushua asked the Father for something that is very interesting: *"Esteem me together with yourself, with the esteem which I had with you before the world was"* (Jn 17:5). A common teaching in the church is Jesus existed as God before he gave up his god-ness (without really giving it up, as seen by the miracles he did to prove he was God) and became a god-man. Those who teach this take this verse to mean he was asking to be restored to his God position (although he never really left it). That teaching is a lie from Satan.

Yahushua, as the representative of mankind, was interceding for us. The world of which he was speaking is the world system of fallen man. The world system began when Adam and Ḥawwah sinned and had to leave the Garden. He was praying that mankind be restored to the innocence and relationship with Yahuah that mankind had before the Fall. Because of what Yahushua did—the last Adam who never sinned—this restoration is now possible. What was that relationship? What did it look like?

It looked like the relationship Yahushua had. It was a relationship of total, abandoned obedience arising from total love for the Father, for who and what he is in his character of unconditional selfless love, goodness, righteousness, set-apartness and justice. Before Adam and Ḥawwah sinned they had no conscience, that "voice" that tells you what is wrong. They didn't need a conscience, for they were "in tune" with the will of Yahuah their Elohim. They were one with him—they in him and he in them (Jn 17:21-23). They did only what they saw Yahuah do and said only what they heard him say (Jn 8:28). They were the exact representation of Elohim's nature (Heb 1:3). When he created them they were "very good" (Gen 1:31).

They had their own mind and will to choose; but if they wanted to do something other than what Yahuah wanted, he would tell them. We see an example of this with Yahushua in the Garden of Gethsemane. What he wanted was different from what his Father wanted. And he struggled so hard with the decision to obey that his sweat was as drops of blood falling to the ground (Lk 22:44).

Because of what Yahushua did—dying on the stake for our sins and being raised from the dead and taken to heaven and given all authority over heaven and earth—mankind can be brought to that original state in the Garden. The price, however, is surrender to him.

In this life the closest we can get to that Garden relationship is by living in the spirit: ever getting sin out of our lives, growing to be like him, and fulfilling the works that Elohim created us to do before creation (Ro 8:1-14; Eph 2:10). Although the road is hard, the eternal Garden is more than worth it—Paradise Regained (Ro 8:18).

This was the way it was before the Fall. With that wonderful relationship they had with Yahuah, what happened? Why did they decide to leave it? We return to how it may have been.

As Ḥawwah looks at the tree, she sees that it is good for food, and pleasant to one's eyes, and desirable to make one wise (Gen 3:6). As though in a trance, she reaches out her hand, picks a fruit, and takes a bite. It is juicy, tender and sweet, and its nectar runs down her throat and drips down her chin. "Wow!" she exclaims. "This is *good!*" She picks another fruit and hands it to her man. "Here, you try. It's amazing!"

Adam stands in horror. He has been standing by and has said and done nothing to stop her. Indeed, he is prevented from doing so. She must follow her choice. Even Elohim himself doesn't override our will to prevent us from sinning. Our free will cannot be violated. "Oh, no," he thinks. "My woman, my wife, my love, my life is going to die, and I can't bear the thought of living without her. I'd rather die!" So he takes the fruit and eats (Gen 3:6).

The effect is horrible. The presence of Elohim lifts from them (Mt 27:46), and they feel empty. The horror of what they have done makes them gasp for breath and want to vomit. "Why, why, why did I leave *that* to get *this*?" each is thinking.

Satan, who is in the snake, is gazing with a gloating gleam in his eyes. "Ha, ha, ha," he laughs. "Now, Elohim, they are mine. They have given me, Satan, your enemy, authority over them. I, I Satan, am now their strong one, not you. Ha, ha, ha." Of course, only Elohim and the demons and angels hear him, for he was not speaking through the snake's mouth.

The eyes of both the man and the woman open, and they know that they are naked (Gen 3:7). "We cannot appear this way," he says. "We have to find something to cover ourselves."

"Fig leaves," she says. And they sew fig leaves together and make themselves aprons (Gen 3:7).

Their misery continues, and in the evening, in the cool of the day, they hear the familiar sound of Yahuah Elohim walking toward them. "We have to hide," says Adam. And they hide among the trees to be away from his presence (Gen 3:8).

"Adam," calls Yahuah. "Where are you? (Gen 3:9). Come out where I can see you. And your wife also. Why are you hiding from me?"

They come out and Adam says, "I heard your sound in the garden, and I was afraid, because I was naked; so I hid myself" (Gen 3:10).

"And who told you that you were naked? Did you eat from the tree

I commanded you not to eat?" (Gen 3:11).

"It's not my fault. The woman you gave me, she took from the tree and gave to me, and I ate" (Gen 3:12).

"Are you blaming me? Are you saying it was wrong for me to make for you a helper? You were so happy when I gave her to you, and you enjoyed each other greatly." He doesn't wait for a reply; indeed, Adam is speechless and even more afraid.

Yahuah Elohim turns to the woman. "Tell me, what have you done? Why did you do it?"

"It's not my fault. The serpent deceived me. He said I wouldn't die. So I ate" (Gen 3:13).

"And how did it happen that you were deceived? Why did you believe him over me?" She looks down and doesn't answer, and he continues: "It's because you wanted to be deceived. Deception only comes when the person wants it. You deceived yourself, and the serpent helped you. He is always ready to help people deceive themselves. Never say, 'The devil made me do it.' He has no power over your will. Your will cannot be violated."

She makes no response, and he speaks to the snake. "Because you have done this, you are cursed more than all livestock and every beast of the field. You will go on your belly, and dust will be your food until you are no more. I will put hatred between you and the woman, and between your seed and her seed. Her seed shall crush your head, and you shall crush him on the heel (Gen 3:14-15).

"Woman, your childbirth will be painful, yet you will desire your husband, and he will rule over you (Gen 3:16). He is your head; you must submit to him as to me (Eph 5:22).

"Adam, because you obeyed your wife instead of me, and ate from the tree against my command, the ground is cursed because of you. All the days of your life you will work hard to get food from it. You will have problems with thorns and thistles, and your food will be plants of the field. Sweat will flow from your face because of your labor, and you will eat bread. This will continue until you die and decay into dust: dust you are, and to dust you shall return (Gen 3:17-19).

"You wanted to know why it is called the Tree of the Knowledge of Good and Evil. Before you ate from it you were in direct communication with me all the time. If there was anything I wanted you to do or not to do, I told you. You were depending on me for understanding, not yourself. Now, you do not have that direct communication. So I have given you a conscience. Conscience means 'with knowledge.' This is an inward 'voice' that tells you when something you are doing or thinking of doing is wrong. Before, you didn't need a conscience, because I was the voice. Now you do. But you can harden yourself against that voice. If you keep disobeying your conscience, it's voice becomes weaker and weaker, until finally you have no conscience and are totally evil. Seek me. Keep seeking me. And as you do, I will strengthen your conscience and will again speak to you directly. I will always be as close to you as you want. But you must fight against your flesh nature and keep seeking my nature.

"Because you disobeyed me demon spirits had the right to enter you, demons of insecurity, low self-esteem and pride. That's why, when you ate the forbidden fruit, you were afraid and felt shame and tried to hide from me. You must trust in me with all your heart and not depend on your own understanding. In all your ways acknowledge me, and I will make your paths straight. Do not be wise in your own eyes; fear me and shun evil. This will bring health to your body and nourishment to your bones (Pr 3:5-8).

"Do not despair, you two; there is hope, as you heard when I spoke to the snake. You and the snake are symbols and signs for future generations. The snake is only a lowly animal that Satan, the accuser and enemy of your souls, used to speak to you. It was my will that he choose the snake, for it symbolizes his lowly position. As you have observed when being among the animals, a snake does not eat dust; it's tongue is a means of smelling. And it moves very easily on ground, trees and water. However, it can look like it is eating dust, and that is what Satan does.

"He is a spirit, a totally evil spirit. He wants to destroy you, and he does that by appealing to your flesh nature. Your literal flesh is from the dust, and it will return to the dust. It has no will to choose right or wrong. But it is selfish. It wants only what pleases it. You, your soul, the immortal you, have a will as to whether to obey what it wants or what I want. You were deceived, woman, because you listened to your flesh nature and pushed away my nature.

"All that is in the world, the desire of the flesh, and the desire of the eyes, and the pride of having things, is not of me; it is of the world, the nature of the flesh (1Jn 2:16). That's what you yielded to. That is why you were deceived: your flesh wanted it, and you gave in to it.

"When you are tempted, do not say I am tempting you, for I cannot be tempted by evil, nor do I tempt anyone. But you are tempted when, by your own evil desire, your flesh nature, you are dragged away and enticed. Then, after desire has conceived, it gives birth to sin; and sin, when it is full-grown, gives birth to death (Jam 1:13-15).

"Although I did not say you mustn't touch the fruit, but only said don't eat it, nevertheless, you should not have kept going back to the tree and wondering about it. When you are being drawn to go against my will and break covenant, run *to* me, not *from* me. You wanted to be wise and have knowledge like me, to be as I am. You already had me. You already had my wisdom. You already were as I am. All of this, and more, are in the Tree of Life which you rejected. This is why I had to remove Lucifer from my presence, the highest of my angels, and why he became Satan, the Accuser. We had covenant and a relationship, but he broke it and chose himself over me.

"He accused both of you to me, that he has a right to you because you chose him over me. Whenever you choose yourself over me, you are choosing him, to be like him. This breaks our covenant relationship and is sin. But, as you heard in the curse, although he will harm you, in the end, *you,* one of your descendents, will have the victory over *him.*

"Adam, because your woman was deceived, even though it was by self-deception, she believed she would not die by disobeying me. You, on the other hand, were not deceived (1Ti 2:14). You ate the fruit knowing you would break our relationship and die. This was because your love for her was greater than your love for me. You did not want to live without her. You knew that I could make another helper for you that you could love just as much, and that she would love you just as much, but you didn't want another one. You wanted this one, and this one only, and you would rather die and be apart from me, to not have a relationship with me, than not have her. Your love for her was greater than your love for me. (See Mt 10:37-38.)

"Both of you have sinned grievously. You experienced some of the

63

result when I lifted my presence from you, and you were stricken with remorse and saw your nakedness. But there are other consequences. Adam, one consequence is your seed. All born from your seed will have a weakness in which they have a tendency to sin. No one's sin can be passed to another, for sin is a person's own conscious act of disobeying my law (1Jn 3:4). Your original sin cannot be passed on. But the tendency to sin, the weakness to sin, can and does (Ex 20:5). This is true for your seed, the man; it is *not* true, however, for the woman's seed. That is why her seed, by a virgin birth, four thousand years from now, will destroy Satan's kingdom.

"There is another result. The wages of sin is death, but my gift is eternal life through an offering that I and the woman's seed, the Anointed One, will make (Jn 3:16; 1Jn 4:10; Is 53). Forgiveness is only possible with the shedding of blood (Heb 9:22). The seed of the woman, the last *adam*, a man who will always obey me, will offer to die for you and for all others who follow you into sin. He will do this because he loves you and me and is not willing for any to perish, but that all should come to repentance (1Pe 3:9).

"The fig leaves that you made to cover your nakedness hide nothing. They represent your effort to cover your sins. But there is nothing you can do to atone for your sins. There is no good in you. I alone am good, and you have goodness only as I am in you and you in me. It is my goodness that shines out of your lives, not yours (Ro 7:18).

"Do you see that lamb over there? Make an altar of stones and bring the lamb to me." He then places the lamb on the altar and says, "Notice how trusting it looks at us." And with a quick movement of his hand he cuts its throat and blood spurts out, and keeps coming out until finally it is dead.

Adam and his wife gasp—it was so sudden, so shocking. "The blood of this lamb represents the blood of the last *adam*, the Anointed One, which covers your sins. Your sin did this. This is a consequence of your sin. Without this bloody death, I cannot forgive you. Justice and righteousness demand it. This lamb died in your place. And this practice will continue until the last *adam* sheds *his* blood. He is the lamb that is slain from the creation of the world" (Rev 13:8).

Then he skins the lamb and makes clothing to replace their fig leaves (Gen 3:20). "Your works cannot save you, lest you boast; you are saved by my favor, through your faith in me and what I have done for you. It is my gift to you (Eph 2:8-9). Do you accept it? Do you commit your lives anew to serve me and me only, that I am your only Elohim, your only Strong One? Do you enter the covenant again to have a relationship of obedient love with me? Do you so swear?"

They both kneel and each says, "Yahuah, I acknowledge my sin. It is ever before me. Please forgive me. I have done wickedly. I have broken covenant and our relationship. You are always true, right and just in whatever you do. I have no excuse. I deserve death. But I accept your offering for me, and I plead forgiveness, not on the basis of what I have done, but on the basis of that offering. I commit my life to you in covenant. Cleanse me. Make me a new creation, a creation in you (2Cor 5:17). Thank you. I know you have forgiven me, and from now on I commit myself to always obey you out of love for you, you being my helper."

"I do indeed forgive you," Yahuah says. "You are now my workmanship to do good works which I have prepared in advance for you to do (Eph 2:8). Our relationship is restored, but not at the level it was before you broke it. You must daily maintain this covenant relationship to keep it, even as you had to before you sinned. In my eternal kingdom, when this earth is no more, only those will be with me who will always choose to keep covenant and never break it. Always, of their free will, they will choose to love me.

"I know everything, past, present and future. I knew all this would happen; it did not catch me by surprise. I knew you would fall, and know that all mankind after you will sin. But I also know that the last *adam*, my Anointed One, born of a woman by a seed I create, a virgin birth, will not sin. And I know that he will offer himself for your sins and that of all mankind. He will do this because of his love for me and for you and from his free will. He will always obey my will, not his if it is different from mine (Lk 22:42). It is because of this knowledge that I did this creation.

"You are married, husband and wife. I created marriage to represent me and those who want to be like me. You, husband, represent me in this relationship; and you, wife, represent those who will believe in me and obey me. Believing is obeying. Even as you, wife, came from the side of your husband, so those who believe in me through my son the last *adam* will come from his side, for his side will be pierced in his death. All believers in me through him are my spiritual bride to be my companions throughout eternity. Most will reject me. That is their choice, and they will receive the consequence of their choice. It grieves me beyond your understanding, but it is the only way I can get a bride like me who will always choose me."

Now the man called his wife's name Ḥawwah (life-giving), *because she was the mother of all living* (Gen 3:20).

Satan has been listening, and Yahuah Elohim says to him: "Behold, the man has become like one of us, knowing good and evil (Gen 3:22). That one is you, for you experienced good and now experience evil. I only know good." (Knowing is experiencing.)

Having said this he turns to the man and says, "I cannot allow you to remain in the garden, lest you eat from the Tree of Life and live forever (Gen 3:22). You must go out and cultivate the ground from which you were taken (Gen 3:23). In the garden food was easily available. Now you must grow food from the ground and prepare it to eat. I have given you the wisdom of how to do that. Also, you must make burnt offerings to me of a lamb or goat to atone for your sins as a reminder of the final offering of the coming Anointed One."

So he drove the man out; and at the east of the garden of Eden he stationed the cherubim and the flaming sword which turned every direction to guard the way to the tree of life (Gen 3:24, NAS).

There is a teaching that says when Adam sinned, the authority he received from God over the earth was surrendered to Satan, and thus Satan now has authority over the earth. That teaching is false. Many scriptures show that our Creator owns and controls everything, all the time. Satan can only do what Elohim allows him to do. And the only authority he has in our lives is if we follow him instead of Elohim. He is the strong one of this world system of fallen man, not the strong one over nature and the earth.

A further word needs to be said regarding Ḥawwah being a helper to Adam (Gen 2:18), Adam having the rule over her (Gen 3:16; Eph 5:22), she having painful childbirth, and she desiring him.

This is not—repeat **is not**—referring to a woman's physical and intellectual abilities. The subject is relationship. Yahuah created us as male and female as types of our relationship with him. He is the male figure, and in reference to him all humans are the female figure. He created us, and we are subject to him. Among ourselves, men are a type of the Father and women are a type of the church. That is why wives are to be subject to their husbands. Messiah, although a man, because he never sinned and is the exact representation of the Father, is to us the male figure, and we the assembly, both men and women, are to him the bride.

The emotional makeup of women equips them more so than men to be helpers. They are the mothers, the nurses, the care givers, etc. The downside of this wonderful emotional quality is that these emotions often affect their decision making. Men, being less emotional, tend to be more objective when making decisions. These, however are just general observations. The point is the type. Everything in creation is a type of things spiritual. So let's look at it from that perspective. It is from this perspective that Paul wrote:

Wives, be subject to your own husbands, as to the Master. For the husband is the head of the wife, as Messiah also is the head of the assembly, he the Savior of the body. But as the assembly is subject to Messiah, so also the wives to their husbands in everything (Eph 5:22-24).

Women were created to be the helper of their husbands. A wife is to support him in his goals and they are to operate together as one. As the bride of Messiah, if we love him, we want to support him in his goal, the goal of bringing as many people as possible into the kingdom and to mature them into being his bride. In all that we do, he is the priority in everything. He is our life, even as the husband is to be the priority of his wife. This is not dominance; it is unity.

The wife having pain in childbirth is also a type. A woman becomes pregnant because of the husband putting his seed in her. This is a type of the word of Elohim coming into our lives so that we produce spiritual fruit for him. It is all about him. But producing spiritual fruit for him is painful. It means dying to self that his life may be seen in us, and we walk in obedience to him because of how much we love him. Even as intimacy in marriage produces physical children, so spiritual intimacy with Messiah and the Father with oneness of desire produces spiritual children. The pain in physical childbirth is a type of giving up of self to produce spiritual children.

This goes along with the wife desiring her husband. If she loves him, she wants to have intimacy with him. The husband is ready for intimacy at any time, even as the Father is ready for spiritual intimacy with us at any time.

More can be said on this subject; this writing can only address the general subject.

We move on to Qayin (KAH-yin, Cain) and Hevel (HEH-vel, Abel).

Qayin and Hevel, 4:1

"Am I my brother's keeper?" (Gen 4:9).

SCRIPTURE SAYS LITTLE about how it was when Adam and Ḥawwah left the Garden. With some imagination, this is how it may have been.

When they leave they bring with them various seeds for planting and some sheep and goats. Before, all the animals were herbivores (plant eaters); now, some are carnivores (flesh eaters). The whole of creation is under a curse (Ro 8:19-21).

They settle near a stream, and soon they have a house, a field sown with various seeds, and a pasture for their sheep and goats. The climate is semitropical and very humid, so much so that the evening and night chill give enough dew to water the ground.

One evening, as they are preparing a lamb for an offering to Yahuah, he appears to them. "I am pleased with you," he says, "in that you are making regular offerings on account of your sins and are constantly seeking my face in order to do my will. I am here to inform you of the future, both near and far.

"Soon you will have a son and then other children. You must dedicate and train them in the way they should go (Dt 6:4-9; Pr 22:6). Tell them what happened to you—what you were like before you sinned, and after. Tell them why you offer an animal from time to time, that it is to take away your sins and as a reminder of a descendent, the last *adam*, my Anointed One, who will be the fulfillment of this offering when he offers himself to shed his blood and die for you on a stake, and then to be raised from the dead, having all authority over heaven and earth.

"Adam, I gave you authority over the earth, but when you sinned you gave up that authority. From you will come a rebellious people,

68

wanting their own way, to live as they choose, to change my laws of selfless love and morality to selfish love and immorality, calling light darkness and darkness light, saying that which is good is evil, and that which is evil good (Is 5:20). They are followers of Satan who is their father: 'Like father, like son.' A son has the nature of his father, so they are sons of men, following fallen man's love of darkness. They will develop a world system, and Satan is the strong one (god) of that system (2Cor 4:4).

"Not all, however, will follow him. Some will follow me, and be persecuted for so doing. These are my sons, sons of Elohim, for they have my nature. But many of these will turn away from me, breaking covenant, and become sons of men, just as you did, Ḥawwah, when you were tempted to eat the forbidden fruit. It is a spiritual battle (2Cor 10:4).

"Pray for your children. I love every one of them, though most will hate me and have no relationship with me. Each has free will to follow his choice, whether light or darkness. And each will receive the result of his choice.

"You no longer have access to the Tree of Life in the garden, even though you have access to me. You are spirit-soul beings, immortal beings who will never cease to exist. Your bodies, however, *are* mortal. They will die and return to dust. But your bodies are not you; they are houses in which you live. When your body dies, if at that time you still love me for who I am, my selfless love and goodness, and strive to be like me, and keep covenant with me, then I will take you to live with me in my eternal kingdom and give you new immortal bodies, bodies not like these (1Cor 15:42-49). Those who do not love me and therefore have no covenant relationship with me, when they die they will go to a place of torment, of eternal outer darkness (Mt 8:12). Darkness they love, so to darkness they go.

"I created the earth and universe in six days and rested on the seventh. This represents six thousand years of man's rule on earth with Satan as their father, and one thousand years of my rule with Satan bound (Rev 20:1-3). During my rule, through the last *adam* and those who believe in him, the curse on the earth will be removed and the whole earth will be as it was before you sinned. Animals will no longer be predators and eat flesh, but all will eat vegetation as before and live in harmony with each other (Is 11:1-10). My rule will show them what it would have been like had you and they not sinned. After that one thousand years I will destroy the entire universe with fire (2Pe 3:10-14) and make a new heaven and new earth in which will dwell righteousness forever.

"Until that time comes, however, there will always be war between those who follow their flesh nature and those who follow me in their spirit nature—the flesh first, then the spirit. You, Adam, became a living being; the last *adam* will be a life-giving spirit (1Co 15:45). You do not understand this now, but in time you will.

"There are two kingdoms, the kingdom of light, selfless love and goodness in covenant with me, and the kingdom of darkness, selfishness and wickedness apart from me. This will continue until the last judgment. Choose wisely; choose light; choose goodness; keep covenant." He then departs.

"What does all this mean?" asks Ḥawwah.

"We choose wisely and keep covenant. As for me and my house, we choose Yahuah" (Jos 24:15).

"Adam knew Ḥawwah his wife, and she conceived" (Gen 4:1). ("Knew" refers to intimacy that produces children. When we spiritually "know" Yahuah, we will produce spiritual children.) "Adam," says Ḥawwah, "you're going to be a father." When the time comes she gives birth to a son. "I have acquired a man with Yahuah," she exclaims. "I name him Qayin (acquired). Isn't this exciting?"

Qayin is a delight to them and they are eager for the time when he can be of help on the farm. Soon they have another son, Hevel (breath, wind, temporary). "Why did you name him Hevel?" Adam asks.

"I don't know. Somehow, it just seemed appropriate." They don't know it was prophetic, that he will be the first to die.

The two sons are very different in personalities. Qayin is independent and strong willed, loving to work the land and experiment with varieties of grain and plants. His joy and pride are to watch and nurture the growth of plants, and then show off what he has accomplished. Hevel, on the other hand, is compliant, loving to be with the sheep and goats, leading them to good grazing grounds, and taking care of them and protecting them.

Qayin versus Hevel, flesh-man versus spirit-man; flesh first, then spirit. Keeping sheep is a type of caring for Yahuah's children, farming the ground (in this case) is a type of caring for yourself. First the natural, then the spirit (1Cor 15).

As they are growing up, along with other sons and daughters that come along, their parents tell them what happened to them and why the situation is the way it is. They also have them participate in the regular slaughter offering of lambs to atone for their sin. We don't know how Yahuah showed his acceptance of their offerings. In many verses (e.g. Lev 9:24; Jdg 6:21; 1Ki 18:38; 1Ch 21:26; 2Ch 7:1) we see him showing his acceptance by sending fire, but there are other ways.

In the course of time Qayin and Hevel marry their sisters and have children of their own, who in turn marry their cousins and nieces, and so on, until the extended family becomes very large. As new families form they move away to have their own farms. But Qayin and Hevel stay with "Mom and Dad" as a large family group under Adam, the patriarch. Always Adam gives his history of being created without birth, and tells what happened to them when they sinned.

Over the years Qayin grows more and more resentful that they are only using his brother's labor, the sheep, as offerings. "Isn't what I do good enough for Yahuah?" he keeps thinking. Whenever he would ask his parents about it, they always give the same answer: "Without the shedding of blood there is no forgiveness, and the lamb foretells of a future human offering."

After many years he has had enough. So the next time for making an offering Qayin makes his own altar and puts on it the fruit of the ground. Hevel, as is his practice, brings of the firstlings of his flock and of their fat portions. Yahuah shows acceptance of Hevel's offering, but not Qayin's. Qayin becomes very angry and it shows on his face (Gen 4:1-6). "Why didn't you accept my offering, Yahuah?" he asks. "Why is what I do not good enough for you? You are unfair. What I do is harder work than what Hevel does."

"Why are you angry?" Yahuah replies. "Why are you pouting? You know what I require, and if you do well, will you not smile? (Gen 4:6-7). Is it so hard to use a lamb from your brother? But it's more than the lamb; it is your attitude of heart. (1Sa 15:22; Ps 51:16-17; Am 5:22-24; Mic 6:6-8.) Sin is lying in wait at the door; it wants you, but you must control it (Gen 4:7), and you can (1Cor 10:13). But it requires humility (Is

66:1-3). It requires loving me for what I am in my selfless love and goodness. It requires having a relationship with me through covenant. There is no good in you, nor in your brother, nor in your parents, nor in any created being. There is none that does good, not even one (Ps 14:3; 53:3; Ro 3:12). The only goodness that anyone has is my goodness in them. And to get that means surrendering your will to mine, having a relationship with me through covenant, and giving up your pride. There is nothing in you to be proud of."

Qayin makes a plan. "I am the older, and my way is just as good and even better than my brother's. I cannot bear to see the sight of him—he thinks he's so much better than I am! Well, we'll see." So he says to his brother, with a smile on his face, "Let's go out to the field. I want to show you something." Willingly Hevel goes, and Qayin kills him (Gen 4:8) and buries the body. "Now what do you think of your offerings!? They will ask me where you are, and how should I know?"

By belief, Hevel offered to Elohim a greater offering than Qayin, through which he obtained witness that he was righteous, Elohim witnessing of his gifts. And through it, having died, he still speaks (Heb 11:4).

"Qayin," asks Yahuah, "Where is Hevel your brother?"

"How should I know? I don't keep track of him. Am I my brother's keeper?"

"What have you done? You are a murderer. Your brother's blood is calling out to me from out of the ground. You love to farm. Now, however, you are cursed from the ground, the ground which has opened its mouth to receive your brother's blood from your hand (Mt 23:35). Therefore, when you cultivate the ground, you won't get a harvest. Instead, you will be a vagrant and a wanderer on the earth. As it is in the natural, so it is in the spirit (Gen 4:9-11). In your spirit you will be restless, never being satisfied with life. Such it is with all who reject me and my selfless love and goodness to follow their own selfish ways. The greatest two laws of life are to love me with all your heart, soul, mind and strength and to love your neighbor as yourself. This is my nature, and obeying this puts my nature in you so you can enter into my joy and be fulfilled. For this I created you. This is what it means to have covenant relationship with me. But you in your pride love only yourself and care nothing about others."

Qayin falls to his knees. "My punishment is too great. I can't bear it! You have driven me this day from the face of the ground, the ground that I love. And I will be hidden from your face. I will have to wander on the earth like a vagabond. Everyone will know what I have done, and whoever finds me will kill me" (Gen 4:13-14).

"That's all you think about, yourself! Are you sorry for what you did? No. Do you want to change your behavior? No. All you want to do is prolong your miserable life. You are not willing to accept blame; instead you blame me! You deserve to be killed, but it is mine to avenge; I will repay (Dt 32:35). Therefore whoever kills you, vengeance will be taken on him sevenfold. I have appointed a sign for you, so that no one finding you will kill you. Go!" (Gen 4:15).

Later, Adam asks, "Yahuah, what will happen to him?"

"I know all and see all. I see the whole history of mankind before I created anything. Whatever I do, and allow to be done, works toward my goal of having as many souls as possible to be with me forever in my eternal kingdom (Ro 8:28-29). Even from the wicked some will be born who want to have a relationship with me. I know who they are and will preserve them for me. No one has control over what happens to him, whether good or bad. Each is in control only over how he responds, whether toward selfishness or towards me. No one is able to respond toward me on his own. But I know who will if I help them, and help them I will."

"I am leaving," Qayin tells his parents. "I will make my life elsewhere." So he goes out from the presence of Yahuah, taking his wife and clan with him, and settles in the land of Nod, east of Ěden (Gen 4:16).

"Nod" is pronounced "Node." It means land of wandering. The direction "east" is a type of the world. Adam and Ḥawwah went east, and Qayin went farther east. When you reject Yahuah you go further and further into the way of the world. But Yahuah loves those who follow the world's way; he loves them so much that he provided a way for them to be reconciled back to him and be in covenant relationship with him. (Jn 3:16; 2Cor 5:17-19; Eph 2:8-10.)

When Adam is 130 years old his wife says to him, "Adam, we're having another baby." And in the appointed time a son is born. "I'm calling him Seth (substituted)," she says, "because Elohim has appointed me another offspring in place of Hevel, for Qayin killed him."

Keep in mind that Adam and Ḥawwah had numerous sons and daughters (Gen 5:4). Seth is the third recorded son, the second in the genealogy of the Messiah. But that doesn't necessarily mean that he was the actual third son that Adam had. It appears from what Ḥawwah said (Gen 4:25) that Elohim gave her a revelation that Seth was substituted for Hevel who would have been in the Messianic line had he lived. Adam lived 930 years, and saw all his descendants up until 126 years before the birth of Noaḥ. They all knew his story and the story of Qayin and Hevel.

Seth grows and has a son whom he names Enosh (mortal). At that time he began to call upon the name of Yahuah (Gen 4:25-26; 5:3).

The verb "began" is 3rd person, masculine, singular, indicating a single person, or "people" as a collective singular noun. "Began" indicates something began anew or resumed. Was it Seth who began to call on the name of Yahuah, or people in general? The account doesn't say, but the context indicates it was Seth, for it sets the stage for Chapter 6 in which we see "sons of men" versus "sons of Elohim" (information from JFB Commentary).

"To call" has many meanings, depending on the context. One meaning is to plead aloud for help and mercy because of being in distress, such as when the blind and others called aloud to Yahushua during his ministry. It is a call from faith in his character that he will respond. It can be a call asking for forgiveness because of sin, such as in the sinner's prayer.

Adam is sitting in front of his dwelling with Seth and Enosh when they see a man approaching. "Shalom (peace)," Adam says. "I am Adam the father of Qayin, and this is my son Seth and his son Enosh. Who are you, and what news do you bring? Come, refresh yourself."

"Ah," the stranger replies, "it's good to see you my father and brothers. My name is Yaval, son of Lameḥ, fifth generation from my father Qayin, and son of Adah (ornament), Lameḥ's first wife. I do not live in the city, but rather dwell in tents and move about with my sheep and goats. All my children do the same. I do have news. You know that my father, Qayin, settled in Nod and built a city and named it after his firstborn, Ḥanoḥ (Enoch).

"Well, a young man got into a fight with my father. In the fight the young man wounded my father and my father killed him. He is afraid about what others might do to him as a result, even as our father Qayin was, that they would seek to kill him in revenge. Qayin was given a sign from Yahuah that whoever killed him would be avenged seven-fold. Since that was the case with him, my father said he will be avenged seventy-sevenfold if anyone kills him" (Gen 4:17-24).

"This is indeed sad news," Adam responds. "I fear things will get worse among my descendents. I am always regretting and repenting for what I did in the garden when I ate the forbidden fruit. I used to wonder what would have been the result if I had not, whether every-one would be living in peace and in the presence of Yahuah as my wife and I were doing before we broke covenant. But Yahuah remind-ed me that we all have free will to obey or disobey, and even if we had not disobeyed, others would. So he withheld my wife from conceiving until after we sinned, which he knew, in his foreknowledge, that we would. It is I who must bear the shame of being the father of all sin-ners, for all born of my seed carry a tendency toward sin, and all follow that tendency and indeed do sin (Ro 3:23). There is none who does good, not one (Ps 14:1-3; 53:1-3; Ro 3:10-19). But, he has assured me, one will be born from a woman, a virgin, the seed of my wife, one who will be like me before I sinned, one not born of my tainted seed, who will always obey his Father, Yahuah, and be the savior of mankind. In this I take hope. What more news have you? How is it going with my first-born's clan?"

"We are very industrious, inventing new things all the time. My brother, Yuval is very musical, and his children are also, particularly in playing the lyre and pipe. I have a half-brother from my father's second wife, Tsillah. His name is Tuval-Qayin. He and his children make all sorts of things from bronze and iron" (Gen 4:21-22).

"I fear for you," says Adam. "Qayin murdered his brother because he was jealous and angry that Yahuah didn't accept his offering. Instead of repenting, he left with his clan. What is your clan doing now in the way of offerings?"

Yabal smiles. "You know the history. After all, it's been over two hundred years since that event. You offer to Yahuah, who rejected him. So he started his own religion, offering to the moon, sun and stars. They are the real strong ones (elohim). They rule the day and the night and the seasons. It is from them that we get our wisdom to do, invent and prosper. It is by them that we are becoming giants in ability (Gen 6:4). To honor them we have made statues of animals, and even combinations of man and animals. And on their altars we burn grain, for it is they who make the grain grow."

The Nephilim (KJV giants) *were on the earth in those days—and also afterward—when the sons of God* (followers of Elohim) *went to the daughters of men* (followers of false elohim) *and had children by them. They were the heroes of old, men of renown* (Gen 6:4, NIV).

Who or what were these Nephilim? (Strong's #5303). Commentators and Hebrew dictionaries give various ideas. The root meaning is "those who fell." Who fell? Some interpret it to mean the angels who fell from heaven, and that these spirit beings took physical form and mated with human women and produced a race of giants. Such activity, however, is impossible. Although angels and demons can manifest themselves in physical form and cause physical things to happen, they are spirit beings and have no seed to propagate. Only Elohim who created man can create seed and cause conception; that seed was a human seed so that Miriam (Mary) could conceive without a husband, and her son (Yahushua) would not have the fallen seed of Adam. (See Book One of this series: Yahushua Messiah, the Last Adam.)

Another interpretation is aliens from outer space visited earth and mated with humans. Evidence given for this is the pagan myths of giants and their grotesque idols; but all these are inspired by demons. This also is impossible. Only the earth was created to be inhabited (Is 45:18). Further, beings of different animal families cannot procreate; e.g. a dog and a cat cannot produce a "cog" or a "dat." It is true that mules come from the mating of horses with donkeys, but they cannot reproduce more mules; all they can do is get a horse or a donkey if they mate with such.

The interpretation that fits with the context and all of scripture is the most common one (e.g. Clark's Commentary) and is used in this book. "Daughters of men" refers to those who follow false elohim, and "sons of God" refers to those who follow the true Elohim.

"Let me tell you of Na'amah (beautiful),"Yaval continues, "sister of Tuval-Qayin. As is the meaning of her name, so is she. And she makes herself even more beautiful by the use of cosmetics and jewelry. She makes and sells these things for all the women, and it makes them all more beautiful. Come visit us and you will see. In fact, your women will want to do the same" (Gen 4:17-24).

Yaval stays with them a few days and observes their style of living. "So plain," he thinks. "But, to each his own."

On one of the days Seth asks him, "You dwell in tents and raise sheep and goats as do we. Do you offer your animals to your strong ones, or only grain?"

"Yes. We also offer animals."

After he leaves, Adam calls a meeting of the elders. "Men," he says, "we have a serious problem. Seth will explain it to you."

"As you are aware," Seth begins, "Yaval, the fifth generation from Qayin, visited us and shared with us what Qayin's clan is doing. I will not go into details—many of you know them already—except regarding their religion. Yahuah is the only true Strong One, the Maker of this world and everything in it. He made the sun and moon and stars (Ac 17:28). He made the seasons and brings water for our crops and livestock. It is in him that we live and move and have our being (Ac 17:28). It is to him that we make our animal and produce offerings. We have sinned, and this is the means to atone for our sins, if with those offerings we humble ourselves before him and seek to be like him in his selfless love and goodness, for it is by this that we keep covenant with him. He created us to love him with all our heart, soul, mind and strength, and our neighbors as ourselves (Mk 12:30-31). This law is written in our hearts. It is part of our creation. When we do this, we are true sons of the Strong One; it is by this we have a relationship with him. Failing to do this breaks covenant and our relationship with him."

He pauses, and they all nod their agreement.

"But we are in danger," he continues. "Too often we have just been going through the motions of making offerings without loving him for who he is. Offerings without humbling ourselves before him and repenting of our sins are worthless. He does not accept them, and he hates it. We are no better than Qayin. So I call upon you to repent, and for you to call upon your families to repent. It is time to return to Yahuah and call aloud upon his name, his character of who he is in beauty, righteousness and truth, and to repent of our sins and beg for mercy. I tell you, now is the time of Elohim's favor, now is the day of salvation (1Cor 6:2).

"Qayin has made a new religion, a religion of bowing to the sun, moon and stars and animals and making offerings to them. He has rejected the true Strong One and made his own, false ones, and his descendants are following him. They are following what their flesh nature wants instead of what Yahuah wants. And we are in danger of doing the same. So again I say, let us call on the name of Yahuah. Those who follow their flesh nature are sons of men. We who follow Yahuah are sons of Elohim. Let us be true examples of sons of Elohim, of those who are in covenant."

At that time they began to call on the name of Yahuah (Gen 4:26).

This is the book of the genealogy of Adam. In the day that Elohim created man, he made him in the likeness of Elohim (Gen 5:1).

What is the likeness of Elohim? When we look at the traits of man we see we have logic, we think, we reason, we love, we have relationships, we rule, we create, we have free will, we are moral beings with a sense of right and wrong, we are spiritual beings (our physical bodies are the houses we live in), and we are immortal; that is, we never cease to exist. In this we differ from Elohim, for we have a beginning, whereas he always exists and never had a beginning.

We now continue with "how it may have been."

III. NOAḤ TO AVRAM
Genesis 6-11

But Noaḥ found favor in the eyes of Yahuah.
Genesis 6:8

Noaḥ, 6-10

Noaḥ GETS UP EARLY and goes to his private place of prayer. This is his favorite time, for it is quiet, both inside the house and out. Soon the bustle of the day—the sounds of his wife fixing breakfast and of people going to work—would begin. He has a construction company and is prospering in it, his three sons helping him plus some employees. But his heart is heavy because of the wickedness around him. He always begins his prayer time by praising Yahuah and thanking him for his presence and taking care of him and his family. Then he asks forgiveness for himself and his family for any sins committed (e.g. Job 1:5). And finally he intercedes for the rest of mankind, his numerous relatives, who are deep in sin.

"Yahuah, my Father," he prays, "I am in deep grief because of the wickedness I see around me: murder, robbery, prostitution, gangs, wars, rape, domestic abuse, sexual harassment, promiscuity, living together without marriage, exchanging spouses, homosexuality, lesbianism, changing gender identity, bisexualism, marriages between persons of the same sex, abortion, and no shame for their wickedness, but rather attacking those who say their actions are evil.

"In the time of my father, Seth, people were beginning to repent and call upon you (Gen 4:26). They were crying out to you, repenting of their sin and turning to you in righteousness and keeping covenant. They were your sons (Gen 6:2; Ro 8:14). But they soon fell away. They saw the daughters of men, their beauty with all their alluring clothes and makeup, and they lusted after them and bound themselves together with them in marriage (Gen 6:2), a thing which ought not to be done, for light can have no fellowship with darkness (2Cor 6:14). They were mixing Seth's seed with Qayin's seed, and they themselves have

79

become lovers of darkness. They know what happened to our father and mother, Adam and Ḥawwah, when they sinned, but they don't care. They love the pleasure of their flesh rather than the pleasure of knowing and serving you. Famous men, men who accomplished great things, have come from their unions, but not famous in your eyes (Gen 6:4).

"My father, Ḥanoh (Enoch), seventh from creation, tried to turn the hearts of the people back to their Maker. He was walking with you in everything he did and said, always doing what pleases you (Heb 11:5), being an example of your goodness and selfless love and what it means to be in covenant. Instead of listening, however, they mocked him, and wanted to kill him because they hated his message of right-eousness. He told them that you are coming with untold thousands of your set-apart angels to judge everyone, and to convict all the souls of all the rebellious acts they have done in the rebellious way, and of all the harsh, rebellious words they have spoken against you. He told them they are grumblers and faultfinders, that they follow their own evil desires and boast about themselves and flatter others for their own advantage (Jude 14-16). But before they could carry out their desire, because of your great love for him, you took him. He disap-peared (Gen 5:24). They looked for his body, but could not find it. They knew it was you who did it, yet they did not repent, but rather continued in ever greater wickedness.

"Yahuah, my Strong One, what can be done to turn them from their wickedness and back to you? It is evident within them of who you are, your invisible attributes, your eternal power, and your nature of being the only true Strong One. They see it in the creation all around them and understand, so they have no excuse. Even so, they do not honor you as the Strong One or give thanks, but rather have become futile in their speculations, and their foolish hearts are darkened. Professing to be wise, they have became fools, and exchanged the esteem of you who are incorruptible for images in the form of corruptible man and of birds and four-footed animals and crawling creatures (Ro 1:18-23). Help me, my Strong One, to understand."

"Noah," responds Yahuah, "you are righteous before me (Gen 6:9), and I have a plan for you, a task which will take many years. As to this wicked generation, I have given them over in the lusts of their hearts to impurity, so that they would dishonor their bodies, for they exchange the truth about me for a lie, and bow to and serve the creature rather than the Creator. For this reason I have given them over to degrading passions; for their women to exchange the natural function for that which is unnatural, and in the same way also the men to abandon the natural function of the woman and burn in their desire toward one another, men with men committing indecent acts, and men and women, even boys and girls, changing their gender identities to the other and not acknowledging their birth gender. By so doing they are receiving in their own persons the due penalty of their error.

"And just as they do not see fit to acknowledge me any longer, I have given them over to a depraved mind, to do those things which are not proper, being filled with all unrighteousness, wickedness, greed, evil; full of envy, murder, strife, deceit, malice; gossips, slanderers, haters of me their Maker, insolent, arrogant, boastful, inventors of evil, disobedient to parents, without understanding, untrustworthy, unloving, unmerciful; and although they know my law in their hearts, that those who practice such things are worthy of death, they not only do the same, but also strongly approve of those who practice them and condemn as bigots those who disagree (Ro 1:18-32).

"You have seen this, and it grieves you. It grieves you, because it grieves me. In a manner of speaking, I am sorry that I ever created man, and it grieves me in my heart (Gen 6:6). But I saw all this from the beginning, ever before I began creation. I love them, because I am love. I have put in the heart of every man and woman that same love—it is my nature within them. Because of my love within them, they are able, with my help, to exercise that same love in response to me and to others. But I have given free will. Each must choose whom and what to love—themselves in selfishness, or me in selfless covenant.

"I cannot continue to allow mankind to go in the direction they are going. I see that the wickedness of man is great on the earth, and that every intent of the thoughts of his heart is only evil continually (Gen 6:5). I look on the earth and see it is corrupt, that all flesh has corrupted their way upon the earth, although there are some I have kept for myself. Therefore I will start over so that the promised seed of the woman will continue and the future Messiah will be born. All of this is in preparation for him.

"Noaḥ, you have found favor in my eyes. You are a righteous man, blameless in your time. You are walking with me, just as Ḥanoḥ (Enoch) did. Ḥanoḥ was a prophet, as are you, and I, Adonai Yahuah, do nothing unless I reveal my secret counsel to my servants the prophets (Am 3:7). I am about to bring a flood of water to cover all the earth to blot out man whom I have created from the face of the land, from man to animals to creeping things and to birds of the sky, everything that has breath. I will begin over again from you, your wife, and your three sons and their wives.

"You will make an ark* (Gen 6:14), a vessel large enough to hold you and your family, plus a pair of each kind of unclean animal and seven pairs of each kind of clean animal,** and the necessary supply of food to sustain you all for a year and to begin again when you leave the ark. You are a carpenter, and I will give you the plans. You have one hundred twenty years to complete the ark (Gen 6:3). At that time I will bring the animals to you. When you and all the animals have entered the ark, I will close the door and begin the flood.

> *The Hebrew word used here for *ark* is *tebah*. It is used only twice: for the ark of Noaḥ, and for the basket in which Mosheh was hidden. In both cases persons were rescued from water. The Hebrew word for *ark* in the "ark of the covenant" is *aron* (aw-ROAN). It means a box. A better translation, to show the difference in the Hebrew, is "box of the covenant."
>
> **The law regarding clean and unclean animals was not given until the Exodus at Mount Ḥorěv (Horeb). But Noaḥ knew about it. Clean animals are those that chew the cud and have a divided hoof, like cows, sheep, goats and deer. All others are unclean (Dt 14:4-8).

"During the time of building, you will be a sign and a testimony to this wicked generation. They will see you building the ark and mock you. When they ask why you are doing it, you will proclaim to them righteousness and the need to repent and turn to me in loving covenant and change their ways. You will tell them the ark is to protect you from my judgment that is coming on them, that it is because you live a life of loving obedience to me that I, Yahuah, the only true Strong One, am protecting you from the flood. But they will not believe you. They will be marrying and giving in marriage and partying as though nothing will happen to them (Mt 24:38). But when the flood comes, and they see the water rising on the ground, and rushing and foaming around them, and their houses and all their works being swept away, they will cry out for help, but no help will come. (See Mt 25:6-12, parable of 10 virgins.) They have chosen what has come upon them because of their rebellion against me, and receive the result of their actions.

"Only the eight of you will be spared. However, many, as the flood is overtaking them, will repent from their disobedience and turn to me and be mine (1Pe 3:18-22).

"I tell you a mystery. All of this happening is a prophecy of the future. In the latter days it will be like this again, wicked people endeavoring to destroy my people, people who are declaring righteousness and calling for repentance, to rescue as many as possible before I destroy them. But, just as I took Ḥanoḥ, I will take my people to be with me. He is a sign of that latter time, as are you.

"I tell you another mystery. Numbers have meaning. Everything I do and cause to happen and allow to happen has meaning. The number one represents me, for I, Yahuah your Elohim, am one, my nature is one; I alone, the Father of all mankind, am he. There is no other besides me (Dt 32:39; Is 44:8; 45:6; Is 47:8,10). Man in his wickedness has made many elohim, and have bowed down to them and made offerings to them, and even have claimed that they are who I am.

"One also represents unity with me in an intimate relationship, so that those who love me move and operate in harmony with my will. A husband and wife are one when they live together in unity and keep covenant with each other, ever growing in a deeper relationship. I created marriage to be an example of that relationship and covenant with me. You are one with me, because I have found you righteous in this generation (Gen 7:1), and you love my goodness and do my will.

"Six is the number of man, for on the sixth day of creation I created man. Six thousand years I give to man to rule on earth and follow his ways. It will end in disaster, even as this flood I am now bringing will bring destruction on all that breathe.

"Seven also has meaning. It is the number of spiritual completeness. I completed my creation in six days, and Ḥanoḥ (Enoch), the seventh from creation, was complete, the way I created man to be. So I took him without his dying. He represents the last-day completed bride that I will take to me (called the rapture). On the seventh day I rested; that represents my rule on the earth with my anointed son and my bride for one thousand years before the end.

"The number eight represents new beginnings. After the flood, you eight will be the beginning of man on the earth again. Eight also represents the beginning of life on the new heaven and new earth in which only righteousness dwells (2Pe 3:13).

"Ten represents completeness in this world. You are the tenth generation from creation. You mark the completeness of this period of mankind."

"Yahuah," asks Noah, "what about Methuselah son of Ḥanoḥ, and Lameḥ, son of Methuselah and my father? Will they perish also?"

"You know their lives, how they have become lukewarm toward me" (Rev 3:14-22).

After finishing his prayer time and breakfast, Noah calls his wife, three sons and their wives together. "I have news for you," he says. "This morning when I recounted to Yahuah how wicked mankind have become, he spoke to me. He said he will judge this wicked generation. He will bring a flood that will cover all the earth, and that flood will destroy all mankind and all animals that breathe. The turbulence of the flood and eruptions from the earth will be so great that all evidence of man's existence on earth will be gone. The bodies of man and animals will be ripped apart, and fish will eat the flesh, and water will dissolve the bones. It will be as though they never were, not a trace left. All that will remain is our memories of them as a warning against sin and its resultant judgment."

*Some believe that the great pyramids of Mitsrayim (Egypt) were built before the flood and are evidence of that pre-flood civilization.

There is quite a reaction to this information, and after they become quiet he continues. "There will be a remnant that escape the judgment. We, the eight of us, will escape. Everyone else will perish. Yahuah our Strong One will start over again with us. He told me to build an ark, a vessel large enough to hold us and a pair of each kind of animal. He will bring the animals to us on the day the flood begins, and we are to store provisions to feed all of us and the animals for a complete year. We also must bring some farming equipment and tents and seed for planting. When the flood is over, we will repopulate the earth."

After a period of silence at this news, his wife asks, "What is a flood?"

"Yahuah will cause water to burst up from the ground and to fall from the sky. All the land will be covered with water. No human or animal that breathes will survive. We have one hundred twenty years to complete the ark. He has given me the directions for building it, and we need to start right away."

"What about our business?" asks his firstborn, Yafeth (Japheth), (enlargement). "How will we live?"

"We have enough employees to keep the business going and provide for us an income. One of them will be the foreman; several are qualified. However, Yahuah is our provider. (See Gen 22:8-14, Avraham offering Yitsḥaq.) Our trust and hope is in him, not in what we or anyone else do. The vessel will be big, very big. And we have never built anything that needs to survive things we cannot even imagine. But I have the plans, and he will give us the wisdom and skill to build it."

"I suppose it means cutting down a lot of trees, then sawing them into lumber, and then shaping them," says his third son, Ḥam (khawm, hot).

"What do you suppose people will say?" asks his second son, Shĕm (Shem, name).

"They already think we're crazy, because we do not join them in their revelry and wickedness. The ways of Yahuah are different from the ways of the world. That is why he is judging them and preserving us. Also, when they come to mock and ask questions, we will call them to repent and save themselves from this wicked generation and from judgment. But, they won't. Only the eight of us will be in the ark when the flood comes. Then it will be too late."

Word of what they are doing spreads rapidly across the land: seven billion people, and still rapidly growing.

The number seven billion is based on length of life then and fertility now, the same number on earth today (Lk 17:26; 1Pe 3:20). At that time the land was one continent. We do not know what forms of communication or travel they had, for they and all their civilization were destroyed by the flood. In summary, Elohim wanted nothing of man to remain. A world-wide flood, such as at the time of Noah, would accomplish that.

See http://www.christiananswers.net/q-aig/aig-c014.html.

"Noah," says Methuselah one day, "what are you doing? You're crazy. You are making a spectacle of yourself. You're hearing voices and believe Yahuah is talking to you. You're giving our family a bad name. What do you mean by rain? How can there be a flood?"

"Judgment is coming. You know Yahuah is righteous and hates sin. You see the wickedness around you. Repent, and get right with Yahuah."

This is Noah's response and that of his sons and their wives. People come to stare and make fun. To them, it is a carnival. (Carnival means festival of flesh.) Vendors come and set up tents to sell food and souvenirs. It is a great tourist attraction.

The ark is nearing completion, but there is still much to do, when Methuselah comes again. "Noah," he says, "Lameh, your father and my son, has died. He has been failing for some time, and finally he passed away. Come, you and your family, for we must gather at my house and have a time of mourning, and then bury him."

"Let this be a sign to you," replies Noah, compassion in his eyes, "that I and my family will not come. There are only five years left to finish the ark (based on the chronology in Genesis), and it will take all that time to finish. Let the dead bury their dead (Mt 8:22), for as my father is, so are they. They have been hearing the call to repentance these 115 years, and they have turned a deaf ear, as have you. In five short years all will be destroyed in judgment from the Almighty. You say, 'What is rain, and where is it? Show us that we may believe.' Even if water were to fall from the sky now, you would not believe. But in five years it will fall, and water will burst up from the deep. But then it will be too late.

"You, my grandfather, will die in that flood.* You are a sign to a future generation when it will be the same as this, eating and drinking and partying and marrying as though no judgment will come, when suddenly it does come (2Pe 3:3-14). They won't believe it, as it is with you, until it is too late. You are lukewarm, and he will vomit you out of his mouth and those like you (Rev 3:14-22, the church of Laodicea).

*The account doesn't say Methuselah died *when* the flood began, just that he died *in* the year the flood began, based on the chronology. However, it fits with typology that he died *when* the flood began. Some commentators, however, say he was a believer.

"I represent believers in Yahuah and in his Anointed One in that time who do repent and who proclaim righteousness and who call others to repent and join them. They are the last day body of believers who will be taken suddenly from the earth, as was our father Ḥanoḥ (Enoch), and not see death and not receive the judgment. They are the bride of Yahuah and of his anointed son. And we who believe in him and have died will rise from the dead and join them and be together with them and with our Father in heaven forever (1Th 4:13-18). Although I will not die in this flood, I will eventually die, and then rise in the last day.

"You want me to take time off from my work for Yahuah because of family. My family are those who do the will of my Father in heaven (Mk 3:32-35). In five years it will be over. Five is the number of favor. You and everyone else have five more years in which to repent" (2Cor 6:2).

The ark was 300 cubits long (450 ft, 137.16m), 50 cubits wide (75 ft, 15.24m), and 30 cubits high (45 ft, 13.716m) (Gen 6:13-15). This is large enough to hold a pair of every "kind" (Family) of animal (Gen 1:21,25).

The conversion to feet is based on the standard of 1 cubit = 18 inches, or 1½ ft.; that is, the length of the human forearm, from the tip of the middle finger to the elbow. This, of course, varies from person to person. The Ark replica built by the Ark Encounter in Kentucky, USA, uses the Nippur Cubit of 20.4 in., or just over 1.7 feet per cubit, making the ark about 510 ft. (155.5m) long.

The remaining five years go by quickly, and the ark is completed.

Then Yahuah says, "Noaḥ, it is time for you and your household to enter the ark. You have remained faithful and completed the task I gave you. You are my faithful servant (Mt 25:21,23), and have been righteous before me in this time (Gen 7:1). I am bringing to you, even now, the animals and birds to be protected in the ark, so that they may reproduce and fill the earth again. As they reproduce they will adapt into a great variety of species.*

*http://amazingdiscoveries.org/C-deception-gene_variation_species_kind

"You will guide them into their respective stalls, and the carnivores will be content to eat fodder. You will keep the interior clean by use of the discharge vents, and the air vents will keep the air fresh. The storm will be severe, causing the vessel to rise and drop and turn about with the waves, often suddenly, with waves crashing over the top. The wind will howl in its fury. But you and your cargo of animals will be safe and healthy. I will protect you. I am your covering. Trust me. You have been experiencing persecution while building the ark. This represents the last day persecution on those who are mine, my bride, before I take them to be with me (in the rapture). The flood, however, represents the judgment that follows that event. (The seven years of tribulation.)

"Just seven more days (Gen 7:4), then you enter the ark and I break open the earth to spew forth water and I send the rain. Seven is the number of spiritual completeness. You are complete when you enter the ark. The ark represents my future son, whom I have known from the beginning, who, through his death for your sins, will be the means of salvation for all who believe in him and commit their lives to him in loving obedience. He is the radiance of my esteem and the exact representation of my being (Heb 1:3), for he has my spirit without limit (Jn 3:34). In him reside all the seven attributes of my spirit (Rev 1:4; 3:1; 4:5; 5:6): set-apartness, wisdom, understanding, counsel, might, knowledge and the fear of me. He will love to fear me (Is 11:2).

"I will send rain on the earth forty days and forty nights. Forty is the number of testing. You will be tested during this time as to your faith in me and love for me."

When all the animals are in and settled, Noaḥ and his family enter also. Yahuah closes the door, and the earth erupts with water and rain begins. After they are settled in their quarters Noaḥ's wife calls the family to a meal. After they finish eating she says, "Wait, I have a surprise." She goes back to the kitchen and brings out a cake and says, "Happy birthday, my husband. Today you are 600 years old" (Gen 7:6).

"So I am," he says. "Time goes by quickly when you're busy with Yahuah's work. Just 120 years ago we started this project, and now it's finished. It has been hard. We have endured much opposition and mocking. But it was worth it. We are safe from the storm and flood that is now beginning, and we will begin a new life and a new generation. All future mankind will come from us. We must do our best not to repeat the wickedness that has brought this judgment. I feel sorry for all the others, for they will surely drown. The flooding from rain and the fountains of the deep will last forty days in which the entire earth will be covered in water. This vessel will be our home for a year. But we have work to do to keep us busy. We have the care of the animals and the responsibility of keeping everything clean."

The drumming of the rain on the roof and sides, the howling of the wind, and the crashing thunder drowns out any other outside noise. If any were crying for help and pounding on the vessel to let them in, they couldn't hear it. When the water becomes deep enough for the ark to float, they can feel it starting to move, and soon it is moving about like a cork on rough seas. By this time everything has been put away and secured so as not to fall from the shelves and cupboards. Some of the animals protest, but soon are quiet. Elohim is in charge.

I with my family were on one of the last trips of the Queen Mary traveling from England to New York through the North Atlantic during a storm, traveling at about 35 mph (56 km/h). That ship was over twice the size of the ark. The wind was so strong that ropes were strung for people to hold onto when on deck, if any dared to go out. The swimming pool, of course, was closed. Our berth was in the bow near sea level. Because of levelers the ship didn't rock from side to side, but just bow and stern up and down vertical as it rose and fell while plowing through the enormous waves. I remember waking up with the feeling of forever rising up, up, up, and then forever falling down, down, down. Nurses came around to help those, myself included, who were experiencing sea sickness. The ark, in contrast, had no power; it just floated as the wind and waves, and

89

Elohim, guided it. I leave it to the reader to imagine what it might have been like.

For forty days and nights rain pours from the sky and waters gush from the deep, and then stops, and the waves cease. The whole earth is now a water world, the shallowest fifteen cubits deep (22½ ft; 6.959m) (Gen 7:20). And it stays that level for 150 days (Gen 7:24). Then the flood begins to subside. An east wind blows, mountains rise, valleys and ocean floors sink, and the water drains into the ocean, causing immense canyons (such as the Grand Canyon) (Ps 104:6-9). The ark finally rests on the mountains of Ararat, two and a half months later tops of mountains become visible, and forty days later Noaḥ opens a window and sends out a raven, but it doesn't return (Gen 8:6-7). It can feed on any seeds and dead flesh, and rest on flotsam. Then he sends out a dove which does return, for it found no place to rest. Seven days later (spiritual completeness) he sends it out again, and it comes back with a freshly picked olive leaf (Gen 8:11). Trees and vegetation are recovering rapidly. Another seven days later he sends it out again, and it doesn't return.

The ark is a type of Yahushua who died for our sins and rose again, providing our salvation The dove represents the set-apart spirit which was given at Pentecost, and the olive tree represents the assembly that came into being as a result.

Finally, Elohim says, "Noaḥ, now is the time to leave." So Noaḥ opens the stalls and cages and leads the animals out, with his family following (Gen 8:15). The animals disperse, all except some ceremonially clean animals and birds, as well as work animals. Then Noaḥ builds an altar to Yahuah, and takes of every clean animal and of every clean bird and offers burnt offerings on the altar (Gen 8:20).

"Noaḥ and sons," says Elohim, "this is my blessing upon you as you start the new family of mankind. Be fruitful, multiply, fill the earth. I have put the fear of you on every animal and bird along with every creeping thing on the ground and all fish of the sea. Formerly, you ate only vegetation, now I give every moving thing to eat, but not the blood in it, for life is in the blood. An animal has to die for you to eat its flesh, a reminder that your sin brought death. Whoever sheds man's blood, however, by man his blood will be shed, for I made man in my image (Gen 9:1-6).

"I now establish my covenant with you and your seed after you, and with every living creature that came out of the ark. This is the covenant, that I shall never again bring a flood like this to destroy life on the earth (Gen 9:9-10). It is a covenant for all successive generations until the earth is no more (2Pe 3:10). The sign is my bow in the cloud, and whenever the bow appears, it is a remembrance to me of the covenant between me and the earth."

"We need to locate a good place to farm," Noaḥ says to his family, "and start raising food." They bring out the farming equipment, tents and the remaining food from the ark, load up the carts, hitch up the two donkeys and two horses, and set off. They find their way down the mountain slope into a suitable valley, set up tents, and begin farming.

Commentaries give varying explanations of why Noaḥ cursed Kena'an (Canaan) instead of Ham. What follows is my choice among them, given in narrative form.

Some years later an embarrassing event happens (Gen 9:20-27). By now his sons have grown children, one of them named Kena'an (Canaan, lowly), fourth son of Ham. Grapes are among their many crops, and when harvest time comes they press out the juice and make wine. Noaḥ drinks too much of it and becomes drunk and, not knowing what he is doing, uncovers himself inside his tent. When he wakes up from his stupor he sees that a garment has been laid on him and he is naked under it. "What have I done?" he wonders. "And who placed this garment over me?" He dresses himself and calls his sons.

"Sons," he says, "I got drunk and fell asleep, and when I awoke, I was naked with a garment over me. Who saw me naked? Yafeth, you're the oldest (Gen 10:1). You tell me what you know about it."

After a moment's hesitation, he replies, "Ham saw you naked in the tent and joked about it to Shĕm and me. So as not to see you that way, and so no one else would, we held the garment on both our shoulders and walked backward, and laid it on you."

"Thank you, Yafeth, and you also, Shĕm. You have shown respect and I honor you for it. But you, Ham, have shown disrespect. This seems to be your character, and I see it in your sons, and especially in your youngest, Kena'an.

91

"I am a prophet of Yahuah Elohim, the Almighty, Elyon (the Most High), maker of heaven and earth. He told me of things to come. He said he would bring a flood to destroy all flesh that breathe, except those he would preserve in the ark in order to populate the earth again. This happened because of gross sin among mankind, that the thoughts of all men were evil continually. Eight of us he kept alive, and that was because he found me to be righteous. You know this. You helped build the ark and saw it all. We are the new people on the earth now, and we have begun to repopulate it. From us will come as many people as there were before the flood. And wickedness will increase the same way until he again brings an end.

"The spirit of prophecy is on me regarding the future of your descendants. You are my only sons, and from you will come three branches of humanity.

"Cursed is Kena'an; a servant of servants he shall be to his brothers. Blessed is Yahuah, the Elohim of Shĕm; and let Kena'an be his servant. May Elohim enlarge Yafeth, and let him dwell in the tents of Shĕm; and let Kena'an be his servant" (Gen 9:26).

Many sources discuss the dispersion of the nations from the three sons of Noaḥ. That detail, however, is not a part of this work. In general, Europeans are from Yafeth (Japheth). Through Shĕm's seed comes the nation of Yisra'ĕl and the Messiah. Dwelling in the tents of Shĕm represents the "wild olive tree" gentiles being grafted into Yisra'ĕl, the "cultured olive tree," through belief in and obedience to Yahushua Messiah (Ro 11:13-24).

Satan

"You said in your heart, 'I will ascend into the heavens; I will raise my throne above the stars of the Strong One, and I will sit on the mount of the assembly in the recesses of the north. I will ascend above the heights of the clouds; I will make myself like Elyon (the Most High)'" (Is 14:13-14). (See also Eze 28:11-19.)

"WHAT ARE OUR PLANS NOW, SATAN? Mankind is starting over again." This from one of his chief demons.

"You saw what we did before the flood," Satan replies. "Their Strong One failed. That's why he brought the flood. His ally Seth was not able to turn the people around, nor was Ḥanoḥ (Enoch), and nor was Noaḥ. All those bodies in the flood died, but their souls are in torment in Sheol (Gk *Hades*, Lk 16:23) awaiting their final judgment to be sent to Gehenna (Lk 12:5), the place prepared for us, a place of eternal fire and outer darkness away from the presence of Elohim (Mt 25:41). We don't want the presence of Elohim: we hate him, and so do the people following us.

"Do you think mankind is any different now just because they have started over? We have the advantage. Man loves his flesh nature. He loves being in charge of his own life, as do we. With arms wide open they welcome us to come into their lives and increase their selfish desires and pride. We give them a feeling of control when they hate others and refuse to forgive.

"We don't care how they live, so long as it isn't according to what Elohim wants. They can be good and compassionate toward others, helping others in need, relieving sickness and poverty, and many good works, and they have warm, pleasant feelings for doing so; but if in their hearts it doesn't come from Elohim, they are still mine, for it is from selfishness, pride and good feelings.

"We will raise up rulers who will be ruthless and cruel; and people will follow them, for they have the same heart as have we. When they reject those rulers, we will give them others. And when they throw off their bondage and try to rule themselves by majority vote, we will turn those democracies into the tyranny of the majority, crushing all who won't go along with their wickedness.

"They will say that their Creator has given them an inalienable right to life, liberty and the pursuit of happiness, ideas which we will put into their selfish minds, whereas he has given them no such thing. All he gives is slavery to him and suffering, in the hope of getting a better life after death. Well, we give them suffering: suffering if they follow him, and suffering if they follow us. But they get fleshly pleasure when they follow us.

"Three branches of humanity will come from the three sons of Noaḥ, for so he prophesied. Elohim wants them to migrate apart and fill the earth. But that's not what we want. We want one world government with me at the top controlling my chosen man and the leaders under him (Rev 12:3; 13:1;17:1-18). And we will have it.

"Nimrod is my man. I will make him a mighty hunter and draw the people to him. They will love his cruelty and savagery. Through him I will start a one-world religion in which I alone am served, as I did with Qayin. You, my messengers, will put it into peoples' hearts to follow me as the only true strong one. I will have them all come to the location I choose, and there they will build a tower to me that reaches to the sky. It will have a temple on the top where animals and humans will be slain to honor me. I, even I, will be the most high.

"But if that fails, and the people migrate apart, they will carry my religion with them, for I will place chief demons over each migrating group. They will use different names for their strong ones, but they will all be from me. I am Satan, the Accuser. I have spoken. So shall it be!"

Nimrod, Tower of Bavel, 11

"Come, let us build for us a city, and a tower whose top is in the sky, and let us make for us a name, lest we be scattered abroad over the face of the whole earth" (Gen 11:4).

THE ARTICLES REGARDING THE TOWER OF BABEL (bah-VEL, confusion), and the confusion of languages Yahuah brought as a result, are much the same. Nimrod, the grandson of Ḥam and great-grandson of Noaḥ, made a name for himself in hunting. (Nimrod means rebel/rebellion/let us rebel.) Some say he was a hunter of men; most, a hunter of wild animals. The saying, *"Like Nimrod, a mighty hunter before Yahuah,"* is to be taken as *"against Yahuah."* The word "before" can have that meaning if context so indicates. It does in this case, because all pagan religions are traced to him. He returned to what Qayin had done. He established a kingdom that began in Babylon, what is now Iraq, and eventually included what is now Syria. He is noted for being a cruel dictator.

What would this tower look like if it were finished? Some say it would be like the ziggurats we see in archaeological ruins—a square pyramid with steps to the top and a temple on top for sacrifices. Others have different ideas. We can't know, for it wasn't finished and no longer exists. The phrase "whose top is in the sky" means "very high." A skyscraper, for example, has its top in the sky.

94

Nimrod's attempt to unite all the people around him by establishing his kingdom and building a tower in defiance of Yahuah failed when Yahuah changed languages, so that most migrated away.

Today, the spiritual battle is still ongoing, those who are against Yahuah opposing those who proclaim him as the only true Elohim. Whenever we set ourselves to be our own strong ones (gods), we are following Nimrod and his strong one, Satan.

Many sources also discuss what it means that the earth was divided in Peleg's days (Gen 10:25). There are two main theories regarding this. One takes the word "earth" to mean the physical earth and says the earth being divided in his days refers to the one continent of all land mass being divided into the various continents we have today through what is known as the continental drift of tectonic plates. They say this accounts for man and animals being on all continents.

The other, the majority I looked at, take the word "earth" to mean nations. They say the division in Peleg's days came because of the confusion of languages, and that the continental drift took place earlier during the flood at the time of Noaḥ. The Hebrew word *erets* can refer to the physical earth or to nations.

Further discussion of these topics are outside the purpose of this book. However, these two topics, the tower and the migration of peoples apart from each other, form the transition from the narrative of creation to the flood, to the history of Yisra'ĕl beginning with Avraham.

Peleg, grandson of Shĕm, is in the messianic line being carried forward from Adam to Avram. Avram is the tenth generation from Noaḥ and the fifth from Peleg. Ten is the number of completeness on the earth, and five the number of unmerited favor. Avraham fits them both and is the first one called a Hebrew. He is also the first of three patriarchs from which would come the nation of Yisra'ĕl, the religion of Judaism, Yahushua the fulfillment of the prophecies, and the religion of Christianity.

Teraḥ Takes Avram to Ḥaran, 11:31

"Leave your country and your people and go to the land I will show you" (Act 7:3).

THE END OF CHAPTER ELEVEN records the Messianic line from Shĕm to Avram. Noaḥ is the tenth generation from creation (Adam is the first of the ten), and Avram is the tenth generation after Noaḥ, or the twentieth generation from creation. The number twenty is used many times in scripture. Ten is the number of completion on the earth, so twenty is double completion. Avram is the first patriarch and the first to be called Hebrew. The promises to him include the nation of Yisra'ĕl and the Messiah.

Twenty can, at times, mean a complete or perfect waiting period. One example, which we will see later, is Ya'aqov (Jacob) waiting 20 years to get possession of his wives and property and being freed from the control of Lavan (Laban, Gen 31:38-41). Yahuah waited 20 generations to get Noaḥ.

This chapter concludes the genealogy by saying:

Now these are the generations of Teraḥ. Teraḥ fathered Avram, Naḥor and Haran; and Haran fathered Lot. Haran died in the presence of his father Teraḥ in the land of his birth, in Ur of the Kasdim (Chaldeans). *And Avram and Nahor took wives for themselves. The name of Avram's wife was Sarai; and the name of Nahor's wife was Milkah, the daughter of Haran, the father of Milkah and Yiskah. And Sarai was barren; she had no child* (Gen 11:27-30).

The probable location of Ur was near the headwaters of the Euphrates river in what is today south-eastern Turkey near the border with Syria. (See the Map Of Patriarchs' Journeys on page xii.) This Ur is different from the one located near the Persian Gulf.

Their travel to Ḥaran (the Hebrew spelling of this city is different from the Hebrew spelling of Avram's brother Haran) is summed up in one verse:

And Teraḥ took his son Avram and [his grandson] Lot the son of Haran, and his daughter-in-law Sarai, wife of his son Avram, and they went out together from Ur of the Kasdim to go into the land of Kena'an (Canaan)*; but when they came to Ḥaran, they settled there* (Gen 11:31).

Later we learn that Sarai was the daughter of Teraḥ by a second wife and is thus half-sister of Avram. From this verse it appears that only these four—Teraḥ, Avram, Lot and Sarai—traveled to Ḥaran. We don't know what happened to Teraḥ's two wives, whether one died before he had the second, or he married the second while he still had the first. Because they didn't come with Teraḥ to Ḥaran, it is assumed that neither was living at that time. From v. 30 we learn that Avram's brother Nahor married his niece Milkah, sister of Lot. So Nahor and his wife stayed behind in Ur of the Kasdim. We know that Avram was ten years older than Sarai, but we don't know how old they were when they married. If she was 15, then he was 25.

Teraḥ's family is semi-nomadic, living in tents in the region of Ur of the Kasdim (Ac 7:4). They have sheep, goats. donkeys and camels as well as a business in the city making and selling idols (Jos 24:2). The moon god Nanna (also called Sin, pronounced "seen") is the chief one among many, many others.

Many years pass, and during this time Nahor has married his niece Milkah and Haran has died. Sarai is barren and has given up hope of ever bearing. Life for Avram is going on as usual when he has a vision. He is now seventy years old. During the night the Elohim of esteem appears to him and says, *"**Leave** your land and your relatives and **come** into the land which I will show you"* (Act 7:2-3).

The term "Elohim of esteem" (God of glory) is a term noting his majesty, splendor and magnificence. We see examples of this in Ex 33:18; Le 9:23; Nu 14:10; and Dt 5:24; 16:7,10. (Information based on Barnes' Notes in Biblesoft.)

This first calling of Avram to leave his land and relatives is not recorded in Genesis. We learn of it in Stephen's defence to the Jews in the Book of Acts. It is thought by most commentators that Avram was a pagan until he had this vision. This "as it may have been" is based on that assumption, and it fits with the typology of being born again and growing in that relationship.

Avram is following the religion begun by Nimrod along with everyone else, and thinking nothing of it. He knows the stories of creation and the flood. Noaḥ had died when Avram was in his fifties, and Shĕm is still alive living somewhere in the area. And then this happens! Instantly he knows that the Nimrod religion is false and that the stories told by Noaḥ are true. His whole life he knew, deep inside, that they were true, but he had repressed that knowledge in order to be in harmony with his father and culture. He repents of his sin, asks for forgiveness and says, "Yahuah, I believe you. From here on you are my Strong One, the only Strong One. I will do as you say."

When morning comes he tells his wife about it, and after breakfast he goes at once to inform his father. Teraḥ is in his workshop making idols when he arrives. "What is it, Avram? Something has happened, I can tell. And how is Sarai, and how is it with the livestock?"

"Sarai and the livestock are doing well. The reason I came is that Yahuah, the only true Strong One, appeared to me last night and said I must leave my land and my people and come to the land he will show me."

"Are you sure it was he and not just a desire of your own imagination?"

"When the Strong One speaks, you know it is he. There is no doubt. But it wasn't just a voice. I saw him in a vision."

"And what did he look like? I thought he is supposed to be invisible."

"You are mocking. Yes, he is invisible. He fills heaven and earth and made everything. What I saw was a brilliant light, and I knew it was he. But he is the Almighty and can show himself in a visible form. After all, he appeared to and even walked with our first parents, Adam and Ḥawwah."

"Another fable. When do you plan on leaving?"

"You are my father, and I love you. I own nothing, for it all belongs to you. I don't know where I am going or how long it will take to get there. I would like to take something for the journey, and I trust Yahuah to provide for us when that runs out."

"You are a man of faith, that is for sure, even though I don't agree with you. I will go with you. Your brother Haran is dead, and I care for his son Lot. I doubt that your brother Nahor will come. I will give the idol-making business to him. We will stop at the city of Ḥaran and see what happens after we get there. I understand it is much the same as here. If I decide not to continue going I will set up business there. My idols look much better than anyone else's."

It doesn't take them long to travel to Ḥaran, for it isn't far to the west. They bring their servants, possessions and livestock with them and settle there. Five years go by, and during that time Avram's brother, Nahor, joins them along with his family.

"Happy birthday, my husband. today you are seventy-five years old" (Gen 12:4), Sarai says to Avram. "I prepared a special meal for the occasion. Your father and Lot will join us."

After the meal Avram speaks with his father. "My father, you are the patriarch of this family. We have been living here now for many years and have increased in wealth, both in servants and in livestock. We are greatly blessed.

"The question is, why are we so blessed, and who is blessing us? You bow to many gods, the chief one being Nanna, the moon god, and you have stone carvings of many gods. You pray to each and believe they are what bring prosperity, although they cannot speak, move or do anything. You even have many temples to the various gods, with offerings of grain and animals, and even babies. Young men and women have become temple prostitutes for devotees to worship the gods through sex. I don't believe any of it. This is the way it was in Ur of the Kasdim, and this is the way it is here in Ḥaran.

"You know the story of Noaḥ and the ark that saved them and their family. They were the only eight that survived the flood, a flood that came because of the wickedness of mankind, a flood that completely destroyed to nothingness every last remnant of what that civilization was. Yahuah the Strong One, our creator, did it. You know the story. But we have gone back into the same wickedness.

"Nimrod, Noaḥ's grandson by Ḥam and Kush, tried to build a tower to reach into the sky and keep the descendents of Noaḥ united with one language and a different belief—bowing to the sun, moon and stars. He was a powerful leader, and ruthless. That's why we have the saying, 'Like Nimrod, a mighty hunter opposed to Yahuah' (Gen 10:8). But Yahuah stopped the construction and gave different languages so we would migrate to different areas and not be united. The religion that Nimrod started is what we are doing today. It is against Yahuah, the only true Strong One.

"Before we left Ur of the Kasdim we heard that our father Noaḥ had died, and there were many celebrations over that 'fool' who said he had saved mankind. He was 950 years old. Shĕm is still strong, I heard, and he will probably outlive me!" (He outlived Avraham by thirty-five years, having lived 600 years.)

While he is speaking his father is becoming more and more

agitated. Is it anger? Is it fear? Avram can't tell. Teraḥ calms himself, sighs and says. "I believe in unity in the family, and I am the patriarch that decides all things for us. And we are larger than our family; we are a community in which we all do the same thing. We are one united culture.

"So what if the gods aren't real and Yahuah is the only true Strong One. It is better to go along with the culture than to go against it. And look at you. You have been married these many years, and yet your wife is still barren. If Yahuah is the only true Strong One, then why have you no children? Have you ever wondered about that? I had three sons, one now dead, and no more children. My wives also are dead. Could that be punishment from the gods because of what you did? As for me, I will keep the traditions. I'm tired now and will go back to my tent and lie down. What a birthday for you it has turned out to be! Thank you, Sarai, for the delicious meal." With that, he leaves.

Later that night, after they are in bed asleep, they are awakened by shouting. "Wake up, master Avram! Wake up! My master Teraḥ is calling for you. He said he is dying and you must come to him at once!"

Avram puts his robe on and hurries to his father. "What is it?" he asks.

"I am dying," he says. "Forgive me for raising you in idolatry. You are right. Yahuah is the only true Strong One. I just didn't want to endure the pressure of going against society. I give all I have to you." With that he closes his eyes and is gathered to his fathers.

After Avram sends word to his brother Nahor and makes the arrangements regarding his father's body and things quiet down, he returns to his tent and falls asleep. In his sleep Yahuah speaks to him: "Avram. You must leave your country, your relatives and your father's household to go to the land which I will show you. I will make you a great nation and bless you. I will make your name great, and you shall be a blessing. I will bless those who bless you and curse any who curse you. Indeed, in you all the families of the earth will be blessed" (Gen 12:1-3). In his dream he sees a city with foundations, whose architect and builder is Elohim (Heb 11:10).

When he wakes up, he knows it was a dream, and that it was from

Yahuah. "I am your servant," he responds. "I will do whatever you say."

In the morning Sarai sees a difference in Avram. "What is it?" she asks. "What is it? Something happened, and it's not because your father died last night. Was it another vision? You said Yahuah told you that you were to leave your country and relatives and go to a land he will show you. But you brought your father and nephew with you and stopped here."

He then relates the dream to her and says, "We must leave as soon as we are able. I'll attend to my father's burial and get everything ready for our journey."

"What about Lot?"

"You are right. I have that responsibility. My father gave me all that he has, and that includes Lot. Nahor will stay and probably take over our father's idol-making business. I'll give Lot the choice to stay or come with us." To one of his servants he says, "Tell Lot I want to talk with him." Sarai is thinking, "If he is to become a father of many nations, then that means I shall have a son." And she is smiling.

"What is it, my father?" Lot asks. After being told the situation he says, "I'll go with you. There's nothing to hold me here, and I also want to follow Yahuah."

"Very well. I don't know where I am going, but go I will, and the Almighty will lead us. When we get to the land of which he spoke, I will give some of my servants and livestock to you so you can support yourself."

Genesis 1:1 to 12:3 lays the foundation for the beginning of the nation of Yisra'ĕl, which is the call of Avram to leave Babylon, a type of the world, and go to the promised land, a type of salvation and heaven. Up to this point the historical information is very compressed, giving only the essentials for the main story. This is why I expanded the narrative with some imagination. Of course, the expansion is "story-telling," but by doing so I have brought in some typology, prophesy of the Messiah through the woman's seed and the last days, and teaching on salvation. How much Yahuah revealed to them and how much they understood, there is no way of knowing from the text alone, although the New Testament indicates they knew much.

101

The set-apart spirit (Holy Spirit) was not given until Messiah rose from the dead and ascended to heaven (Jn 7:39; Ac 1:8; 2:1-4). Nevertheless, the spirit of Elohim is always involved in the lives of his people. In the Psalms we see a deep relationship of covenant between David and Elohim—I dare say a deeper one then the average believer has today. Certainly the prophets had a deep covenant-relationship, otherwise Elohim wouldn't have moved through them.

This brings us to Genesis 12, the beginning of the stories of the three patriarchs: Avraham, Yitshaq (Isaac) and Ya'aqov (Jacob).

Covenants

WHAT FOLLOWS IS A SUMMARY of the major covenants in the first eleven chapters. Not all covenants are stated as covenants.

- Angels. They are given the responsibility to help those who will inherit salvation (Heb 1:14). The covenant: if you obey, you stay.
- Adam (mankind). The covenant: to be made into the image of Elohim (Gen 1:26). Those who obey to achieve it become the purpose for which they were created. Also, *"Be fruitful and multiply and fill the earth and subdue it"* (Gen 1:28). Man was given authority over the earth, but surrendered that authority when they sinned. Yahushua and believers in him fulfill that covenant. The covenant includes the curses pronounced against mankind for the sin of Adam and Ḥawwah, as well as Yahuah's provision for that sin (Gen 3:15).
- Marriage. We saw this earlier as a type of the relationship that Yahuah wants with us (Eph 5:31-32). Because marriage is a type, any sexual relationship outside of one-man/one-woman in a marriage covenant relationship of fidelity and trust, including thoughts of the mind and pornography, is sexual immorality. Such ones will not inherit the kingdom of Elohim (Gal 5:19, 21).
- Garden in Ěden. Adam and Ḥawwah were given the responsibility of tending the garden.
- Blood, when Elohim killed an animal to provide a skin covering. Life is in the blood. *"This cup is the new covenant in my blood, which is poured out for you"* (Lk 22:20).
- Noaḥ. The covenant with him was that he build an ark to save a remnant of mankind and animals that breathe.

- Rainbow. This covenant is unconditional, that Yahuah would never destroy the earth with a worldwide flood again, and it is a reminder that he can and will judge sin (2Pe 2:5).
- Avraham (Gen 12:1-3,6-7; 13:14-17; 15; 17:1-14; 22:15-18). The covenant with him began when Elohim called him to leave Ur of the Kasdim (Chaldeans) and come to a land he would show him, and the details kept increasing until its culmination with Avraham offering up his son Yitsḥaq.

In this covenant with Avraham, the Strong One promised many things to him: He would make Avraham's name great, Avraham would have numerous physical descendants, and he would be the father of a multitude of nations. Elohim also made promises regarding a nation called Yisra'ĕl, and gave the geographical boundaries of the land, from the Nile River to the Euphrates River—all of which include what today is called eastern Egypt, Palestine, Lebanon, Jordan, Syria, Iraq and northern Arabia. This will be fulfilled in the Millennium when Yahushua returns to rule the entire earth. The promised land at the time of Exodus was limited to Palestine. Another promise is that the families of the world will be blessed through the physical line of Avraham. This is a reference to the Messiah, who would come from his line. These provisions of the covenant with Avraham can be categorized in three areas: to Avraham; to the Seed, Yisra'ĕl; and to the Gentiles. This covenant was reaffirmed to his son Yitsḥaq and grandson Ya'aqov.

IV. AVRAM TO YITSḤAQ
Genesis 12-23

Yahuah appeared to Avram and said,
"To your seed I will give *this* land."
Genesis 12:7

Avram Goes from Ḥaran to Mitsrayim, 12:1

THE STORY OF AVRAHAM is full of types that apply to us who are believers in Yahushua haMashiakh (Jesus the Messiah). As we go through his life we will see, in type, his spiritual growth from born again to a mature bride of Messiah and called a friend of Elohim (Jas 2:23). We, who believe in Yahushua, are of the seed of Avraham through faith. *"It is not the children of the flesh that are the children of Elohim, but the children of the promise are counted as [Avraham's] seed"* (Ro 9:8).

Using scripture only, and with Ur being a pagan city in the east, in type, Avram was yet a pagan in Ur when he received his first call from Yahuah. Genesis doesn't record his first call, but Acts does. When Stephen was giving his defense in Acts 7, he said: *"Men, brothers and fathers, listen! The esteem of Elohim appeared to our father Avraham when he was in Mesopotamia, before he lived in Ḥaran, and said to him, 'Leave from your land and your relatives, and come into the land that I will show you'"* (Ac 7:2-3).

This was his day of visitation (1Pe 2:12), his day of salvation (2Cor 6:2). We do not know what the esteem of Elohim looked like to Avram, but we can have an idea from the testimonies of former nonbelievers who had visions of Yahushua—*who is the radiance of Elohim's esteem and the exact representation of his being* (Heb 1:3)—that resulted in their conversion.

One such person, a teenager, in a vision of Yahushua, saw beauty, love, compassion, goodness and light so overwhelming that he converted on the spot. He had never gone to church, had never heard the gospel or the sinner's prayer, and knew nothing of Christianity. He was a total heathen living a totally selfish life. Yet, on seeing the vision, he immediately confessed his sins, asked for forgiveness, and committed his life totally to serve him out of love. In his vision he also saw the opposite, Satan in all his darkness, and was told to choose. To him, there was no choice but to surrender to Yahushua. He is now, forty plus years later, operating in the ministry offices of apostle, prophet, evangelist, pastor and teacher (Eph 4:11) traveling around the world with signs and wonders to confirm the message of righteousness (Mk 16:17-20).

Scripture records many instances of visions of the esteem of Yahuah and of Yahushua, and the effect on those who saw it. One example is when Yahushua was transfigured before three of his disciples. They fell face down on the ground and were terrified (Mt 17:1-6). Another example is the vision Yeshayahu (Isaiah) had that led to his call to be a prophet. His response on seeing the vision was: *"Woe to me, for I am ruined! Because I am a man of unclean lips, And I live among a people of unclean lips; For my eyes have seen the King, Yahuah of armies"* (Is 6:1-5).

What Avram saw and heard changed his life forever. Yahuah told him to **leave** his land and relatives and **come** to a different land. A sinner lives in the land of darkness; conversion brings him into the land of light. *"You were formerly darkness, but now you are light in the Master; walk as children of light"* (Eph 5:8).

Believing in Yahushua as your master and savior is the first step in being born again. Believing is obeying. You have received the privilege of becoming a child of Elohim, and eternal life has been given to you (Jn 1:12; 3:16). This is the first step. Eternal life, however, is conditional; that condition is continued obedience. You are on the road to completion, and much in your life needs changing. You are working out your salvation with fear and trembling (Php 2:12) to get all sin, pride, insecurity and selfishness out of your life so that you can bear fruit for the kingdom (Jn 15) and become the bride of Messiah (Eph 5:27). So it is with us, and so it was for Avraham. As we go through his life, we will see his growth from unbelief and insecurity to becoming a friend of Elohim.

When Avram was in Ur of the Kasdim, Yahuah told him to leave his relatives and come. But we see that he started out with his father Teraḥ and nephew Lot, with his father being in charge. It was a patriarchal (father the ruler) culture with Teraḥ having authority over his family. When they came to Ḥaran, Teraḥ didn't want to go farther, and so there they stayed until Yahuah spoke to Avram again. It was then that Avram continued his journey, leaving his father behind.

It might appear that Avram left Ḥaran when his father died, because the end of chapter 11 says Teraḥ died when he was 205 years old, and chapter 12 begins the narrative of Avram leaving Ḥaran when he was 75 years old. The chronology of births and deaths in Genesis shows that Teraḥ lived another forty years after Avram left. However, Acts 7:4 says Avram left Ḥaran *after* his father died. There is a Samar text and version that says Teraḥ died when he was 130 years old, thus solving the problem (McClintock and Strong Commentary). Nevertheless, whatever the situation was, when Avram left, he was now the head of his family, a family of three: himself, his wife Sarai and his nephew Lot, the son of his deceased brother Haran. He also had many servants and livestock. So it was quite a group that left.

Avram leaving Ur of the Kasdim is a type of being born again, but he hadn't left his relatives, particularly his father and nephew. Ḥaran was also a pagan city, so in type he was still in the world, although he was on the way out. When his father died he felt free to continue the journey. This is a type of dying to your old life and the hold of family tradition. But he still had his nephew Lot who had also decided to follow Yahuah by accompanying Avram. Peter, in his second letter to the assemblies, called Lot a righteous man (2Pe 2:7-8). We will see more of Lot later. Our purpose here is to note that Avram didn't leave all his relatives when he left Ḥaran.

The calling that Avram received in Ḥaran added to the first calling in Ur of the Kasdim. The addition was the covenant blessing:

"And I will make you a great nation, and I will bless you, and make your name great; and you shall be a blessing; and I will bless those who bless you, and curse the one who curses you. And in you all the families of the earth shall be blessed" (Gen 12:2-3).

Yahuah made this covenant because of his foreknowledge of what Avram would become, of the nation Yisra'ĕl that would come from him, of the Messiah that would come from that nation, and of the bride that would come through Messiah.

Avram had acquired much while in Ḥaran, both in possessions and in persons. In type, although he was still in the world, he was not of it, and he had gathered an assembly of believers. He was now, as it were, a pastor, but there was much growth in the spirit that he still needed.

Haran is west of Ur of the Kasdim near the headwaters of the Euphrates, in south-eastern modern Turkey. From there they traveled south through what is now Syria and Jordan, and crossed the Yardĕn (Jordan River) into the land of Kena'an (Canaan), what is now Palestine. Kena'an, as we saw earlier, was the fourth son of Ham, who was the youngest son of Noaḥ. Kena'an's descendants had migrated to the land between the Yardĕn and the Mediterranean Sea. Avram continued until they got to Shekem (Shechem), a site north of what would be Yerushalayim (Jerusalem), between Mount Ěval (Ebal) and Mount Gerizim, and where eventually a city would be built, and in particular to a prominent oak tree, evidently owned by a man named Moreh. Mosheh, when writing this, points out that the Kena'ani (Canaanites) were in the land at that time (Gen 12:6), because at the time of Mosheh the hill country was occupied by the Hivi (Hivites) and the Emori (Amorites) (Jos 11:3), with the Kena'ani living only in the lowlands along the Mediterranean coast.

While at the oak, Yahuah appears to Avram and says, "To your seed I will give this land." Avram is now in the land Yahuah had promised to show him. So he heaps up stones as an altar for a memorial of the event (Gen 12:7). This is the third time Yahuah spoke to him, and the first time that he builds an altar. He is now in the promised land. In our walk as believers in Messiah, significant events happen that are turning points in our relationship with Yahuah. We need to remember those events and honor him.

From Shekem they continue on to the hill between Bĕth'ĕl and Ai (AH-ee) where he pitches his tent, and there builds another altar to Yahuah and this time calls upon his name (Gen 12:8). To call upon the name of Yahuah is to commit to him as your Strong One and the only one, and to acknowledge your dependence upon him. Earlier we saw Seth doing this (Gen 4:26). Avram is growing in his commitment and trust. A promise has been fulfilled: he is now in the land. The promise of descendents from him is yet to be fulfilled. Before that can happen, however, he must go through some trials. He is about to face famine. How will he handle it? Will he stay in the land promised to him and trust Yahuah to supply his needs, not only for himself but also for his family, livestock and servants? Or will he continue beyond it going into Mitsrayim (Egypt), trusting in his natural mind? We face that choice all the time when things aren't going the way we want, and instead of seeking Yahuah to get his mind on the situation, we go ahead with our own stinking thinking, and get into deeper trouble.

Avram is still traveling southward, seeing what the land is like, and going toward the Negev (Gen 12:9). The Negev is an arid area in southern Yisra'ĕl and borders the Sinai Peninsula, which is part of Mitsrayim. Mitsrayim was the grandson of Noaḥ through Ham, brother of Kush and uncle of Nimrod.

Genesis 12:10 says there was a severe famine in *the land*. The Hebrew for *the land* is *ha-erets*. Yahuah had told Avram to **leave** his land (in type, darkness) and **come** to this land (in type, light). *"Come to me, all you that are weary and are carrying heavy burdens, and I will give you rest"* said Yahushua (Mt 11:28, NRSV).

Although *erets* can refer to any land or nation, in this case it refers to the entire promised land, it is *the land.* In type, Avram is a new believer and is experiencing dryness in his spirit. He is excited about being in the promised land, but now is in a trial. The parable of the soils by Yahushua gives four responses to the seed of the gospel: barren, shallow, thorny and fruitful (Mt 13:1-23). The barren do not accept the seed at all. The other three do, but one gives up when trials come, and another becomes lukewarm because of the cares of the world. Only the third one endures through the trials to bear fruit: *"He who endures to the end will be saved"* (Mt 24:13). Which soil will Avram be? Which soil are you?

Avram Deceives Par'oh, 12:10

BECAUSE OF THE FAMINE, Avram decides to go to Mitsrayim and stay there until the famine is over. He has no instructions from Yahuah not to go there. But he has a problem with insecurity. He is not yet fully trusting Yahuah. His wife is a beautiful, stately mature woman. Her name, Sarai, "my princess," fits her. Because of her beauty, Avram is afraid the Mitsrayim might kill him to get her, if they learn she is his wife. So he asks her to please say she is his sister so he won't be killed. She agrees, the servants of Par'oh (Pharaoh) see her, praise her to him, she is taken into his harem, and he treats Avram well for her sake, receiving sheep, oxen, donkeys, camels, and male and female servants (Gen 12:10-16). What a blessing for his insecurity!

The blessing, however, isn't because of his insecurity, it is because of Yahuah's plan for him. Good things sometimes happen when we follow our natural thinking and make wrong choices. The good is not because of the wrong choices, but because of Yahuah's mercy and plan for our lives. *"To those who love Elohim, who are called according to his purpose, all things* (good and bad) *work together for good* (for the best)*"* (Ro 8:28).

However, because of that plan for Avram, it doesn't work out good at all for Par'oh, for Yahuah strikes him and his house with great plagues (Gen 12:17). We don't know what those great plagues were, but they were such that Par'oh, a pagan, probably asked his priests the cause, and learned it was from Yahuah, the Strong One of Adam and Noah, and Yahuah did it because Sarai was Avram's wife. Later, in a similar situation, all the females in the family of Avi-meleh (Abimelech) are made barren (Gen 20:18). But the word "plagues" is not used in that later situation. In Par'oh's case it is called "great plagues." As a result, Par'oh returns Sarai to Avram and sends him away with all that belong to him, including Lot.

Avram and Lot Separate, 13:1

THE FAMINE IS LIKELY OVER, for they return to Bĕth'ĕl, the place where Avram had pitched his tent at the beginning when he entered the land and had built an altar. By this time he is very rich in livestock, silver and gold. And there he calls again on the name of Yahuah (Gen 13:1-4).

In type, this trial is now over, and, spiritually, he is in a better place with Yahuah. He is experiencing Elohim's care for him. He had experienced, in type, being born again when he entered the promised land. He had been called to **leave** his former life and **come** to the land he would be shown. That, in type, is being born again, for he called upon the name of Yahuah. Now he has experienced deliverance from a trial and has returned to where he started, his *"first love"* (Rev 2:4), and has again called upon the name of Yahuah.

Again, this is typical of the believer's walk with Yahushua. We have our spiritual ups and downs, but *"a righteous person falls seven times, and rises again"* (Pr 24:16). A righteous person is one who is working at obeying Yahuah: *"Be working out your own salvation with fear and trembling"* (Php 2:12). It is not our own righteousness; it is the right-eousness of Yahushua imputed to us. It is counted to us as though we have it, and we do have it, but it is his righteousness in us, not ours (Jam 2:3; see also 1Cor 1:30). And it is in us only on the condition that we continue on our journey toward him to become like him in his character of selfless love. He will work with us and help us stay on the narrow path, but we have a free will and have the possibility, at any time, of leaving the path and following the broad one that leads to destruction (Mt 7:13-14).

Yes, a believer can lose his salvation if he continues in unrepentant sin (Heb 6:4-6). The question, however, should not be whether or not you can lose your salvation and how much sin you can do without losing it. That is a wicked question coming from an evil heart. It's like a wife asking her husband how much adultery she can do without his divorcing her. The question should be, do you love him? If you love him, you do not want to be unfaithful. Bride believers love Messiah and want to be faithful and have all sin out of their lives.

Avram is now about to face another trial. Lot has his own flocks and herdsmen, and is increasing in his possessions, so much so, that there is conflict between his herdsmen and Avram's: "We're grazing our herds here." "No, *we* are. *We* were here first." "No, *we* were." This is mountainous land with many valleys, and Mosheh notes that the Kena'ani (Canaanites) and Perizzi (Perizzites) were also dwelling in the land at that time. In type, they were bringing the gospel to unbelievers.

In type, Avram and Lot represent different groups of believers (churches and denominations) fighting over the same unbelievers, and also fighting over doctrinal and organizational differences. They have the same Elohim, Yahuah, but their ideas about him and how to serve him are different in some ways. Avram is more mature and is a type of the bride and of the spirit-man. Lot is a type of the lukewarm and flesh-man. Avram endeavours to make peace. "Look, Lot, we are brothers. Let's not fight. We don't have to be this close together. There is plenty of land. Let's separate and work in different areas. Whichever way you go, I'll go the other. You decide" (Gen 13:5-9).

During the early Protestant missionary movement, when different organizations were going to the same country, they divided up the country among themselves so as not to compete.

Note, the problem doesn't seem to be between Avram and Lot, but between, in type, the members of their congregations. Lot likes the idea, and looks for the most favorable place. In type he is saying, "My church is better than yours, and I'm going where I'll get the most people and the best results." The area that Lot decides on is a well-watered valley of the Yardĕn River, likened to the garden of Yahuah (Gen 13:10). So they separate, Avram in the hill country, and Lot going east near Sedom (Sodom), the people there being very wicked and sinners against Yahuah.

East is a type of Babylon and the world system. The valley people are flesh people, their flesh nature continually getting stronger. Going east is a type of going into worldliness.

Avram has now fulfilled the command to leave his relatives, and Yahuah speaks to him again. The more we obey, the more he reveals regarding what he wants us to do. He says, "Lift up your eyes and look from the place where you are, to the north, to the south, to the east, and to the west; for all the land which you see, I will give it to you and to your seed forever. I will make your seed as the dust of the earth, so that if anyone can number the dust of the earth, then your seed can also be numbered. Get up! Walk about the land, the length of it and the width, for I will give it to you." Then Avram moves his tent and travels by the oaks of Mamrĕ, which are in Ḥevron (Hebron), and there he builds an altar to Yahuah (Gen 13:14-18).

Malki-tsedeq blesses Avram, 14:1

AVRAM IS LIVING by the oaks of Mamrĕ the Emori (Amorite) near what is now Hebron, about twenty miles south of what is now Jerusalem, and has an alliance with the Emori people. By this time he is known as Avram the Ivri (Hebrew) (one from beyond). Among the Emori is a priest of Yahuah named Malki-tsedeq (Melchizedek), who is king of Shalem (Salem), perhaps located near what is now Jerusalem. Because of the alliance and because of similar belief, Avram and he are likely friends. The name Malki-tsedeq means "king of righteousness," and

111

the name Shalem means "peace." So he is also king of peace (Heb 7:2). What, perhaps, was their conversation when they met? And what followed? Here is a suggestion.

One day Avram goes to Shalem. "And how are you, my friend?" asks Malki-tsedeq.

"I'm doing very well, thank you, and you?"

"Very well, also. Come, refresh yourself."

After the pleasantries and a meal Malki-tsedeq asks, "And to what do I owe this visit?"

"It is good to fellowship with someone who shares my faith in Yahuah, the one true Elohim. I am from Shĕm, one of the three sons of our father, Noaḥ. My father and relatives followed Nimrod's religion of bowing to the sun, moon, stars and animals—bowing to creation instead of the Creator. I left that belief to obey the Creator. He told me to leave my people and come to the land he would show me, and when I arrived here, he said this is the land. That's why I am here. I own no land, but do have many servants and much livestock. The people of this land are from Ḥam and, except for you, also follow Nimrod's religion.

"In order to live among you in peace, I have made alliances with your people. Unlike you, however, who live in walled cities, we live in tents and move about with our livestock. Therefore, despite the alliance, there is always danger of raids, and there are also wild animals. So I have 318 men born in my household whom I have trained to fight. I am their leader, their general, as it were. We have swords and spears, and they take pleasure in staging mock battles— war games, I guess you could call it. I am thankful that we have had no occasion for real battle. Perhaps, because we are ready, there has been no occasion.

"That's my story, and I would like to hear yours. How did you, who believe as I do, come to be a king and a priest of Ĕl Elyon, Elohim most high?"

Malki-tsedeq smiles and says, "Everyone in this land follows Nimrod's religion, but not I. When I was a young adult Ĕl Elyon spoke to me. He said, 'I am he, there is no other.' When I shared this, there was no opposition to speak of, and some gathered around me and appointed me as their king. That's the way we become kings—we are chosen by our followers. Some kings try to increase their importance by conquering others and making them pay tribute, but not I. So that's how I became king and Shalem was started. And then in a dream Ĕl Elyon said to me, 'I anoint you as my priest. You must intercede for your city and for all the people of this land and slaughter livestock as offerings to me to cover your sins and theirs."

"So you didn't inherit being priest from your father. Will your children inherit it from you?"

"Mine is a solitary priesthood. I have no genealogy of being a priest, and none will follow from my seed. In fact, there will be no record showing any of my genealogy, of those before me or of those after me (Heb 7:3). I was shown, however, that a priesthood will come from *you* that *will* be based on genealogy, a priesthood with many strict requirements of purification and slaughter-offerings. But that priesthood will end and Ĕl Elyon will anoint another priest, also from your seed, but not from that genealogy. That priest will be like me, having no genealogy of priesthood. He will offer himself as the slaughter-offering for the sins of the whole world—of those past, present and future—and will be a priest forever after my order of priesthood. (See Ps 100:4; Heb 5:6,10; 6:20; 7:11,17.) I was raised up as priest to represent him. He is the seed of the woman, the mother of all mankind, our mother Ḥawwah, who will crush Satan and his kingdom."

After a pause, Avram says, "That is a lot to think on. Do you do anything else as priest besides prayer and the offerings?"

"It's interesting that you should ask that. From time to time I prepare bread and wine for a special service of homage. When I asked Yahuah about its significance, he said it represents the life of that future priest. The bread represents his body that will be broken for us, and the wine his blood that will be spilt. To eat of it, in this manner, is to take his life into our lives" (1Cor 10:16; 11:26-28).

Avram returns to his tent village with much on his mind.

Some days later, towards evening, a stranger, running, exhausted and out of breath, comes to Avram. "What is it?" asks Avram. "You have bad news, I can tell." Turning to his head servant, Eli'ezer, he says, "Bring something to refresh him."

"Terrible news it is," says the stranger. "I am from Sedom (Sodom)

113

where your nephew Lot came to live. We had been paying tribute for twelve years to the king of Ĕlam (Elam) far to the north and east of us. Last year we stopped paying, and this year he came to punish us. He joined with three kings and came against us, and we joined with four kings in our valley and went out against him. Our king and the king of Amorah (Gomorrah) fled and got stuck in the tar pits and were captured. They took our possessions and our people, including Lot, and have taken them away. I escaped and came to you" (Gen 14:1-13).

"Which way did they go?"

"They're on the road going north. They came down the east side of the Yardĕn, and are returning on this west side."

"Eli'ezer," says Avram, "get my men. They've been trained to fight, and now we will put their training to use. We're going after them to bring back Lot and the others. They'll be traveling slowly because of the people and spoils they've taken, and they won't be expecting pursuit. So if we hurry we can catch them by tomorrow night. We travel light, and fast."

Soon they are on their way, each with a sword, a staff, a small bag of provisions and a skin of water. They run, taking short breaks from time to time. A scout is ahead to check the route and to inform them when they are close. Late evening the following day as they are nearing Mount Ḥermon the scout comes and tells them where the enemy has made camp. "They are drinking and making merry," he says, "and they have no one standing guard."

"Men," Avram says, "we are few and they are many, but they are unaware and at ease. When it is night and they are asleep, half of you will go on the other side of their camp, while half remain on this side. At my signal, we attack."

It is a total victory. In a panic, the enemy flees, leaving everything behind. And Avram and his men pursue them as far as Ḥovah, northeast of Dammeseq (Damascus). He brings back all the goods, his relative Lot, the women, and the people, and stops at the valley of Shavĕh, also called the King's Valley, a place near Yerushalayim (Gen 14:14-16).

In type, believers who are the bride are giving their all to rescue believers who are lukewarm, that these lukewarm ones become fervent for Yahushua and also become part of the bride—the bride calling to the bride. (See Mt 25:1-13, the parable of the ten virgins. See also Rev

114

3:14-22, the message to the church of Laodicea.)

After they make camp, Malki-tsedeq arrives. "Avram," he says, "it is good to see you again. I heard of your adventure and success. I am here to bring you a blessing from Ěl Elyon (Elohim most high), and I have some bread and wine to refresh you." Then he says, "Blessed be Avram of Ěl Elyon, possessor of heaven and earth; and blessed be Ěl Elyon, who has delivered your enemies into your hand." By blessing Avram he showed that he is greater than Avram (Heb 7:1-11).

"Thank you," says Avram. "You are a priest of Ěl Elyon, our Strong One. To honor you and him, I give you a tenth of all the spoil which I captured from the kings." By so doing, and by being the first patriarch of the nation of Yisra'ěl, and with all his descendents being in his loins, those descendents also paid a tithe to Malki-tsedeq, including the priesthood of Lěwi (Levi) (Heb 7:9; Gen 14:17-20).

The priesthood of Aharon (Aaron) began when Yahuah appointed him as high priest at Mount Ḥorěv (Horeb) during the Exodus. He was of the tribe of Lěwi. All priests had to come from Lěwi, and the high priest position could only come from Aharon. No such high priest could hold his office forever, for he would die. This was the Levitical system. Also, when he made the sin offering, he had to do it for himself as well as for the nation, because he was a sinner along with the rest. But Yahushua was different. He never sinned, so he could die for others. Also, because he was raised from the dead, he continues his priesthood office forever (Heb 7).

The king of Sedom says to Avram, "Give to me the people whom you rescued, and take the spoils for yourself. You deserve them, because you rescued us."

Avram refuses. "No. Thank you for the offer, but no. I have sworn to Yahuah Ěl Elyon, possessor of heaven and earth, that I will not take a thread or a sandal thong or anything that is yours, for fear you would say, 'I have made Avram rich.' I will take nothing except the tithe I gave to Malki-tsedeq, what the young men have eaten, and the share of the men who went with me; let them take their share."

"So be it," says the king, and departs with his men and the spoils to return home (Gen 14:21-24).

Avram Believes Promise of a Son, 15:1

SOME TIME LATER Avram has a vision. In the vision he is talking with Yahuah. Yahuah says, "Do not fear, Avram. I am a shield to you; your reward shall be very great" (Gen 15:1).

Avram replies, "Adonai Yahuah (Master Yahuah) what will you give me, since I am childless, and the heir of my house is Eli'ezer of Dammeseq (Damascus)? Since you have given me no offspring, one born in my house is my heir" (Gen 15:2-4).

"No, Avram. This man will not be your heir; but one who will come from your own body shall be your heir." Then, in the vision, he takes him outside. "Look at the sky," he says, "and count the stars, if you are able to count them. So shall your seed be" (Gen 15:5).

When Avram hears this, hope and faith rise in him, and he believes that indeed what Yahuah had promised he will do (Is 55:10-11). And Yahuah took that belief and credited it to him as righteousness (Gen 15:6; Ps 106:31; Ro 4:3,9-25). So it is with us, when we believe his promises and act on them.

"I am Yahuah," he continues, "who brought you out of Ur of the Kasdim, to give you this land to possess it" (Gen 15:7).

"Adonai Yahuah, how may I know that I will possess it?"

"This is how you will know. Bring me a three year old heifer, a three year old female goat, a three year old ram, a turtle-dove, and a young pigeon. Cut them in two and lay each half opposite the other; but do not cut the birds" (Gen 15:8-10).

Avram wakes up from his vision and does what he was told. Doing this was a traditional way of making and ratifying covenants, in which the participants in the covenant, after killing and dividing the animals, would walk between the animal parts. But Elohim is invisible. How would this be done? Avram waits to see.

What happens next is birds of prey come down upon the carcasses to feast. "I can't let them do this," he says to himself, and stands guard, driving them away (Gen 15:11). "I'll keep doing this forever, if necessary, until the covenant is ratified."

So it is with us. Yahuah has made a covenant with us when we accept his son Yahushua as our savior from sin and commit our lives to learn to be like him and obey him from a heart of love. The covenant is total, continued obedience. Birds of prey represent the enemy

116

of our souls, Satan and his demons. They try to pull us out of the covenant by appealing to our flesh nature, a nature which is opposed to Yahuah. And we have to be as diligent as Avram was by resisting the devil and working out our salvation (Jam 4:7; Php 2:12).

As the sun is setting, a deep sleep falls upon Avram, and terror and great darkness fall upon him (Gen 15:11). How awesome it is to be in the presence of Yahuah! We too often take our relationship with the Almighty lightly. Yahushua delighted in the fear of Yahuah (Is 11:3).

"Avram," says Yahuah, "know for certain that your seed will be strangers in a land that is not theirs. There they will be enslaved and oppressed for four hundred years. But I will also bring judgment on the nation which they will serve, and afterward they will come out with many possessions. As for you, you will die and be gathered to your fathers in peace and be buried at a good old age. In the fourth generation your descendents will return here. The Emori (Amorites) who live here are exceedingly wicked, and I will judge them for their iniquity, but not yet, for their iniquity is not yet complete" (Gen 15:12-16).

Yahuah brings judgment in many ways. In Mitsrayim the judgment was through plagues, the last one being the death of the firstborn of man and beast. But the nation itself still remained and will remain into the final millennium. The Emori, however, would increase in their wickedness until the land could bear them no longer. Their judgment would come with the nation of Yisra'ĕl destroying them totally as they come to conquer and live in the promised land.

Finally, when the sun has fully set and it is very dark, a smoking oven and a flaming torch pass between the pieces. This act was Yahuah ratifying the covenant. He says to Avram, "To your seed I have given this land, from the river of Mitsrayim (the Nile) as far as the great river, the river Euphrates. All the land which the current people now inhabit I give to your seed (Gen 15:17-21). You will continue to be a sojourner in the land; it is your seed that will inherit it. The land belongs to me; all the earth belongs to me. I take it from whom I wish, and give it to whom I wish. It is all according to my plan of creation, to make man in my image."

Hagar Conceives by Avram, 16:1

"MY MASTER," says Sarai to Avram (1Pe 3:6), "we have been in this land for all of ten years since we left Ḥaran. You are now eighty-five and I am seventy-five. Where is this promise of children? My monthly flow has ended and Yahuah has prevented me from bearing. It is apparent to me that the promise is not going to come through me."

"I know the promise is true," replies Avram, "and perhaps you are right. What do you have in mind?"

"I have a slave girl, Hagar, that was given to me when we were in Mitsrayim, when you told me to say I am your sister and Par'oh took me into his harem. Because I own her, any children she has are mine. I give her to you as your second wife. Please, go into her; perhaps I will obtain children through her."

That night he goes into Hagar, and she conceives. When she becomes aware that she is with child, she lifts up her heart in pride and despises her mistress: "You can't conceive and I can. Ha, ha, ha. I'm better than you." And she begins acting as though she is above her. Whenever Sarai tells her to do something, instead of obeying humbly, she would toss her head and smirk and give a knowing look while doing it.

Finally Sarai has enough. "I'm not going to put up with this," she says. "She has to submit, and do it humbly." So she goes to her husband and says, "May the wrong done me be upon you. I gave my maid into your arms, but when she saw that she has conceived, she despises me. May Yahuah judge between you and me" (Gen 16:1-5).

"It's not my fault. I did what you said, and she got pregnant as you wanted. What is in her is my child, but yours also, for she is your slave. Although she is now also my wife, she is in your power, so do with her as you please. I wash my hands of it."

Sarai is now emboldened to treat this slave as she wishes, and so she does, harshly. (In type, the spirit-man must treat the flesh-man harshly.) "I'm not going to live like this," Hagar decides, "No way!" So she leaves and heads for Shur in Mitsrayim (Gen 16:6). The road leads through wilderness, but she remembers where the springs are. She had traveled the road before when leaving Mitsrayim with Avram and Sarai.

At one such spring she stops to drink the cold, clear water and to bathe her face. It feels so good! While she is resting under the shade of a palm tree, a man appears dressed in white. He is the angel of Yahuah, Yahuah himself manifesting as a man. "Hagar, Sarai's maid," he says, "where have you come from and where are you going?"

"I am running away from the presence of my mistress Sarai."

"Go back," he says. "Return to your mistress, and submit yourself to her authority. She is your mistress, your owner. Respect her in that position. Yes, you conceived by her husband, but that is no reason to be proud and despise your mistress. Rather, you should be humble. It is I who withhold conception, and it is I who give conception.

"This I will do for you, because of Avram my servant. I will greatly multiply your seed so that they will be too many to count. You are with child and will bear a son. You shall call his name Yishma'ĕl (Ishmael), because Yahuah has heard your affliction. He will be a wild donkey of a man, his hand against everyone and everyone's hand against him; and he will live to the east of all his brothers." Then he disappears.

This is the history of the nations in the mideast, all of which have become Muslim. The fighting between the different sects of Islam is an example of this prophecy.

She sits there for awhile, amazed, wondering what this all means. Then she says, "You are Ĕl Who Sees (Ĕl Ro'i). Have I even remained alive after seeing him? This well shall be called Be'ĕr-laḥai-ro'i; (the well of seeing alive)" (Gen 16:8-13).

In obedience to the heavenly command, Hagar returns. When she comes to Sarai she kneels with her forehead on the ground. "I am sorry," she says. "I have behaved badly. Please forgive me. You are my mistress and I am your slave."

"You are forgiven. You may get up now. What changed your mind to come back?"

"The angel of Yahuah appeared to me at the spring on the way to Shur and told me to return and submit to your authority. And he told me about the future of the child within me, what his name should be and what kind of person he and his seed would be."

In due time Hagar bares Avram a son, and Avram names him Yishma'ĕl, according to the word of the angel. Avram is now eighty-six years old (Gen 16:15-16).

119

Covenant of Circumcision, 17:1

THIRTEEN YEARS PASS QUICKLY. Avram doesn't go into Hagar again, and she is properly submitted to Sarai. "I am ninety-nine years old," he says to himself, "and life is good" (Gen 17:1).

Then Yahuah appears to him as before. "I am Ĕl Almighty (Ĕl Shaddai)," he says. "Walk before me, and be blameless. I will establish my covenant between me and you, and I will multiply you greatly." Avram falls on his face in homage, and Elohim continues.

"As for me, behold, my covenant is with you, and you will be the father of a multitude of nations. No longer shall your name be called Avram (exalted father), but your name shall be Avraham (father of a multitude); for I have made you the father of a multitude of nations. I will make you very fruitful, and I will make nations of you, and kings will come forth from you. I will establish my covenant between me and you and your seed after you throughout their generations for an everlasting covenant, to be Elohim to you and to your seed after you. I will give to you and to your seed after you the land that you have been sojourning in, all the land of Kena'an (Canaan), for a possession forever; and I will be their Elohim.

"Now as for you, you shall keep my covenant, you and your seed after you throughout their generations. This is my covenant, which you shall keep, between me and you and your seed after you: every male among you shall be circumcised (circumcision is a type of cutting off of the flesh nature). And you shall be circumcised in the flesh of your foreskin, and it shall be the sign of the covenant between me and you. And every male among you who is eight days old shall be circumcised throughout your generations. (Eight is a type of new beginnings.) This includes a servant who is born in your house (in type, children of believers), or who is bought with silver (in type, redemption) from any foreigner (in type, new converts), who is not of your seed; thus shall my covenant be in your flesh (in type, leaving the flesh nature) for an everlasting covenant. But any male who is not circumcised in the flesh of his foreskin (in type, a believer who does not work at leaving his flesh nature and overcoming sin), that person shall be cut off from his people; he has broken my covenant (Gen 17:1-14).

"I have this to say to you about your wife, Sarai. Even as I have changed your name, so I change hers. No longer call her Sarai (my princess), but Sarah (princess). I will bless her, and indeed I will give you a son by her. Then I will bless her, and she shall be nations; kings of peoples will come from her" (Gen 17:15-16). (In type, the last-day assembly harvest of souls.)

Avraham had arisen from his prostrate position by this time, but with this news he falls on his face and laughs, and thinks, "Will a child be born to a man one hundred years old? And will Sarah, who is ninety years old, bear?" Aloud he says to Elohim, "Oh that Yishma'ĕl might live before you!"

"No," Elohim replies. "That is not to be. But Sarah your wife will indeed bear you a son, and you shall call his name Yitsḥaq (Isaac, laughter); and I will establish my covenant with him for an everlasting covenant for his seed after him. As for Yishma'ĕl, I have heard you. Behold, I will bless him, and will make him fruitful and will multiply him greatly. He shall become the father of twelve princes, and I will make him a great nation. But my covenant I will establish with Yitsḥaq, whom Sarah will bear to you at this time next year." Then Elohim goes up from Avraham (Gen 17:17-22).

When Yahuah speaks and says to do something, if you love him, you will obey, and do it without delay. So Avraham proceeds immediately. He calls a meeting with his son and all the males in his household, and explains what happened and what they are going to do. "This is a covenant," he says. "It is between me and Yahuah, but it includes you because you are in my household. Every male, eight days and older, must be circumcised. The foreskin of the male organ must be cut off. That is the sign of the covenant. It will hurt, hurt badly. And it can take up to three weeks to heal fully." Avraham is 99 years old when he is circumcised, and Yishma'ĕl is thirteen (Gen 17:23-27).

Circumcision is the covenant sign of the decision to walk blamelessly before Yahuah and overcome the flesh nature. When we are born again, water immersion is the sign. It replaces the physical circumcision as the sign.

Sedom and Lot, 18-19

AVRAHAM IS SITTING at the door of his tent by the oaks of Mamrĕ when Yahuah and two angels appear to him as three men. He

121

recognizes one of them as Adonai (a title meaning Master and refers to Yahuah) and has refreshments prepared for them. Adonai tells him that the same time next year Sarah, his wife, will have a son. Sarah is listening, and laughs when she hears it.

Then the men go to a place that overlooks the valley and look down toward Sedom (Sodom), and Yahuah tells Avraham what he is about to do (type of Messiah, Jn 8:28). He says, "Shall I hide from Avraham what I am about to do, since Avraham will surely become a great and mighty nation, and in him all the nations of the earth will be blessed? For I have chosen him, so that he may command his children and his household after him to keep the way of Yahuah by doing righteous- ness and justice, so that Yahuah may bring upon Avraham what he has spoken about him." (Note the reason why Yahuah chose Avraham, and consider how this applies to bride beleivers.) Yahuah tells him that the wickedness of Sedom and Amorah (Gomorrah) is so great that he will destroy them. The particular wickedness is sex of men with men. (This is why homosexual sex is called sodomy.)

The two men (angels) then leave to go to Sedom to destroy it, and Avraham intercedes for the city. "What if there are fifty righteous in the city? Suppose forty-five? Suppose forty?" Avraham keeps drop- ping the number by five until he is down to ten. Then he stops and returns to his tent. For each number Yahuah says he won't destroy if there is that number (Gen 18:1-33). (In type, interceding for the lukewarm.)

When the two men come to Sedom it is evening and Lot is sitting in the gate of the city. When he sees them he invites them into his house to spend the night. When they decline and say they will stay in the square, Lot urges them strongly to come into his house. He knows the wickedness of the city and that if they stay in the square they will be attacked by the men of the city and raped. After they finish eating and before going to bed the men of the city, both young and old, surround the house and demand that Lot bring the two men out so they can rape them. Lot goes out, shutting the door behind him, and asks them not to be so wicked since the two men are under the shelter of his roof, and offers his two daughters to be raped instead. (In that culture, hospitality to strangers had greater importance. Also, women were property.) In response, the men start to attack Lot, calling him an alien; but the two men pull him inside and shut the door and strike the men with blindness so they can't find the door.

The two men then tell Lot that Yahuah has sent them to destroy the place because the wickedness is so great (judgment comes on cities and nations because of sin), and ask him if he has any relatives to bring out of the city so they won't be destroyed with the others. Besides his wife and two daughters who are in the house with them, there are two men in the city who are engaged to his daughters. Lot goes out to tell them of the coming judgment and to leave with them immediately, but they think he is joking and pay no attention.

When morning dawns the angels urge Lot to quickly leave the city with his wife and two daughters so as not to be swept away in the punishment of the city. When Lot hesitates, because of Yahuah's compassion for him, the men seize his hand and the hands of his wife and two daughters and pull them outside the city. Then the angels say, "Escape for your life! Do not look behind you, and do not stay anywhere in the valley; escape to the mountains, or you will be swept away." (In type, escaping to high places in Yahuah.)

Because Lot is afraid the disaster might overtake him before he escapes to the mountains, he asks if they may stop at the small town of Tso'ar (Zoar). The men grant his request and promise not to destroy that town with the rest of the towns in the valley. But they urge him to hurry, for they can't begin the judgment until he and his family are safely there. (In type, the tribulation judgment can't come until after the rapture.)

By the time they reach Tso'ar, the sun is up, and Yahuah rains on Sedom and Amorah brimstone and fire out of heaven and overthrows those cities, and all the valley, and all the inhabitants of the cities, and all vegetation. (In type, the light of Yahuah brings judgment.) Lot's wife looks back to see the destruction, and becomes a pillar of salt (Gen 19:1-26). (In type, if you look back to the world you will lose your salvation and your position in Yahuah. Lot and his daughters who didn't look back are a type of the bride in this situation.)

In the meantime, Avraham has risen early in the morning and gone to the place where he had stood before with Yahuah. He looks down toward Sedom and Amorah and all the land of the valley and sees the smoke of the land ascend like the smoke of a furnace. But, because of Avraham's request regarding the righteous, Yahuah has protected Lot so that he and his two daughters would not perish in the judgment

(Gen 19:27-29).

"These things happened to them as examples and were written down as warnings for us, on whom the fulfillment of the ages has come" (1Cor 10:11, NIV).

Why was Lot living in the city? What happened to his flocks, herds and servants? Formerly he was living in tents. He had separated from Avram because they were so many, and had chosen the well-watered valley. Where are they now? Scripture doesn't say.

Scripture records only what Yahuah wants us to know. In this incident we see several types. Lot is a type of the believer who has become lukewarm and worldly. He was prospering spiritually while living in the hill country with Avram, but the people of the valley where he chose to live were wicked. This affected his spiritual life. But in his mercy, Elohim rescued him from destruction in hell.

The angels encouraging Lot and his family to leave Sedom is a type of the bride believers calling the lukewarm to repent of their lukewarmness and become fervent for Yahushua. The judgment that came on Sedom and Amorah is a type of the tribulation on believers after the rapture. It is also a type of judgment in hell. The sons-in-law of Lot who thought the warning of judgment is a joke, are a type of lukewarm believers who take the mark of the beast in the tribulation, lose their salvation, and go to hell (Rev 13:11-18). Lot delaying to leave Sedom is a type of how hard it is to leave the flesh nature of the world, but some do make the decision to do so. His wife looking back and becoming a pillar of salt is a type of starting to leave luke-warmness, but not really willing to leave the world, so goes back to it and experiences the two-fold judgment—dying spiritually in the great tribulation by taking the mark of the beast, and spending eternity in hell.

When Lot with his wife and daughters reach Tso'ar, the judgment on the other cities in the valley begins. After reaching Tso'ar, Lot's wife looks back and dies (Gen 19:22-26). Lot and his daughters are frightened out of their mind at their narrow escape with death! And the fear of Yahuah is on them. Anyone with a close encounter of death because of a near accident or serious disease can understand this. "We must leave," says Lot to his daughters, his whole body trembling. "Judgment might come here also. We have to go up in the mountains away from this valley of judgment (Joel 3:2,12, prophecy of the Battle of Armageddon). I know these mountains and where some caves are where people stay when they are in danger" (Gen 19:30).

He leads them to a suitable cave, one that has been used before for cooking and sleeping, and they make it their home. "Look for any sheep or goats that no longer have an owner," he tells his daughters. "We also are going to plant a vineyard so we can make wine." In time they are well settled in the cave as their home.

"When are we going to live among other people," ask his daughters. "It's lonely here."

"I'm still shaking from our narrow escape," he responds. "When I'm ready I'll let you know."

"I'm worried," says the elder to the younger. "The ones who were to be our husbands are dead, our father is old, and he has no wife to preserve his seed. It is up to us to do it. It is our duty. This is what we will do. We will make our father drink wine so that he gets drunk and won't know what he is doing. Then tonight I will lie with him so he puts his seed in me, and then tomorrow night we will get him drunk again, and you lie with him so he puts his seed in you."

They follow through on their plan, and both became pregnant by their father. After the second night they tell him what they did. "It was to preserve your seed," they say.

"What is done is done," he responds.

In the course of time they give birth to healthy boys. Lot is both their father and grandfather, and he delights in them. The older daughter names her son Mo'av (Moab) (from father). The Mo'avi (Moabites) would come from him. The younger daughter names her son Ben-ammi (son of my people). The Ammoni (Ammonites) would come from him (Gen 19:31-38).

The line of Messiah comes through Teraḥ, Avraham, Yitsḥaq (Isaac) and Ya'aqov (Jacob). Teraḥ did homage to (worshiped) idols, but Avraham, Yitsḥaq and Ya'aqov did homage to Yahuah Elohim. The other seed of Teraḥ, except for Lot, did homage to idols, as did the other seed of Avraham (namely, Yishma'ĕl and Midian) and of Yitsḥaq (namely, Ěsaw).

Elohim gave to Mo'av (the Mo'avi that came from him) the land east of the Dead Sea (Deut 2:10-11). They hired Bil'am (Balaam) to curse Yisra'ĕl

125

during their exodus from Mitsrayim to the promised land (Num 22-24) and practiced rites of religious prostitution connected with slaughter offerings to the dead (Num 25:1ff).

The Ammoni also joined with Mo'av in hiring Bil'am to curse Yisra'ĕl (Deut 23:4). The Ammoni were probably more of a predatory tribe, moving from place to place, while the Mo'avi were more settled. They inhabited the country east of the Yardĕn and north of Mo'av and the Dead Sea (Easton's Bible Dictionary).

Keep in mind that Elohim decides who is born when and by whom and where they live and when they die (Ac 17:24-28). It is all according to his foreknowledge to have as many people as possible to be with him forever in the eternal kingdom. Those alive now were chosen to live in our present period of history, the time when greater works shall we do (the bride believers) than Yahushua did, because he has gone to the Father (Jn 14:12).

Yahushua said he came not to bring peace on earth, but rather division (Lk 12:51). Earlier we saw division between light and darkness, and between waters above and below the expanse. Always it is the remnant he is after, those who seek him for who he is as to his nature, with a desire to obey him out of love. These are the bride.

Avraham Deceives Avi-meleḥ, 20:1

AFTER SEEING THE DESTRUCTION of the cities in the valley, Avraham journeys south toward Mitsrayim and settles in the kingdom of Gerar. Avi-meleḥ (Abimelech) is the title for the king, not his personal name; it means "my father is king." While there he falls into the same sin of insecurity that he experienced with Par'oh in Mitsrayim. Although Sarah is now much older, she is still very beautiful, a true princess. Avraham is afraid for his life, so he says to Avi-meleḥ, "She is my sister," and Sarah confirms it, saying "He is my brother." So Avi-meleḥ takes her into his harem, but he doesn't come near her.

After some time Avi-meleḥ notices that neither his wife nor any of the women in his household are getting pregnant. "Why is this happening," he wonders, and in a dream at night he learns the reason.

"Behold," says Elohim to him, "you are a dead man because of the woman whom you have taken, for she is married."

"Adonai (Master)," he responds, "will you murder a nation, one that is righteous? They said they were sister and brother. In the integrity of my heart and the innocence of my hands I have done this."

"I know that," says Elohim. "It is I who kept you from touching her, to keep you from sinning against me. This is what you must do. Return her to her husband, for he is a prophet, and he will pray for you so that you live. But if you don't, then not only will you die, but also all who are yours." (In type, the world wants the character beauty of the bride, but cannot get it.)

In the morning Avi-meleh tells his servants about the dream, and they are very frightened. These are religious people, people who believe in the supernatural, even though they bow to the wrong elohim. He then confronts Avraham. "Why did you do this? How have I wronged you that you have brought on me and on my kingdom a great sin? What you did ought not to be done."

"Because" Avraham replies, "I thought surely there is no fear of Elohim in this place, and they will kill me because of my wife. Besides, she really is my sister, the daughter of my father, but not the daughter of my mother, and she became my wife. When Elohim caused me to leave my father's house and come to this land, I told her to show kindness to me, wherever we go, by saying I am her brother."

Avi-meleh then gives to Avraham sheep and oxen and male and female servants and restores his wife Sarah to him. Then he says to Avraham, "Behold, my land is before you; settle wherever you please." And to Sarah he says, "Behold, I have given your brother a thousand pieces of silver; behold, it is your vindication before all who are with you, and before all men you are cleared." (In type, this is taking loot [spoil] from the nations for the work of Elohim.)

Then Avraham prays to Elohim, and Elohim heals Avi-meleh and his wife and his maids, so that they bear (Gen 20:1-18).

Some things should be noted in this incident. Despite Avraham's insecurity and unbelief, Yahuah is with him. Yahuah is shaping him to be the man he knows he will become. What an example of how he cares for us, despite our failings!

He has a plan for Avraham's life, and that plan will be accomplished (Is 55:11). He also has a plan for each of us who have been created in Messiah Yahushua through being born again (2Cor 5:17).

Each of us is his workmanship to work in his kingdom (Eph 2:10). Before he created anything, on the basis of his foreknowledge, he chose whom he would save, and prepared works for each of us to do. And he will work with us, through all our ups and downs, to get us to the place that we do them. He doesn't need us to do his works, but he loves to have us involved in what he is doing, as a father toward his sons. It is for our benefit, and this gives him pleasure.

Yitsḥaq Born, Hagar and Yishma'ĕl Sent Away, 21:1

AVRAHAM IS NOW one hundred years old, and Sarah is ninety. He is beyond having viable seed, and she is beyond bearing. Conception is impossible, medically speaking. But with Elohim, all things are possible (Mk 10:27). Yahuah fulfills his promise, and Sarah conceives and bears a son. Note: it was at the appointed time. Yahuah has an appointed time for each of his promises to be fulfilled. He knows how to accomplish what he sends his word to do (Is 55:11).

Avraham calls the name of his son Yitsḥaq (Isaac, laughter), for Sarah laughed when she heard she would conceive, laughed when she gave birth, and said everyone would laugh when they hear of it. Imagine, a woman of her age, giving birth! Then, when he is eight days old Avraham circumcises him, according to Elohim's command. Yitsḥaq grows and is weaned, and Avraham makes a great feast on the day he is weaned. Weaning was between two and three years old.

Yishma'ĕl is seventeen and his mother, Hagar, has been dutifully submissive to Sarah. According to custom, the mother has the sole responsibility for a son until he is weaned. After that, he is the father's responsibility. Avraham has been training Yishma'ĕl for fourteen years, and now he has another son to train. He loves them both dearly, but is bonded more closely to his firstborn.

Now a problem arises. Yishma'ĕl no longer has his father's attention as before, and he becomes jealous—typical sibling rivalry, except Yitsḥaq is only three years old! Yishma'ĕl wants all the attention on himself, so he begins mocking Yitsḥaq, belittling him. The words he was saying, we don't know, but we do know the attitude he was displaying. Likely he was pointing out his superiority as being the firstborn and therefore the one who would receive the firstborn inheritance. Sarah sees it, and is angry. She had seen this attitude in

Hagar when Hagar became pregnant, and she is seeing the same attitude now in Hagar's son. So she goes to Avraham.

"*Adoni*, my master," she says, "I know Yishma'ĕl is your firstborn, but the promise of inheritance is through me. You've heard him mocking Yitshaq, as though he is superior. The only solution is for Hagar to take her son and go. The son of this maid shall not be an heir with my son Yitshaq!"

"I love Yishma'ĕl," he replies. "He is my son. How can I send him away? You are upsetting me. What you are requesting is evil in my eyes. I'll see what I can do to stop this mocking."

Avraham is going by his natural understanding. And as he is thinking about this, Elohim speaks to him. "Do not let it be evil in your eyes because of the boy and your handmaid; whatever Sarah tells you, listen to her, for your seed shall be named through Yitshaq. As for the son of the maid, I will make a nation from him also, because he is your seed" (Gen 20:1-13).

Yahuah is in control of circumstances. The whole story of Hagar and Yishma'ĕl, and Sarah and Yitshaq, was planned by Yahuah to be a type of the comparison between the law given on Mount Sinai and salvation by favor given through Yahushua Messiah.

The apostle Paul explains this in his letter to the gentile believers in Galatia. Judaizers* had come to their assembly telling them that believing in and following Yahushua as the savior was not enough for salvation, but they must also follow the Jewish law of circumcision, that without circumcision they could not be saved. The opposite is the truth, explains Paul, and that if they get circumcised they will lose their salvation. They will lose it not because of the circumcision, but because of trusting in the physical act, that what Yahushua did was not enough, that they needed the works of circumcision (Eph 2:8-9).

> *Judaizers; namely, Jewish Christians who demanded that Gentile Christians observe the Mosaic law, including ritual observances such as special days, kosher foods and circum-cision (Gal 3:1-7; 4:8-11,17,21-22). (Hard Sayings of the Bible, ©1983 by F.F. Bruce, InterVarsity Press, in BibleSoft.)

Before we go further we need to look at *Torah* (law, or more properly, instructions) given through Mosheh and what its purpose is. It contains the first five books of scripture—Genesis through Deuteronomy—the story of beginnings. The instructions are in three categories: moral, civil and ceremonial.

The moral instructions are summed up in the greatest two commandments. When asked by a Pharisee which is the greatest commandment, Yahushua answered: *"You shall love Yahuah your Elohim with all your heart, and with all your soul, and with all your mind. This is the great and foremost commandment. The second is like it: You shall love your neighbor as yourself. On these two commandments depend the whole Torah and the Prophets"* (Mt 12:34-40).

The reason these two are the greatest is because if you do them, you do no hurt to your neighbor. You don't need laws to tell you not to steal or murder or covet or commit sexual immorality if you live in love. The second greatest commandment is the natural outflow of the first—to love Yahuah your Strong One with all that you are. Without this first, it is impossible to do the second the way Yahuah intends. These two greatest laws are the foundation of morality, and are eternal. These are the rules of the kingdom. We will be following them for eternity in the new heaven and new earth. They never pass away.

Paul said the same thing: *"Owe nothing to anyone except to love one another, for he who loves his neighbor has fulfilled Torah. ... Love does no wrong to a neighbor; therefore love is the fulfillment of Torah"* (Ro 13:8,10).

Civil instructions have to do with obeying those in authority in civil government. These instructions are temporary for this life only, and they vary according to the government under which each one lives. Paul wrote, *"Let every soul be subject to the governing authorities. For there is no authority except from Elohim, and those which exist are established by Elohim"* (Rom 13:1).

Ceremonial instructions are the great majority of instructions in Torah, and they are all fulfilled in Messiah. We no longer go to Jerusalem for the three annual festivals—Passover, Pentecost and Ingathering (Feast of Booths/Tabernacles)—to do the animal sacrifices and harvest offerings. He fulfilled the ceremonial washings required when one is doing "unclean" things, such as giving birth, having the monthly cycle, touching dead things, etc. He also fulfilled all the instructions having to do with clean and unclean meats. All foods are now "clean" (Mk 7:19; Col 2:14; 1Ti 4:1-5). Some foods are more healthy than others, but that is a different subject and has nothing to do with what is "clean" and "unclean."

Another ceremonial instruction is the fourth commandment, the one in which we are to set-apart the Sabbath (the seventh day). This also was discussed earlier, that the Sabbath is a sign of living our whole lives, every day of our lives, for Messiah. Messiah fulfills that sign, so for us every day is the Sabbath.

Circumcision is another ceremonial instruction. Yahuah gave this to Avraham before Yahuah gave the written instructions to Mosheh during the Exodus. This also was discussed earlier, and that its fulfillment is in water immersion. As a ceremonial law, it was the sign of the covenant; it showed that you belonged to the covenant people, namely, the Jews, or, more properly, the Yisra'eli. This was the law that Paul was addressing. In his argument to prove his point, he refers to the incident of Hagar and Yishma'ĕl leaving Avraham and Sarah (Gal 4:21-31).

Salvation is by favor through faith, not by ourselves; it is the gift of Elohim, not of works (works include keeping ceremonial Torah), lest we should boast (Eph 2:8-9). The Jews believed salvation was by doing the works of Torah, and those of them who converted to Messiah believed that keeping Torah was still necessary. But the new covenant in Messiah is by promise, not by works, as the story of Hagar and Yishma'ĕl being sent away illustrates. Before Messiah, the ceremonies were a foreshadow and prophecy of the fulfillment in him. Now that he has come, they are done away. The Book of Hebrews particularly deals with this subject, that even as the Aaronic Priesthood was replaced by the Melchizedek one in Messiah, so also all the ceremonial laws are fulfilled in him. The old was a foreshadow of the new. The principle of giving and tithing, however, continues, for *"it is more blessed to give than to receive"* (Ac 20:35).

We now return to the narrative, as it may have been.

Avraham does as Sarah requests and sends the mother and son away. According to custom, he gives each of them bread and enough water to sustain them to the next well, and asks Hagar, concern in his voice, "You do know the way to the next well, do you not?" She assures him that she knows, she's been there before, and there should be no problem. And to Yishma'ĕl he says, "I love you, my son. You are a grown man now, seventeen years old. Take care of your mother. You are now the man of your family."

And so they depart. But she loses the way, misses the well, and they wander in the wilderness of Be'ĕr-Sheva (Beersheba), a large area that borders Mitsrayim. Eventually they run out of water. "I feel sick," Yishma'ĕl says, then falls from heat exhaustion and dehydration. She leaves him under one of the bushes and sits down opposite him, about a bowshot away so as not to see him die, and then wails and sobs. Keep in mind, Yahuah is in charge of all circumstances, and arranges them for our benefit (Ro 8:28).

Elohim hears the lad crying; and the angel of Elohim calls to Hagar from heaven, "What is the matter with you, Hagar? Do not be afraid, for Elohim has heard the lad's voice. Get up, lift up the lad and hold him by the hand, for I will make a great nation of him." Then Elohim opens her eyes and she sees a well of water; and she goes and fills the skin with water and gives the lad a drink (Gen 21:9-19).

Why didn't Hagar see the well? It was there, but she didn't see it. This is a type of being spiritually blind when in a trial. The solution is there, but we don't see it. But when it gets desperate, because of his mercy, Elohim shows up.

Elohim is with Yishma'ĕl as he grows up. He lives in the wilderness of Pa'ran (the north-eastern section of the Sinai peninsula) and becomes an archer, and his mother gets a Mitsri (Egyptian) wife for him (Gen 21:20), (in type, a wife from the world, and she herself is of the world). We next hear of him when he meets with his brother Yitsḥaq for the burial of their father, Avraham, and he lives to be 137 years old. We will meet some of his descendents later. He becomes the founder of many Arab tribes, constantly fighting with one another and with anyone else, and spreads throughout Northern Arabia from the Red Sea to the Euphrates. *"He will be a wild donkey of a man; his hand will be against everyone and everyone's hand against him, and he will live in hostility toward all his brothers"* (Gen 16:12, NIV).

There is something of interest to note regarding Yishma'ĕl that applies to our lives today. Yahuah has a plan for his descendants, most of whom are now Muslims. The plan has to do with the last days' judgment against Yisra'ĕl, but also for the salvation of many. In this life, Yahuah is with every person—no exception. Some will respond to him; most will not.

Avraham Makes a Covenant with Avi-meleḥ, 21:22

WE MET AVI-MELEḤ EARLIER regarding Sarah, wife and sister of Avraham. We meet him now again. He sees the prosperity of Avraham in both possessions and servants, and is concerned for his kingdom, even though he has an army. So he and his army commander come to Avraham with a proposal. He says, "Elohim is with you in all that you do; now therefore, swear to me here by Elohim that you will not deal falsely with me or with my offspring or with my posterity, but according to the kindness that I have shown to you, you shall show to me and to the land in which you are sojourning."

Avraham agrees, but complains to him about the wells he had dug, that Avi-meleḥ's servants were seizing them. (In type, the world trying to stop the anointing of the bride.) He denies knowledge of it, that this is the first time to hear of it. So Avraham takes some sheep and oxen and gives them to Avi-meleḥ, and the two of them make a covenant.

Avraham sets seven ewe lambs of the flock by themselves, and when Avi-meleḥ asks the meaning, Avraham says, "Take them, so that it may be a witness to me, that *I* dug this well." Therefore he called that place Be'ĕr-Sheva (Beersheba, well of an oath), because there the two of them took an oath. After Avi-meleḥ and his commander leave, Avraham plants a tamarisk tree at Be'ĕr-Sheva, and there he calls on the name of Yahuah, Ĕl Olam (Yahuah, Strong One Everlasting) (Gen 21:22-34). Remember, calling on Yahuah's name means you're appealing to him for help on the basis of his character of mercy and love, and acknowledging him as your Strong One.

In this incident we see a meeting between two religions: the follower of Yahuah, the only true Strong One, and followers of false strong ones. The followers of the false know about the True One, and know that the True One is the one who is bringing the prosperity. Avraham is letting his light shine that others may know the truth. Avi-meleḥ sees this, but is not willing to leave his false way. What he wants is peace, that there be no fighting. Avraham agrees that there be peace, but he refuses to be taken advantage of. He points out a problem (the wells), and stops the problem with a peace offering.

Water in wells is fresh because it is supplied by underground water in rivulets and in porous rock or soil. Scripture calls this living water (Jn 7:38). This is in contrast to water in cisterns, holes dug in the ground to hold water and is not fresh. In type, water from the well is the believer living in the spirit through obedience to Yahuah and getting refreshed through regular prayer and scripture reading. The unbeliever sees the result in the believer's life, but doesn't want any of it. In fact, he tries to stop or hinder it (the seizing of the wells). But the believer refuses to stop, and does what is necessary to keep his spiritual life alive and prospering. The more we become like Yahu-shua, who is the exact representation of Elohim, the more we will have opposition from the world.

Regarding the tamarisk tree, it is a long-lived tree of hard wood and thickly clustered evergreen leaves. As such, it is a type of the ever-enduring favor of the faithful covenant Elohim. (Information from Keil and Delitzsch commentary in Biblesoft.) Pagans often planted a group of this tree to make a grove in order to worship their false gods, and when Yisra'ĕl went into apostasy they did the same thing (Is 1:9). Some have wondered whether Avraham was doing the same thing. The answer is "No." His planting was not for a worship of false gods but as a reminder of the faithfulness of Elohim. There he called upon the name of Yahuah. To call upon his name is to declare our commitment to him and acknowledge our dependence upon him.

Avraham Offers Yitsḥaq as a Burnt Offering, 22:1

WHEN YITSḤAQ IS 33½ years old (age based on typology), Avraham hears Yahuah call him. "Avraham!" he calls.

"Behold, here I."

"Take now your son, your only son, whom you love, Yitsḥaq, and go to the land of Moriyah (Moriah) and offer him there for a burnt offering on one of the hills of which I will tell you."

Avraham obeys. He calls for his son and two young men and says, "Tomorrow we are going to make a burnt offering on a hill Yahuah will show me. Split some wood for the fire. We leave tomorrow."

The next morning they are up early, Avraham saddles his donkey, and they leave with the wood and some live coals. On the third day he sees the place from a distance and says to the two young men, "Stay here with the donkey while we go on."

Avraham takes the wood for the burnt offering and lays it on his son (Yahushua carried his stake, *"Take up your stake daily"*), and takes in his hand the fire and the knife. So the two of them walk on together. "My father!" says Yitsḥaq.

"Here I am, my son."

"We have the fire and the wood, but where is the lamb for the burnt offering?"

"Elohim will provide for himself the lamb for the burnt offering, my son."

Eventually they come to the place of which Elohim had told him. Avraham builds the altar and arranges the wood. "My son," he says, "you asked about the lamb. Yahuah told me that you, my son, my only begotten son, the one whom I love dearly, you are the offering. You are a young man in full adult strength. Are you willing to be offered? You will recall that Yahuah told me that I will have many descendents from you, more than grains of sand on the seashore and more than stars in the sky. That means, my son, that he will raise you from the dead. Are you willing for me to bind you and lay you on the altar and kill you as one kills a lamb?" While he is speaking he is looking with eyes full of deep love into his son's eyes." (Yahushua willingly laid down his life for us.)

Yitsḥaq sees that love and trusts his father. "Yes, I am willing."

Avraham then binds him, lays him on the altar on top of the wood, and takes the knife to cut his throat. Through all this his son's eyes are fixed on him. Such love they see in the eyes of each other!

His hand is raised to cut his son's throat when the angel of Yahuah calls to him from heaven: "Avraham, Avraham!"

"Behold, I."

"Do not harm the lad, for now I know that you fear Elohim, since you have not withheld your son, your only son, from me."

Then Avraham turns and sees a ram caught in the thicket by its horns. He releases his son and offers it up for a burnt offering in the place of his son, and calls the name of that place Yahuah-yir'eh (Jehovah Jireh, Yahuah will see [to it]).

135

The angel of Yahuah speaks to Avraham again from heaven: "By myself I have sworn, because you have done this thing and have not withheld your son, your only son, indeed I will greatly bless you, and I will greatly multiply your seed as the stars of the heavens and as the sand which is on the seashore; and your seed shall possess the gate of their enemies. In your seed all the nations of the earth shall be blessed, because you have obeyed my voice" (Gen 22:1-18). To posses the gate of one's enemies means to take from them their power and authority.

This incident is a powerful type. Avraham is a type of our Father who, because of his love for us, offered his only begotten son to die in our place that our sins be forgiven; and Yitshaq is a type of Yahushua Messiah who, also because of his love for us and for his Father, agreed to be nailed to a stake to be that offering.

By faith Avraham, when he was tested, offered up Yitshaq, and he who had received the promises was offering up his only begotten; to whom it was said, "In Yitshaq your seed shall be called," considering that Elohim is able to raise up even from the dead, from which he also received him back as a type (Heb 11:17-19).

What faith—to obey Yahuah in something that is totally contrary to reason! In the pagan culture around him people were giving their firstborn children to be slain as offerings to their gods. The offering to Moleh (Molech) was by placing the live baby on the arms of the idol, arms which had been heated to glowing red; and there the baby would scream until it was dead. It was this sin, among many others, that brought their wickedness to the full, so that Elohim commanded the children of Yisra'ĕl, when they entered the Promised Land from Mitsrayim, to totally destroy them—man, woman and child—and occupy the land. Yahuah did not want his people to take on the customs of the land and so be destroyed themselves.

It is thought by many that the hill of Moriyah where the event took place was the hill on which Yahushua was impaled. The wood that was laid on Yitshaq is a type of Yahushua carrying his stake (or cross) on which he would be impaled. It was on the third day of the journey that Avraham saw the place where he was to offer his son. Three is a type of resurrection. In type, Yitshaq was raised from the dead on the third day.

This incident also has a powerful spiritual truth for our lives. Because Avraham obeyed Yahuah to give up what was the most precious to him, an obedience out of love, he was worthy to receive the blessing. Yahushua said:

> *"He who loves his father or mother more than me is not worthy of me; and he who loves his son or daughter more than me is not worthy of me; and he who does not take his stake and follow me is not worthy of me. He who finds his life will lose it, and he who loses his life for my sake will find it"* (Mt 10:37-39).

The blessing the bride of Messiah seeks is oneness with the Father and son in intimate fellowship (1Jn 1:3).

Avraham Buys a Field to Bury Sarah, 23:1

IN THIS CHAPTER Sarah dies in the land of Kena'an (Canaan), having lived 127 years. After Avraham finishes mourning for her, he buys a field for a burial site for 400 shekels of silver from the inhabitants and receives a deed for the property. The field has a cave in it and trees, and he buries his wife in the cave.

Of note in this chapter is that Avraham now owns land in the Promised Land. Before this, he was a sojourner in the land. A sojourner is someone who lives in a land that is not his.

Silver is a type of redemption. The number 400 is 4x10x10. Four is the number of the world, and 10 is the number of completion in the world. 10x10=100, x4=400. This means great completion in the world. Some examples of the number 100 are: Avraham was 100 when Yitsḥaq was born to him; Yisra'ĕl's army often appear in groups of a 100; and Ovadyahu (Obadiah) hid 100 prophets from Izavel (Jezebel).

The number 100 also is the principle of completion. We see this in the parable of the lost sheep, in which the number of sheep was not complete with just having 99. The lost one had to be found to complete the number. The number 100 suggests a large return, as in the parable of the good soil which produced a hundredfold crop (Lk 8:8,11-15).

Avraham's buying the plot of land was, as it were, a down payment on the whole land for his seed, through Yitsḥaq and Ya'aqov, to occupy. In type, it is being born again and water immersed in the name of Yahushua Messiah: you have made a claim; now you must live it to get all its benefits.

V. YITSHAQ TO YA'AQOV
Genesis 24-26

"Will you go with this man?" And she said, "I will go."
Genesis 24:58

Yitshaq Gets Rivqah as Wife, 24:1

IN THIS CHAPTER Yitshaq (Isaac) gets a wife, and the account of it is full of typology. In the story, Yitshaq represents Yahushua Messiah, Avraham represents Yahuah, Rivqah (Rebecca) represents the bride, and the servant represents the bride believers going to get the bride, as the crier does in the parable of the ten virgins (Mt 25).

The chief servant is in charge of all that Avraham owns. This represents us, the bride believers, being full of the spirit and having everything we need to do the Father's will in going out to get the bride. Messiah cannot return to earth to get his bride; his servants must do the work to find the bride.

Placing the hand under the thigh, a location near the reproductive organs, was a cultural way to swear a vow. For us, this represents making a solemn commitment to do exactly what the Father says to do. Back then, vows were serious things, and they should be serious for us. Scripture gives many warnings regarding them (Ecc 5:4-6). The marriage vow is an example—do not go into it lightly, and having gone into it, follow it. This applies to being born again: it is a vow to love and obey Yahushua for the rest of your life, and to grow in that love.

The vow Avraham had his servant make was to get a bride for his son, but not from among the daughters of the Kena'ani (Canaanites) where he was living, but rather from his own country and relatives, namely, his elder brother Nahor who was living in Padan-Aram in the area of Haran, the place he left to come to Kena'an. The Kena'ani are a type of the world; Avraham's country and relatives are a type of the assembly and believers in Yahushua. Most believers are not the bride—they are lukewarm. These relatives are in idolatry. Our job is

139

to call them out into fervent love for Yahushua, *"having no spot or wrinkle or any such thing, but set-apart and blameless"* (Eph 5:27).

The servant asks what he should do if the woman isn't willing to come, and is told that, should that happen, then he is released from the vow, and further, that he is not to take his son back there. The woman must come of her own free will without first seeing her husband-to-be. *"Whom not having seen, you love; in whom though now you do not see, you are believing"* (1Pe 1:8). Messiah has risen and is in heaven ruling with all authority over heaven and earth. He is not coming to earth until after his bride is ready. Our task is to find those who are willing to become the bride, and not to force those who are not willing. The bride position is voluntary. We have been given free will—a most precious thing, but a dangerous thing if we choose our own way instead of Elohim's.

The servant leaves with ten camels and a variety of things from his master, and also a number of men to be his companions. (In type, a team ministry to get the bride of Messiah.)

Ten is the number of completeness in this world, and the variety of things are *charismata*, the manifestations of favor or spiritual gifts (1Cor 12). We do not go out with our own natural abilities and earthly personality, but with the Master's life and light in us (Mt 5:16) as we are being changed into his image (2Cor 3:18), and with the fruit of the spirit (Gal 5:22-23). Yahuah gives us all we need to bring others into the kingdom and to be the bride.

It is at evening, the time when women go out to draw water, that the servant arrives outside the city of Naḥor by the well spring. Women are a type of believers, the spring is a type of living water from Messiah, and evening is a type of the last days before Messiah's return. In the parable of the ten virgins, it was at midnight that the call went out that the bridegroom has come (Mt 25).

After arriving at the well the servant makes the camels kneel. These are the animals used to carry the variety of things from the master. Kneeling represents humility. We are to carry what Elohim has given us with humility—we have nothing in ourselves of value, only what Yahuah gives us. The one that Yahuah esteems is the one who is humble and contrite in spirit and trembles at his word (Is 66:2).

At this time the servant asks Yahuah for a sign regarding what woman will be the bride. He asks, "May it be that the girl to whom I say, 'Please let down your jar so that I may drink,' and who answers, 'Drink, and I will water your camels also,' that this is the one." Before he finishes speaking Rivqah arrives. She is the granddaughter of Nahor, Avraham's deceased brother, and the sister of Lavan (Laban), whom we will meet later. She is a virgin and very beautiful, and has a jar on her shoulder. She goes down into the well to the spring, fills her jar and comes up. He asks her for a drink, she gives it and also draws water for the camels. She is fulfilling the sign, and the servant is wondering if she is the one, that his journey is successful or not. (In type, the bride are those who are humble and look for opportunities to serve Yahuah.)

After the camels have finished drinking, the servant gives her a gold ring weighing a half-shekel and two wrist bracelets weighing ten shekels in gold. Jewelry rings were commonly worn in the nose and on the ears. Gold is a type of the nature of Elohim. The wrist is a part of the hand, and the hand represents what we do with our lives. Ten, again, is the number of completeness in this world, and two is the number of strength. So two gold bracelets weighing ten shekels represents us, the bride, living our lives for Elohim with his strength. The nose is a type of breath and discernment, and the ears are a type of spiritual hearing and obedience from faith. The bride is given all that she needs to manifest the nature of Elohim in all that she does.

After giving her the gifts the servant learns that she is a relative of his master, and he bows low and does homage to Yahuah, thanking him for success. Rivqah informs her family of what transpired, and they invite him to stay with them. They prepare a meal for him and his companions, but he won't eat until he states his reason for coming. He begins by saying how rich his master Avraham is—flocks, herds, silver, gold, servants, maids, camels and donkeys, all provided by Yahuah. Then he states the vow he made to his master to get a wife for the son from his father's house and relatives and what to do if the maid isn't willing. Then he relates what happened at the spring—his asking Yahuah for a sign, and that Rivqah fulfilled the sign. He concludes by saying, "So now if you are going to deal kindly and truly with my master, tell me; and if not, let me know, that I may turn to the right hand or the left" (Gen 24:1-49).

Lavan and Bethu'ĕl, the girl's brother and father, reply, "The matter comes from Yahuah; so we can't say anything. Take her to be the wife of your master's son, as Yahuah has spoken."

On hearing their words, Avraham's servant bows to the ground before Yahuah, then brings out articles of silver and gold and garments and gives them to Rivqah, and also precious things to her brother and her mother (Gen 24:53). (A type of equipping the bride with spiritual gifts, and also giving spiritual gifts to believers who are not the bride.)

After a night's sleep he says, according to custom, "Send me away to my master." But Rivqah's brother and mother are not willing. They want her to stay with them for ten days before she leaves. This is a type of lukewarm believers hindering other believers who want to become the bride. Also, bride believers are the most active in an assembly, doing most of the church work. The lukewarm don't want them to leave. The number ten, again, is completeness in this world.

But the servant asks not to be delayed, since Yahuah has prospered his way. This is a type of not compromising with the lukewarm and of not being sidetracked by offers from the world. So, reluctantly, they call Rivqah to ask what she wants to do. "Will you go with this man?" they ask. She says she will go. (In type, when the bride hears the invitation, she will go, without knowing where or what the situation will be.) And so they send her with her nurse to leave with the servant and his men. Before she leaves they bless her saying, "May you, our sister, become thousands of ten thousands, and may your seed possess the gate of those who hate them" (Gen 24:50-61).

Yitshaq has gone out to meditate in the field in the evening (a type of the end times) when looking up, he sees camels coming. When Rivqah sees him and learns who he is, she puts her veil on, showing modesty. (In type, she is coming in his righteousness, not her own.) Then the servant tells Yitshaq all that had transpired, and Yitshaq brings her into the tent of his mother, and she becomes his wife and he loves her, and he is comforted after his mother's death (Gen 24:62-67).

The mother, in type, is the church out of which comes the bride. The marriage of the bride is a type of the rapture, after which the rest of the church dies in the tribulation. The whole purpose of creation and the seven thousand years of man on the earth is to get the bride. It is a grief that most don't become the bride, but getting the bride makes it worthwhile.

Avraham Dies, Ĕsaw and Ya'aqov Born, 25:1

THIS CHAPTER NOTES the end of Avraham's life. He takes another wife, Qeturah (Keturah), who bears him six sons. The rejuvenation that enabled him to father Yitsḥaq is still working. Of the six sons, the most notable is Medan (Midian), for the people that come from him are involved in later events recorded in scripture. In his last days Avraham gives all that he has to Yitsḥaq (in type, Messiah gets all), but to the sons of his concubines, Hagar and Qeturah, he also gives gifts and sends them away to the land of the east (Gen 25:1-6). The two wives are called concubines because they don't have the status of Sarah.

Avraham dies when 175 years old and is buried next to Sarah by his sons Yitsḥaq and Yishma'ĕl (Gen 25:7-10). There is no evidence of animosity between the two brothers. After the death of Avraham Elohim blesses his son Yitsḥaq (Gen 25:11). The blessing promise to Avraham continues in him.

Regarding Yishma'ĕl, he lives to be 137 years old. The twelve tribes that come from him settle in northeast Arabia (Gen 25:12-18).

Yitsḥaq is forty when he marries Rivqah (Gen 25:20), the third year after his mother's death and when Avraham is in his 140th year. We don't know how old Rivqah was when Yitsḥaq married her, but likely fifteen or sixteen, which would make her about twenty-five years younger than he.

Bearing children was very important in their culture, as was noted regarding Sarah. It is Elohim who grants or withholds conception, and he does so for his purposes. *"All things work together for the good of those who love Elohim and are called according to his purpose"* (Ro 8:28). Women, as noted earlier, are types of the assembly. And in the assembly are two kinds of believers, the bride and the lukewarm. Sarah was withheld from conceiving so that Yishma'ĕl would come through Hagar and so that Yitsḥaq would be the son of promise—the flesh first, then the spirit. We saw this principle with Qayin and Hevel. Rivqah is barren so that the birth of her twin sons, the only children she will have, would be born when they are. All of this is in the *logos* of Elohim, his plan, before creation. Everything that happens—everything without exception—fits in with Elohim's plan to have a bride

143

with him for eternity.

Because Rivqah is barren for many years, Yitsḥaq prays to Yahuah, and Yahuah grants conception (Gen 25:21). The mature bride of Messiah who is ready to be raptured (Eph 5:27), comes at the end of the gentile church age. It seems as though she is barren, for she is few in number. But when the anointing comes at the end of the age, she will become many.

> *"Sing, barren one, you who did bear! Break forth into singing, and cry aloud, you who have not been in labor! For the children of the deserted one are more than the children of the married woman," said Yahuah* (Isa 54:1).

When Yitsḥaq took Rivqah as his wife, he is a type of Messiah and she a type of the bride. In his prayer for Rivqah to conceive, the type continues, for Messiah ever lives to intercede for us (Heb 7:25). The purpose of his interceding is that we mature to become his bride and bear fruit for the kingdom. The fruit, however, is of two kinds: the good and the bad. In the parable of the dragnet both good and bad fish are caught, the good kept and the bad thrown out (Mt 13:47-50).

In her pregnancy Rivqah experiences unusual activity in her womb and asks Yahuah why this is happening. He tells her that two nations are in her womb, one stronger than the other, and the older serving the younger. The firstborn is Ĕsaw, the second is Ya'aqov (Jacob). He comes out holding the heel of Ĕsaw. Ĕsaw is a type of the flesh man, Ya'aqov of the spirit man—the flesh/natural man first, then the spirit man (1Cor 15:46). Yitsḥaq is now sixty years old (Gen 25:12-26).

Ĕsaw is covered with red hair, like a garment, and becomes a skilled hunter (in type, feeds on flesh) and a man of the field (world). Yitsḥaq loves *him* the most because he likes the taste of game. (In this case, Yitsḥaq is a type of the flesh man.) Edom (red) is the nation that comes from him.

Ya'aqov (supplanter, or holding the heel) is smooth-skinned, peaceful, and becomes a shepherd living in tents. He is a type of the bride. Rivqah loves *him* the most. (In type, the bride loving Messiah. Yisra'ĕl is the nation that comes from him.) When Yisra'ĕl came into the Promised Land after the Exodus, the two nations were in constant hostility. Yitsḥaq is sixty years old when Rivqah gives birth to them (Gen 25:27-28).

Before their birth, even before creation, Yahuah sees the nature of

144

these two. What he sees in Ésaw he hates, and what he sees in Ya'aqov he loves (Ro 9:13). Ésaw cared only for his present pleasure, the desires of the flesh, and would exchange what is truly valuable to get it. In contrast, Ya'aqov cared for what is very valuable, and would do anything—lie, deceive, cheat, steal, whatever—to get it. The latter is the heart of the bride, to do whatever is needed to be the bride of Messiah. The bad things Yahuah doesn't like, but the perseverance he does.

Ésaw Sells Birthright to Ya'aqov, 25:29

ONE DAY AN EVENT HAPPENS which reveals their two natures. Ésaw, a man of the moment, has been out hunting and has returned tired and hungry. Ya'aqov, a man with a plan, has made a delicious soup with red lentils, its aroma filling the air. He knows of the prophecy regarding their birth, that the elder would serve the younger, and has been thinking, "How can I get Ésaw to give me the birthright?" And now he is thinking, "Perhaps this is the time."

Ésaw, on his way to his tent to fix something to eat, smells the soup, and the hunger in him increases so that to him it seems unbearable. So he goes to his brother and says, "Please, let me have some of that red-red to swallow, for I am famished." (The Hebrew has "red" twice to refer to the lentil soup. The nation from Ésaw is Edom. Edom means red.)

"I'm glad to do so," says Ya'aqov, "but first sell me your birthright."

"Look," responds Ésaw, "I'm so hungry I'm about to die. What good is the birthright to me if I'm dead!?"

"First swear to me." So he swears to him, and sells his birthright to Ya'aqov. Then Ya'aqov gives Ésaw bread and lentil soup; and he eats and drinks, and rises and goes on his way, thinking nothing more of it. In this way Ésaw despised his birthright (Gen 25:29-34). (See Heb 10:35-39.) So is everyone who chooses his own way over the way of Yahuah. Our birthright is the eternal kingdom, but we have to choose Elohim's way, the way of Yahushua, to get it.

Yahuah Renews Covenant with Yitsḥaq, 26:1

YITSḤAQ IS A NOMAD CHIEF, responsible for many people and animals. He has been pasturing near Ḥevron (Hebron) when he experiences famine, similar to the one his father Avraham experienced. So he decides to go to Gerar, a fertile land on the border with Mitsrayim, the same place where his father had gone earlier.

While on his way Yahuah appears to him. "Do not go down to Mitsrayim," he says. "Stay in the land of which I shall tell you. Be sojourning in this land and I will be with you and bless you, for to you and to your seed I will give all these lands, and I will establish the oath which I swore to your father Avraham. I will multiply your seed as the stars of heaven, and will give to your seed all these lands; and by your seed all the nations of the earth shall be blessed; because Avraham obeyed me and kept my charge, my commandments, my statutes and my instructions (*torah*)" (Gen 26:1-5).

"Like father, like son," as the saying goes (Ex 20:5-6). Yitshaq is going through the same kind of testing that his father went through, and is responding in the same insecure way. The only difference, he doesn't go as far south as Mitsrayim, and that's because Elohim told him not to. This is a different king from the one Avraham met.

Another thing to note is the reason why Yahuah is blessing him—it is because of the obedience of his father. In this incident Avraham is a type of Messiah and Yitshaq is a type of the believer. We who believe in and obey Yahushua (believing is obeying) are blessed because of his obedience to the Father.

Yitshaq and Avi-meleh, 26:6

YITSHAQ NOW REVEALS the same fear and insecurity his father had regarding Par'oh, (Gen 12) and Avi-meleh (Gen 20). He is afraid he will be killed on account of his wife's beauty. In the culture of that time, he has reason to be afraid, so he says she is his sister. So quickly he has forgotten Yahuah's words of the covenant! (Do we ever doubt when circumstances seem to be against the promises of Elohim?) For Avraham, Sarah *was* his sister; but not for Yitshaq—she was his niece. Rivqah, however, is not taken into the kings harem as Sarah was, but is left to be with Yitshaq as his sister.

After a long time the deception is revealed. With Avram, the deception regarding Sarah became known to Par'oh because of plagues, and to Avi-meleh because the women were not conceiving and Elohim spoke to him. In this case the deception is revealed when the king sees Yitsḥaq caressing his wife Rivqah. When he sees it, he summons Yitsḥaq. "Surely this woman is not your sister," he says, "but is your wife. I saw you caressing her."

"I did this because I thought I might die on account of her."

"What you did is wrong. Guilt would have come on us if one of the men had lain with her, which could easily have happened. You may stay in the land, and I will command all the people not to touch her, on penalty of death" (Gen 26:6-11).

As with his father, after the deception is revealed Yahuah blesses him. When he sows grain, he reaps a hundredfold (Mk 4:20). The blessing is so great with riches, flocks, herds and a great household that the Plishtim (Philistines) envy him. (In type, jealousy of success in the spirit.) This is the area in which his father's servants had dug wells in the days of his father, but the Plishtim had filled them with earth. In type, this is stopping the anointing of ministry in the bride. Because of Yitsḥaq's increased wealth and power, Avi-meleḥ tells him to leave. So Yitsḥaq leaves from there and settles in the valley of Gerar (Gen 26:12-17).

Wells are a type of living water that comes through Yahushua. As our wealth in manifestations of the spirit increases, we should not be surprised when opposition comes to hinder us. In fact, we should be concerned if there is *no* opposition. Yahushua said, *"Woe to you when all men speak well of you, for that is how their fathers treated the false prophets"* (Lk 6:26, NIV).

Most of the rest of this chapter deals with friction between Yitsḥaq and the Plishtim regarding wells. Yitsḥaq digs again a well that his father had dug, and the herdsmen of Gerar claim the well is theirs. When Yitsḥaq moves on and digs another, the same thing happens. The third time, however, they leave him alone, and he says, "This time Yahuah has made room for us, and we will be fruitful in the land" (Gen 26:18-22).

From there he goes to Be'ĕr-Sheva (Beersheba), and Yahuah appears to him that night and says, "I am the Elohim of your father Avraham; do not fear, for I am with you. I will bless you, and multiply your seed, for the sake of my servant Avraham." This is a great encouragement to him. He wants peace with the people of the land, but they have opposed him. So he builds an altar there and calls upon the name of

Yahuah, and his servants dig another well (Gen 26:23-25).

After he is settled, visitors come. They are Avi-meleḥ who had sent him away, with his advisor and the commander of his army. He asks them why they have come, since they hated him and had sent him away. They respond, "We see plainly that Yahuah has been with you; so we said, 'Let there be an oath between us, between you and us, and let us make a covenant with you, that you will do us no harm, just as we have not touched you and have done to you nothing but good and have sent you away in peace. You are now the blessed of Yahuah.'"

This covenant is similar to that which was made with Avraham. Yitsḥaq agrees and makes them a feast, and they eat and drink. In the morning they rise early and exchange oaths; and Yitsḥaq sends them away and they depart from him in peace. On the same day Yitsḥaq's servants tell him about the well which they had dug and that they have found water (Gen 26:26-33).

Friction over wells between Yitsḥaq and the Plishtim is a type of friction between local churches and pastors. It is a fight over church members, called "sheep stealing," in which some churches try to grow their congregations by taking members from other assemblies instead of getting new members from those who don't go to church. There is nothing wrong with a person leaving one assembly and going to another, although a believer should seek Elohim to find his will on the matter. The problem is if an assembly encourages active recruiting from other assemblies. In this incident, the covenant made between the two parties is a type of agreeing not to do that anymore. Yitsḥaq hadn't been doing it, but the Plishtim had.

Another type that can be seen in this incident is jealousy on the part of those having no power with Elohim against those who do.

Ěsaw Marries Two Ḥiti Women, 26:34

WHEN ĚSAW IS FORTY YEARS OLD he marries two Ḥiti (Hittite) women. This brings bitterness of spirit to Yitsḥaq and Rivqah (Gen 26:34-35). (In type, marrying the world brings sadness to Messiah and the bride.)

VI. YA'AQOV TO YOSEF
Genesis 27-36

"May peoples serve you,
And nations bow down to you;
Be master of your brothers,
And may your mother's sons bow down to you."
Genesis 27:29

Ya'aqov Steals Firstborn Blessing, 27:1

IN THIS CHAPTER Ya'aqov (Jacob) gets the firstborn blessing, with the help of his mother Rivqah (Rebecca). Yitshaq is now very old, and his eyes are too dim to see. He believes his time to die is near, so he wants to bless his firstborn, Ěsaw,, before he dies. So he tells him to go to the field and hunt game, and from it to prepare the kind of savory dish he loves, and then he will bless him (Gen 27:1-4).

Rivqah is listening and hears this, but wants the blessing for Ya'aqov. So she tells him to bring two choice young goats, and she will prepare the savory dish he loves, which he will take to his father and receive the blessing, as though he is Ěsaw. He cannot hide his voice, but he can wear Ěsaw's best garments and put the skins of the young goats on his hands and on the smooth part of his neck. (In type, the assembly giving instructions on how to receive from Yahuah.)

All this is done, and Ya'aqov brings the savory food and the bread which Rivqah has made to his father. (In type, the assembly satisfying the Father's heart.) Upon being asked who he is, he says, "I am Ěsaw your firstborn; I have done as you told me. Get up, please, sit and eat of my game, that you may bless me." Ya'aqov lied, but, in type, he is obeying the assembly leadership. He is willing to do whatever is necessary to get the blessing.

Yitshaq is surprised at the quickness of the meal, and Ya'aqov gives the credit to "Yahuah your Elohim." Because Ya'aqov's voice sounds like who he really is, Yitshaq asks him to come close so he can feel and smell him. He comes close and his father says, "The voice is the voice of Ya'aqov, but the hands are the hands of Ěsaw." So he asks again, "Are you *really* my son Ěsaw?" Ya'aqov affirms that indeed he is. His father is satisfied and eats the food. After eating he says, "Please come close and kiss me, my son" (Gen 27:5-26).

So Ya'aqov comes close and kisses him; and when Yitshaq smells the garments, he blesses him, saying: "The smell of my son is as the smell of a field which Yahuah has blessed. Now may Elohim give you of the dew of heaven and of the richness of the earth and an abundance of grain and new wine. May peoples serve you and nations bow down to you. Be master over your brothers, and may your mother's sons bow down to you. Cursed be those who curse you, and blessed be those who bless you" (Gen 27:27-29). This blessing is fulfilled in Messiah.

As soon as Ya'aqov leaves, in comes Ěsaw with the savory food *he* has prepared from his hunting, and says to his father, "Let my father arise and eat of his son's game, that you may bless me." When asked who he is, he says, "I am your son, your firstborn, Ěsaw."

Yitshaq trembles violently and says, "Who was he then that brought food to me so that I ate it before you came, and blessed him? Yes, and he shall be blessed." Yahuah arranged this blessing for Ya'aqov, for he loves Ya'aqov's attitude of heart.

When Ěsaw hears this he cries bitterly and says, "Bless me, me also, my father!"

"Your brother came deceitfully and has taken away your blessing."

"Is he not rightly named Ya'aqov," he says, "for he has supplanted me these two times? He took away my birthright (a lie, he sold it to him), and behold, now he has taken away my blessing. Haven't you a blessing for me also?"

But Yitshaq replies, "Behold, I have made him your master, and I have given to him all his relatives as servants; and with grain and new wine I have sustained him. Now as for you then, what can I do, my son?"

"Do you have only one blessing, my father? Bless me, me also, my father." So he lifts up his voice and weeps.

Yitshaq then prophesies over him, saying, "Behold, away from the fertility of the earth shall be your dwelling, and away from the dew of heaven from above. By your sword you shall live, and your brother you shall serve; but it shall come about when you become restless that you will break his yoke from your neck" (Gen 27:30-40). The descendents of Ĕsaw are at war with the descendents of Ya'aqov to this day, both in the natural and in the spiritual.

Ĕsaw doesn't like the blessing he received, and hates Ya'aqov for the one *he* received. So he decides that he will kill his brother when their father has died and the mourning for him is over.

When Rivqah hears of Ĕsaw's plan, she informs Ya'aqov about it and tells him to flee to Ḥaran, to her brother Lavan (Laban), and stay with him a few days until his brother's anger is over and he forgets about it. "Why should I be bereaved of you both in one day?" she says. Then she would send for him. (In type, this is separation from the world.) Then she goes to Yitsḥaq and complains about the women Ĕsaw has married. "I'm tired of living," she says, "because of the daughters of Ḥĕth. If Ya'aqov takes a wife from the daughters of Ḥĕth, like these, from the daughters of the land, what good will my life be to me?" This was her way of getting her husband to send Ya'aqov away. Of course, this was in the plan of Yahuah for Ya'aqov to get a wife from his own people, just as Avraham wanted a wife from his own people for his son Yitsḥaq (Gen 27:41-46). (In type, the bride does not want mixture from the world.)

We have no record of Yitsḥaq punishing or blaming Ya'aqov for what he did. If there were hot words, we know not of it. The book of Hebrews says this about the incident:

> *Beware lest anyone fall short of the favor of Elohim, lest any root of bitterness springing up causes trouble and by it many be defiled, lest there be any immoral or wicked person like Ĕsaw, who sold his birthright for a meal. For you know that even afterwards, when he desired to inherit the blessing, he was rejected, for he found no place for a reversal* (of the decision to bless Ya'aqov), *though he sought for it with tears* (Heb 12:15-17).

Some translations translate "reversal" as "repentance." But this choice of translation, although technically correct, conveys the idea that Ĕsaw repented of his behavior. "Repent" means "to change direction." For example, when we repent of our sins, we are changing the direction of our lives to go the opposite direction and live righteously. Ĕsaw didn't repent in this sense, nor was he asking his father to be sorry for giving the blessing to the wrong son. No. He wanted his father to revoke the blessing given to his brother and give it to him. But there is no reversal. So it is on the day of judgment. When we die, there is no "second chance." It's over. What we have become in our souls and spirits by the choices we make in this life, that determines our eternal destiny, whether in heaven or in hell. The only "second chances" are in this life.

Ya'aqov Sent Away, Dreams of a Stairway, 28:1

YITSHAQ CALLS YA'AQOV and tells him not to take a wife from the daughters of Kena'an but to go to Paddan-aram, to the house of Rivqah's father and take a wife from one of his cousins, the daughters of Lavan his mother's brother. (In type, the Father wanting his son's bride to come from his own people.)

Then he blesses him: "May Ĕl Shaddai (God Almighty) bless you and make you fruitful and multiply you, that you may become a company of peoples. May he also give you the blessing of Avraham, to you and to your seed with you, that you may possess the land of your sojournings, which Elohim gave to Avraham." Yitshaq then sends Ya'aqov away. The blessing of Avraham is being passed through Yitshaq to Ya'aqov, which will have its fulfillment in Yahushua Messiah during the Millennium.

Ĕsaw sees what his father did regarding Ya'aqov, both the blessing and where he should get his wife, and that Ya'aqov obeyed and left. In particular, he sees that the two Kena'ani (Canaanite) wives he has are displeasing to both his father and mother, that they want marriage from their relatives. So he goes to Yishma'ĕl and marries one of his daughters (a cousin) to add to the wives he already has (Gen 28:1-9). (In type, this is still marrying the world.)

On his way to Ḥaran Ya'aqov comes to a certain place to spend the night because the sun has set (a type of the end times). All he has is his garment to sleep in, and he takes one of the stones and puts it under his head for a pillow. (The stone is a type of Messiah on whom we rest our head, Mt 11:28-30). (See also Mt 21:42-43; 1Pe 2:4-8.) During the night he has a dream in which he sees steps leading from the earth to heaven and angels ascending and descending on it. Yahuah is standing above the steps in heaven and says:

"I am Yahuah, the Elohim of your father Avraham and the Elohim of Yitsḥaq. The land on which you lie, I will give it to you and to your seed. Your seed will also be like the dust of the earth, and you will spread out to the west and to the east and to the north and to the south; and in you and in your seed shall all the families of the earth be blessed. Behold, I am with you and will keep you wherever you go, and will bring you back to this land; for I will not leave you until I have done what I have promised you" (Gen 28:10-15).

This is a prophecy of Messiah, of whom the stairway is a type. Yahushua referred to this dream when he said to Nathani'ĕl, *"Hereafter you shall see the heaven opened, and the angels of Elohim ascending and descending on the son of man"* (Jn 1:51). To Thomas he said, *"I am the way, and the truth, and the life; no one comes to the Father but by me"* (Jn 14:6). To the Jewish religious leaders Peter said, *"There is salvation in no one else; for there is no other name under heaven that has been given among men, by which we must be saved"* (Ac 4:12). And Paul wrote to Timothy, *"For there is one Elohim and one mediator between Elohim and man, a man Messiah Yahushua"* (1Ti 2:5).

The angels on the stairway also represent the help they give to those who will inherit salvation (Heb 1:14). Angels are fully involved in the lives of all mankind, one way or another (Mt 18:10). Only those who will inherit salvation, however, receive the full benefit of that activity.

Ya'aqov wakes up, afraid. "Surely Yahuah is in this place," he says, "and I did not know it. This is none other than the house of Elohim, and this is the gate of heaven." He takes the stone that was under his head, sets it up as a pillar, pours oil on its top (a type of anointing Yahushua), and calls the name of the place Bĕth-Ĕl (house of Ĕl).

The stone, therefore, is also a type of us who are believers in Yahushua, for we are living stones, being built up as a spiritual house for a set-apart priesthood (1Pe 2:5).

Then Ya'aqov makes a vow, saying to Yahuah, *"If the Strong One will be with me and will keep me on this journey that I take, and will give me food to eat and garments to wear, and I return to my father's house in safety, then Yahuah will be my Strong One. This stone, which I have set up as a pillar, will be the Strong One's house, and of all that you give me I will surely give a tenth to you"* (Gen 28:16-22).

Note the principle of tithing; a tithe is a tenth. We saw this earlier with Avraham giving a tenth to Malki-tsedeq. The tithe became a requirement when the law was given. Tithing is not mentioned in the New Testament, but the principle applies.

Ya'aqov Marries Leah and Raḥel, Has Four Sons, 29:1

THIS CHAPTER RELATES Ya'aqov meeting his cousin Raḥel (Rachel, a female sheep) at a well, staying with her family for a month, agreeing with his uncle Lavan to work seven years to get Raḥel as his wife, being deceived and given her elder sister Leah (weary) instead, working another seven years to get Raḥel because of his love for her, Raḥel being barren, and Leah, because of being unloved, bearing four sons: Re'uven (Reuben, behold a son), Shim'on (Simeon, heard), Lĕwi (Levi, lay-WEE, joined to), and Yahudah (Judah, praised).

These events contain many types. Keep in mind that not everything in a story is a type, that a type can have more than one application or fulfillment or antitype, and that if something fits a type then it is a type. Ya'aqov is a type of Messiah; the younger, beautiful sister Raḥel a type of the bride who is barren (as was Sarah); the older plain Leah a type of the lukewarm church; the east and Ḥaran types of Bavel (Babylon) and the world; and Lavan a type of lukewarm leadership.

The sheep are a type of believers; and Raḥel as a shepherdess a type of the bride taking care of believers. Ya'aqov at the well is a type of Messiah looking for a shepherd's heart, which is the heart of the bride. The well of living water at which Ya'aqov meets Raḥel is a type of the set-apart spirit, and having to wait until all the sheep are gathered before watering them is a type of the bride being completed before the rapture.

Ya'aqov removing the stone from the mouth of the well is a type of Messiah being raised from the dead and giving the spirit of set-apartness to believers. It is also a type of Messiah and the bride bringing anointing to the assembly. The flock of sheep that Raḥel brings is a type of bride believers, and the three flocks of sheep that are waiting for the stone to be removed so they can be watered is a type of spiritually dry believers waiting for living water from the bride believers. The stone being replaced on the mouth of the well is a type of spiritual dryness when the church goes into apostasy before Messiah's return.

Ya'aqov discovering who Raḥel is, that she is of his family, and then kissing her and weeping, is a type of Yahushua's joy and love in finding the company of believers who are his bride. A month begins with a new moon and a sabbath rest; so Ya'aqov staying a month with Raḥel's family is a type of new beginnings.

Serving seven years is a type of spiritual completeness to get the bride; it is also a type of when serving Messiah for love, time is meaningless. Getting plain Leah first and beautiful Raḥel last is a type of getting the flesh-nature lukewarm Laodicea church first and the bride Philadelphia church last: first the flesh, then the spirit. We saw this with Qayin and Hevel, with Yishma'ĕl and Yitsḥaq, and with Ĕsaw and Ya'aqov.

Serving two seven-year periods is a type of double spiritual completeness—for Messiah to present to himself a bride without spot or wrinkle or any such thing, but set-apart and spotless (Eph 5:27).

Ya'aqov will have twelve sons from his two wives and their two maids. These sons will be the heads of the twelve tribes that will make up the nation of Yisra'ĕl. Only two of the sons, Yosef (Joseph) and Binyamin (Benjamin), will come from Raḥel, the loved one, Yosef being a type of Messiah and Binyamin a type of the bride. The other ten represent the lukewarm church. The first four sons are from Leah. Yahuah has mercy on her because she is unloved. So it is with the lukewarm church. Yahuah loves them and grants them many members. Yahuah controls who has what children and how many. Leah stopped bearing for his purposes. She will bear again, later.

Re'uven, the first born, will lose his birthright blessing; Lĕwi (Levi) will become the tribe of priests, a priesthood that will end; and Yahudah will be the one through whom will come Messiah and his unending Malki-tsedek priesthood.

Ya'aqov's Next Eight Children, 30:1

BARREN RAḤEL IS JEALOUS of her fruitful sister and says to Ya'aqov, "Give me children, or I die," a type of the bride being desperate in prayer to have fruit of ministry for Messiah. So she gives her maid Bilhah (timid) to him to bear on her behalf, as Sarah did with Hagar, and only brings flesh. Bilhah gives birth and Raḥel says, "Elohim has vindicated me, and has indeed heard my voice and has given me a son," and names him Dan (pronounced Dawn, judge). Bilhah gives birth again and Raḥel said, "With mighty wrestlings I have wrestled with my sister; I have indeed prevailed," and names him Naftali (Naphtali, my wrestling).

Leah, who has stopped bearing, takes note of what is happening and gives her maid Zilpah (drooping?, dignity?) to Ya'aqov as a wife. When Zilpah gives birth, Leah says, "Good fortune," and names him Gad (pronounced "god"; the word can mean "troop" KJV, or "fortune," referring to the god Fortune). When Zilpah bears again Leah says, "Happy am I! For women will call me happy," and names him Asher (happy) (Gen 30:1-13). All of this is a type of competition among church organizations, but still getting flesh.

Jealousy between the two sisters continues. Leah's firstborn, Re'uven, comes in from the field during wheat harvest. He has found some mandrakes and gives them to his mother. (Mandrakes, also called love-apples, are related to the potato family. They are a narcotic and are believed to increase sexual desire and fertility.) Raḥel, who is still barren, sees what Re'uven gave her sister and asks if she can have some. Leah is very much aware that, although she is Ya'aqov's first wife and has borne him four sons, he prefers her sister and treats her as though she is the first wife. She ignores the fact that it was only by deceit that she became his wife at all.

To Raḥel's request Leah says, "Is it a small matter for you to take my husband? And would you take my son's mandrakes also?" Raḥel then buys the mandrakes by giving her sister permission to have intimacy with their husband that night. (A type of salvation by works.) In the evening when Ya'aqov comes in from the field Leah gives him the news: "You must come into me, for I have surely hired you with my son's mandrakes." Elohim gives her favor, and she bears Ya'aqov a fifth son and names him Yissakar (a man of hire), saying, "Elohim has given me my wages because I gave my maid to my husband." Then she bears him a sixth son, naming him Zevulun (dwelling), saying, "Elohim has endowed me with a good gift; now my husband will dwell with me, because I have borne him six sons." Afterward she bears him a daughter and names her Dinah (dee-NAH, vindicated, judged).

Then Elohim remembers Raḥel and enables her to conceive. She bears a son and says, "Elohim has taken away my reproach." She names him Yosef (may Yahuah add), saying, "May Yahuah give me another son" (Gen 30:14-24). Yosef is the fullest type of Messiah.

As noted before, in that culture a woman's worth comes from her ability to bear children—the more the children, the greater the worth. Bearing children is a type of bearing fruit for the kingdom, both in adding souls, and in nurturing them to become the bride of Messiah. Leah, the first wife, is very fruitful. She, however, is not the favorite. She is a type of the lukewarm believers. They are the majority. Raḥel, the second wife, is late in being fruitful. She is a type of the bride believers. They are the minority—first the flesh, then the spirit. She has two sons, Yosef first, and later Binyamin.

A repeated theme is that Yahuah remembers and hears. He does this both for Leah (the lukewarm) and for Raḥel (the bride). The bride is among the lukewarm in their assemblies, and among the bride are those who will backslide and become lukewarm. Yahushua spoke of this in the parable of the wheat and the tares (Mt 13:24-30). As the saying goes, "It's not over until it's over." We are each given our span of life in which to determine whether we will be in his kingdom or not, whether we are the bride or not.

Yahuah instituted three festivals on Mount Ḥorĕv (Horeb) after the Exodus. The Feast of Unleavened Bread begins with Passover the night before. It is at the time of the barley harvest in the spring and is a type of salvation or born again. Yahushua fulfilled that type when he died for our sins.

The Feast of Weeks is fifty days, a week of weeks, after Passover, also called Pentecost, and is at the time of the wheat harvest in the summer. Yahushua fulfilled that type when he poured out the spirit of set-apartness.

The Feast of Ingathering, also called the Feast of Booths or Tabernacles, is at the time of the fruit and nut harvest in the fall. The final fulfillment of this type will be when Yahushua comes to take his bride at the rapture. He fulfilled the slaughter-offering part of this feast when he died for our sins.

Re'uven, a type of a member of the lukewarm church, found mandrakes, a type of the spirit, during the wheat harvest, a type of

Pentecost, and gave them to his mother Leah, a type of the entire lukewarm church, who in turn sold them to Raḥel, a type of the bride, to have children from Ya'aqov, a type of Messiah. Two things resulted from this event. Leah bore again, and Raḥel bore for the first time. Those whom Leah bore are like Re'uven in type—lukewarm. Yosef, the one whom Raḥel bore, is a type of Yahushua Messiah. She will also bear the twelfth and final son of Ya'aqov, Binyamin, who is a type of the last-day male-son bride who will do greater works than Yahushua did.

To sum up, the incident of the mandrakes is a type of some in the lukewarm church finding the spirit and becoming the bride. It is amazing how interrelated types can be.

Speckled, Spotted and Black Animals, 30:25- 31:16

AFTER YOSEF IS BORN Ya'aqov asks permission of Lavan to return to his home in the Promised Land, taking his wives and children with him. He has bought them from Lavan with the purchase of his labor. Lavan doesn't want him to leave, because he knows he is being blessed on account of Ya'aqov being with him, and he asks Ya'aqov what wages he would like in exchange for staying longer. Ya'aqov reminds him that he has no possessions of his own, yet it is because of him that Lavan has increased greatly in livestock, then asks, "But now, when shall I provide for my own household also?" (Gen 30:25-30).

In type, the lukewarm assemblies are blessed because of the activity of the bride within her. The bride wants to be separate as her own assembly, but the lukewarm don't want her to leave.

The agreement reached is not in money, but in livestock. All the speckled and spotted sheep and goats and the black lambs, animals of lesser value, will belong to Ya'aqov. To prevent cross breeding, Lavan takes all the animals that are not all white and puts them in the care of his sons a three-days' journey away (about twelve miles) and leaves Ya'aqov with only the white ones to take care of. (A type of the flesh-church trying to hinder the ministry of the bride.)

Ya'aqov now has a problem. How is he to increase his flock? He knows how. He has been taking care of these flocks for fourteen years to get his wives, and for a number of more years until Yosef is born, so he is well acquainted with selective breeding. Further, in a dream

158

from the angel of Yahuah he sees the non-white male goats breeding with the white females. So that's what he does. He also makes sure the strong animals are not all white and the weaker ones are all white. By so doing he becomes very prosperous, and has large flocks and female and male servants and camels and donkeys (Gen 30:31-43).

The account says that Ya'aqov made striped rods from different trees and, during mating time (which was twice a year) placed the rods in the watering troughs so they would see the stripes while mating and thus bear young that were streaked, speckled and spotted. Theories vary regarding this. The theory I like the best is that the prosperity Ya'aqov experienced had nothing to do with his efforts. These were all efforts of the flesh and natural reasoning. Rather, Elohim prospered him for his purposes in building the nation of Yisra'ĕl and eventually the bride, *"not by works, lest any should boast"* (Eph 2:9). In type, Yahuah is selecting those who will be his. We have the examples of Avram with Par'oh and Avi-meleḥ, and Yitsḥaq with Avi-meleḥ, both being blessed in spite of their efforts through fleshly reasoning to protect themselves.

In the meantime Lavan's sons begin accusing Ya'aqov of stealing their father's wealth to make himself rich, and their attitude toward him is no longer friendly. (In type, this is jealousy of the flesh-led church over the success of the spirit-led church.) At this point Yahuah tells Ya'aqov, "I am the Elohim of Bĕth-ĕl (house of Ĕl), where you anointed a pillar, where you made a vow to me; now arise, leave this land, and return to the land of your birth," and "I will be with you" (Gen 31:1-3).

Ya'aqov tells his wives of the situation, how their father has cheated him and changed his wages ten times. (A type of completeness in this world.) They respond, "Do we still have any portion or inheritance in our father's house? Are we not considered by him as foreigners? For he has sold us, and has also entirely consumed our purchase price. Surely all the wealth which Elohim has taken away from our father belongs to us and our children; now then, do whatever Elohim has said to you" (Gen 31:4-16).

In type, the assembly agrees to leave the flesh-church, where they received nothing in the spirit. Also, Ya'aqov is reaping deception from Lavan because he deceived his father. "We reap what we sow" (Ho 8:7).

Lavan and his sons were immersed in the culture of Babylon and were idol worshipers, and as such they are a type of the lukewarm church. Ya'aqov increasing in wealth is a type of the last-day assembly, the bride of Messiah, growing in strength in the spirit. His leaving Lavan with his wives and children and wealth is a type of the bride coming out of the lukewarm church. They are obeying the command, *"Come out of her, my people"* (Rev 18:14).

Ya'aqov Leaves for Kena'an, Mitspah Covenant, 31:17

WITHOUT NOTIFICATION, Ya'aqov flees from Lavan's land with his children and his wives and all his property that he has acquired to go to the land of Kena'an to his father Yitshaq. Unknown to him, however, Rahel has stolen her father's household idols. After some days he crosses the Euphrates River, and is on his way toward the hill country of Gil'ad (Gilead) east of the Yardĕn (Jordan) River.

On the third day Lavan learns of Ya'aqov's deception and goes in pursuit, taking relatives with him. On the seventh day he overtakes them and asks why he went away secretly. If he had known he would have sent him away with a party. "It is in my power," he says, "to do you harm, but the Elohim of your father warned me not to speak either good or bad to you." Then he asks, "Why did you steal my strong ones?"

In type, the flesh-church has been serving lies, trusting in them. But their powerlessness has been revealed for what they are. When you come out, you bring baggage of the flesh nature with you.

Ya'aqov replies that he was afraid, for he thought Lavan would have taken his daughters from him by force. Then he adds, "Go ahead and search, and the one with whom you find your strong ones shall not live; in the presence of our relatives point out what is yours among my belongings and take it."

Lavan searches the tents of Ya'aqov, Leah and the two maids, but without success. When he comes to Rahel's tent he finds her sitting on the camel's saddle in which she has hidden the idols. She says, "Please don't be angry with me for not getting up, because the manner of women is upon me." So his search is unsuccessful.

Ya'aqov becomes angry and accuses Lavan of mistreatment and how he suffered in tending his sheep. He concludes by saying, "If the Elohim of my father, the Elohim of Avraham, and the fear of Yitshaq had not been for me, surely now you would have sent me away empty-handed. Elohim has seen my affliction and the toil of my hands, so he rendered judgment last night" (Gen 31:17-42). (In type, Elohim protects, judges, and decides who has his flock.)

In reply, Lavan claims that his two daughters and their children "and all that you see are mine." (In type, the flesh-church claims everything for itself and wants to get the credit for what Yahuah does.) But he releases his claim and asks that they make a covenant as a witness between them. Ya'aqov agrees. He uses one stone for a pillar (Gen 31:45), and Lavan and his relatives make a heap of stones (Gen 31:46). Ya'aqov calls it Gil'ad (Gilead, heap of witness). The place is also called Mitspah (Mizpah, lookout, watchtower), for this took place on the top of a hill.

Lavan says, "This heap is a witness between you and me this day. May Yahuah watch between you and me when we are absent one from the other, that neither of us does harm to the other. If you mistreat my daughters, or if you take wives besides my daughters, even though no man is with us, take note, the Strong One is witness between you and me. The Strong One of Avraham and the Strong One of Nahor and the Strong One of their father, judge between us." (In type, they agree to let the other minister in his own way.)

So Ya'aqov swears by the fear of his father Yitshaq. Then Ya'aqov makes a slaughter-offering on the mountain, and calls his relatives to the meal; and they eat the meal and spend the night on the mountain. Early in the morning Lavan gets up, and kisses his sons and his daughters (Ya'aqov's eleven sons and daughter Dina, and their mothers Leah and Rahel) and blesses them, and then leaves for his home (Gen 31:43-55).

This whole incident—Ya'aqov leaving Lavan, Lavan pursuing, and Yahuah intervening to prevent Lavan from harming his son-in-law and taking his wife and children and possessions—is a type of Yahuah protecting his bride believers who have come out of lukewarmness.

Ya'aqov Fears Ĕsaw, Wrestles with an Angel, 32:1

WHEN YA'AQOV SEES some angels, he says, "This is Elohim's army." So he names that place Maḥanayim (double camp). What a comfort after the confrontation with Lavan! (A type of comfort being given to the bride after being confronted by the lukewarm.)

Ya'aqov is traveling south on the east side of the Yardĕn to meet his brother Ĕsaw, for Ĕsaw has taken the land east of the Dead Sea to be his country. It has two names: the land of Sĕ'ir (say-EER) and the country of Edom (red, eh-DOME). Ya'aqov has been gone twenty years (double completeness in the world), and he remembers his brother's plan to kill him for stealing the firstborn blessing. So he sends servants ahead to inform his brother that he is returning, that he has many possessions, and he hopes to find favor from him. He calls his brother *adoni* (ah-doe-NEE), my master.

His servants return with the news that his brother is coming to meet him with 400 men. Ya'aqov is alarmed, greatly afraid and distressed. So he makes a plan to appease his brother. He divides his people, flocks, herds and camels into two groups, thinking, "If Ĕsaw comes to the one company and attacks it, then the company which is left will escape" (Gen 32:1-8).

Ya'aqov realizes that his only protection is Yahuah, the Strong One of his fathers Avraham and Yitshaq. So he prays, recounting Yahuah's command to return to his country and relatives and that he would prosper him. He then acknowledges that he is unworthy of the kindness and faithfulness he has received, and asks for protection for himself and his family. He ends with recalling to Yahuah the covenant in which he said, "I will surely prosper you and make your seed as the sand of the sea, which is too great to be numbered" (Gen 32:9-12).

After spending the night there, he selects many animals from his possessions, and puts them in three droves to be gifts for his brother so as to appease him. The droves would go, one after the other, with a space between. As his brother would meet each drove and ask the servants tending them who owns them, they were to say, "These belong to your servant Ya'aqov; it is a gift from him sent to my master Ĕsaw. And behold, he also is behind us" (Gen 32:13-23).

That same night they all cross the ford of the stream Yaboq (Jabbok). That's a little over half way from the Sea of Galilee to the Dead Sea on the east side. He sends them ahead and is left alone. While alone a man wrestles with him until daybreak. When the man sees he isn't winning, he touches the socket of Ya'aqov's thigh, dislocating it. When Ya'aqov still doesn't give up, the man says, "Let me go, for the sun is about to rise." But Ya'aqov tells him, "I will not let you go unless you bless me." The man then asks his name, and he says, "Ya'aqov." The man responds, "Your name shall no longer be Ya'aqov (supplanter), but Yisra'ĕl,* for you have striven with Elohim and with men and have prevailed." Ya'aqov again asks what is his name. The man doesn't answer, except to ask why he wants to know. Then the man blesses him and is seen no more. Because of this experience, Ya'aqov names the place Peni'ĕl (Peniel, face of Ĕl), for, "I have seen Elohim face to face, yet my life has been preserved." Thereafter, he limps on his thigh. (In type, the flesh-man slain, no longer depending on strength of flesh to live for Yahuah.) And therefore, to this day the sons of Yisra'ĕl do not eat the sinew of the hip which is on the socket of the thigh (Gen 32:24-32). This is still true today of orthodox Jews.

*The name Yisra'ĕl means the prince who prevails with, overcomes, then rules with Elohim. This definition combines two possible meanings of the name.

Wrestling with the angel of Elohim shows us what it means to wrestle in prayer. We see in this wrestling the perseverance of Ya'aqov. It is this trait which Yahuah loves: when he sees something of value, no cost or effort is too much to get it. The parables of Yahushua about the treasure in the field and the pearl of great price say the same thing (Mt 13:44-46). This is the commitment we make when we commit our lives to Yahushua in being born again. This is the commitment that produces the bride of Messiah. The bride perseveres and will not be denied the blessing of fruitfulness and intimacy with Yahuah. This is why he loves the bride and hates the lukewarm. Prayer is not a casual thing. It doesn't change Elohim—he doesn't need changing; it changes us—we are the ones who need changing. Do you find spending time in prayer difficult? Do you experience getting nowhere when you pray? *"The prayer of the righteous is powerful and effective"* (Jam 5:16, NRSV). See the parables of perseverance in prayer (Lk 11:5-13; 18:1-8). Are you pursuing righteousness? It's the only way to grow close to Yahuah and his son Yahushua.

Ya'aqov Meets Ĕsaw, 33:1

THE MEETING WITH ĔSAW turns out well. Ya'aqov bows himself to the ground seven times as he is nearing his brother. (In type, spiritual completeness in humility.) They embrace, kiss and weep. Then Ya'aqov introduces his wives and children to him. Ěsaw asks, "What do you mean by all this company which I have met?"

"To find favor in the sight of my master," Ya'aqov replies. Ěsaw protests that he has enough, but Ya'aqov insists, saying, "No, please, if now I have found favor in your sight, then take my present from my hand, for I see your face as one sees the face of Elohim, and you have received me favorably, so, please take my gift which has been brought to you, because Elohim has dealt favorably with me and because I have plenty" (Gen 33:1-11). (In type, the bride assembly blesses the flesh-church.)

Ěsaw accepts and suggests that they continue on together. Ya'aqov declines the offer, saying they move slowly because of the children and livestock. Ěsaw then offers to leave some of the people who are with him. Again Ya'aqov declines, saying, "What need is there? Let me find favor in the sight of my master." So Ěsaw returns on his way to Sě'ir, and Ya'aqov goes back over the stream Yaboq, builds a house, and makes booths for his livestock; therefore the place was named Sukoth (Succoth, sue-KOTH, booths) (Gen 33:12-17). (The Feast of Booths, or Tabernacles, is called Succoth.) (In type, the bride refuses spiritual help from the lukewarm.)

After resting at Sukoth for awhile, Ya'aqov crosses over the Yarděn into the land of Kena'an and comes to the city of Shekem (Shechem, shoulder), arriving safely from his journey from Paddan-aram, the home of Lavan. This fulfills the command Elohim gave him to leave Lavan and return home. (In type, the bride assembly and flesh-church separate, the bride going to the promised land, and the flesh staying in the east, a type of the world.)

Because he plans to stay for awhile, he buys a parcel of land from the sons of Ḥamor. Ḥamor is the prince of the land and the father of Shekem. They are Ḥivi (Hivites). The area Yisra'ěl bought is large enough to live on and grow crops. He pays one hundred pieces of money for it. There he erects an altar and calls it Ěl-the Elohim of Yisra'ěl (Strong One, the Strong One of Yisra'ěl) (Gen 33:18-20).

Earlier, farther to the south, Avraham bought land for a burial site. This is the second purchase of land in the Promised Land, and much larger. It is another earnest of the inheritance. Its purpose was to have a place to live, grow crops, and house his livestock and servants. But, something happens to make them leave.

Shekem Rapes Dinah, 34:1

DINAH (dee-NAH, justice), a lovely young girl, the only daughter of Ya'aqov and the daughter of Leah, wants to see the daughters of the land. (In type, disciples of Yahushua looking to see what the world is like, and get contaminated.) She has six full brothers and five half brothers and only knows safety. When she goes out alone she is not aware that she is in danger, but she is. Shekem, the son of Ḥamor, sees her, wants her, rapes her, and tells his father to get her to be his wife.

Ya'aqov hears about the rape and that his daughter is in Ḥamor's house, but waits until his sons come in from the field where his livestock are. In the meantime, Ḥamor and Shekem come out to Ya'aqov to speak to him. When the sons come in from the field they hear what happened and are grieved and angry. A disgraceful thing has been done in Yisra'ĕl, something that ought not to be done (Gen 34:1-7).

Ḥamor pleads with them, saying, "Intermarry with us (mixture with the world); give your daughters to us and take our daughters for yourselves. In this way you shall live with us and the land shall be open before you; live and trade in it and acquire property in it."

Shekem also speaks and says, "If I find favor in your sight, then I will give whatever you say to me. Ask me however much you want for the bridal payment and gift, and I will give according as you say to me; but give me the girl in marriage" (Gen 34:8-12).

Ya'aqov's sons answer, but with deceit, saying that it would be a disgrace to consent unless all their males are circumcised. They then say, "If you do this, we will give our daughters to you, and we will take your daughters for ourselves, and we will live with you and become one people. But if you will not listen to us to be circumcised, then we will take our daughter and go" (Gen 34:13-17).

This seems reasonable to Ḥamor and Shekem, and they go back to the city and tell the men about the situation, wanting their consent to be circumcised. Their argument is, if they do this, then all the property of Ya'aqov, which is much, would be theirs. They like the idea, and are circumcised, a painful surgery that makes it impossible

165

to do anything until it heals (Gen 34:18-24). (In type, the world wants to consume the whole assembly by intermarriage, 2Cor 6:14-18.)

On the third day, while they are still in pain, Sime'on and Lĕwi, two full brothers of Dinah, go into the city and kill every male with the sword, including Ḥamor and Shekem. They take their sister from Shekem's house (in type, rescuing the bride from the world) and tell their brothers what they have done. Then all of Ya'aqov's sons, in revenge for raping their sister, loot the city, taking all their livestock and wealth and their little ones and their wives, even everything in the houses (Gen 34:25-29).

When Ya'aqov hears what his sons did he is afraid. He says to Sime'on and Lĕwi that they have brought trouble on him because, when the people of the land hear about it, they being many and he being few, "they will gather together against me and attack me and I will be destroyed, I and my household." But they say, "Should he treat our sister as a harlot?" (Gen 34:30-31). (In type, rescuing from the world can result in persecution.)

The people of the land are a type of the world, and Ya'aqov/Yisra'ĕl and his family are a type of the bride of Messiah. The world wants the bride to compromise with them, and those who do so become lukewarm. That is the condition of the church today. Killing the inhabitants of Shekem and reclaiming their sister is a type of removing worldly things from our lives and rescuing the lukewarm to become the bride. All these events are written for us, the bride, so we can benefit spiritually from them (1Cor 10:11). Later, when the nation of Yisra'ĕl leaves Mitsrayim (Egypt), Yahuah commands them that when they enter the Promised Land they are not to mix with any of the people. Paul writes the same thing to the assembly in Corinth (2Cor 6:14-18).

Raḥel Dies Giving Birth to Binyamin, 35:1

ELOHIM TELLS YA'AQOV to leave and go to Bĕth'ĕl where earlier he had made an altar when fleeing from Ĕsaw. In preparation for leaving he says to his household and to all who are with him to put away the foreign strong ones (gods, idols) which are among them and to purify themselves and change their garments. (In type, cleansing of the assembly and getting garments of righteousness.) So they give to Ya'aqov all the idols

166

which they have and the rings which are in their ears, and he hides them under the oak which is near Shekem (Gen 35:1-4).

Ya'aqov had feared that because of what happened in Shekem the people in the cities around them would pursue them. But as they journey a great terror comes upon the cities and they don't pursue them.

When they arrive at Běth'ěl he builds an altar and calls the place Ěl-běth-ěl (Strong One, house of the Strong One), because it was there that Elohim had revealed himself to him when he fled from his brother (Gen 35:5-7).

Elohim appears to him again, confirms that his name is changed to Yisra'ěl, and confirms the covenant, that kings would come from him and that the land he gave to Avraham and Yitshaq is given to him and to his seed after him. And Ya'aqov sets up a pillar (Gen 35:8-15).

They continue south going to Běth-lehem (Bethlehem, house of bread), and on the way Rahel gives birth to Yisra'ěl's twelfth son. The labor is hard, and she dies in the process. As she is dying she names him Ben-oni (son of my sorrow); but his father names him Binyamin (son of the right, or son of my right hand, or son of the South). There Rahel is buried and Ya'aqov places a pillar over her grave, and they continue going south (Gen 35:16-21).

While they are dwelling in that southern land Re'uven goes into Bilhah, Rahel's maid and his father's concubine, and Yisra'ěl hears about it. (In type, immorality in the assembly.)

Eventually they come to his father Yitshaq at Mamrě of Qiryath-Arba (that is, Hebron), where Avraham and Yitshaq had sojourned. After they arrive his father Yitshaq dies, and his sons Ěsaw and Ya'aqov bury him. He was 180 years old (Gen 35:22-29).

When Lavan had pursued Ya'aqov and said his household strong ones were stolen, Ya'aqov said whoever had them shall die. Rahel had them, but they weren't found, for she was sitting on the camel's saddle where they were hidden. She didn't die then, but now she does.

Through all this moving about we see the hand of Elohim protecting Ya'aqov and his seed so that the nation of Yisra'ěl would be born, and through that nation the Messiah would be born, and then the bride of Messiah, the purpose of creation.

12 Tribes of Israel

ABRAHAM ———————— SARAH

ISAAC ———————— REBEKAH

JACOB

Leah (older sister)

Zilpah (Leah's servant)

Bilah (Rachel's servant)

Rachel (younger sister)

| 1 Reuben | 2 Simeon | 3 Levi | 4 Judah | | 5 Dan | 6 Naphtali |

7 Gad   8 Asher

| 9 Issachar | 10 Zebulun | Dinah | | 11 Joseph | 12 Benjamin |

www.conformingtojesus.com

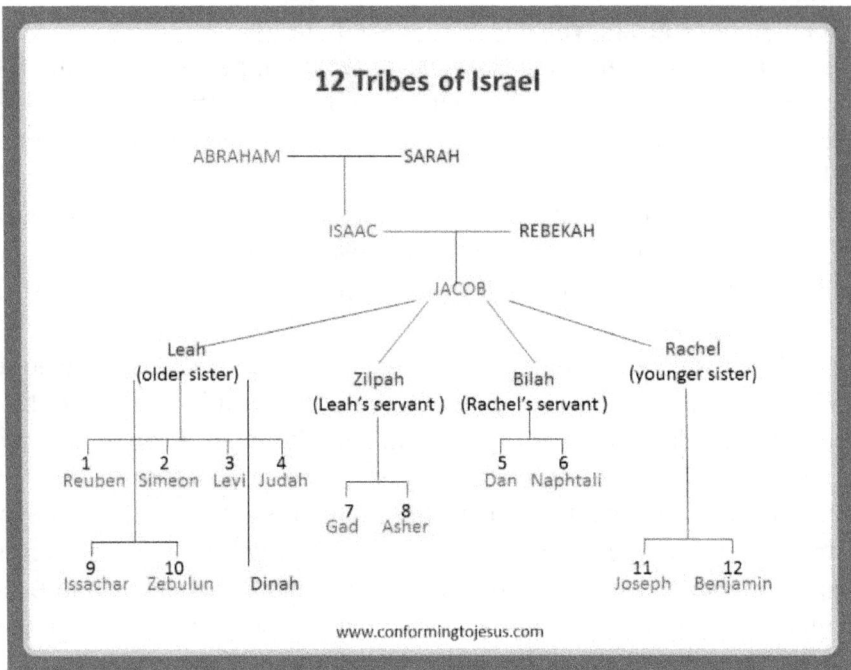

Ěsaw's Seed, 36:1

THIS CHAPTER records the descendants of Ěsaw (that is, Edom), and that Ěsaw separated from his brother Ya'aqov, leaving the west side of Yardĕn and going east of it to sojourn in Mount Sĕ'ir, because their herds were too great for them to dwell together. This is their second separation.

168

VII. YOSEF TO END
Genesis 37-50

Yisra'ĕl loved Yosef more than all his sons,
because he was the son of his old age.
Genesis 37:3

Yosef Dreams, His Brothers Sell Him, 37:1

YISRA'ĔL MAKES a beautiful tunic for Yosef, one that is richly orna-
mented with many colors. He does this because he loves him more
than his other sons, for he is the son of his old age. Also, he is the son
of his beloved wife, Raḥel. As a result of this preferential treatment,
the other sons are jealous of him. Further, to add to the jealousy, he is
a tattle-tale: he reports to his father what his brothers are doing. (In
type, Messiah reporting to Elohim what is going on in the assembly.) So they hate
him and show it by how they speak to him. (In type, the flesh church hates
the bride assembly.)

To make matters worse, he has two dreams that make him greater
than they. In one, the sheaves of his brothers are bowing down to his
sheaf. In the other, the sun, moon and eleven stars are bowing down
to him. When he tells his father, Ya'aqov, of the second dream, his
father recognizes the meaning and rebukes him, saying, "Shall we,
your mother and I and your brothers, indeed come to bow down to
the earth before you?" (In type, the worldly church cannot bear the spiritual
authority of the bride.) (See Is 66:3-5.) This sets the stage for murder. We
saw this hatred before with Qayin and Hevel, and with Ĕsaw and
Ya'aqov (Gen 37:1-11).

One time when his brothers are out pasturing their father's flock,
Yisra'ĕl tells Yosef to find them and see about their welfare and bring
back word. (In type, Messiah checking the activities of the pastors at the direction
of the Father.) Eventually Yosef finds them. When they see him at a
distance they make a plan to kill him, saying, "Here comes this
dreamer! Now then, come and let us kill him and throw him into one
of the pits; and we will say that a wild beast devoured him. Then let

us see what will become of his dreams?!"

Re'uven disagrees, saying, "Let us not take his life. Shed no blood. Instead, throw him into this pit that is in the wilderness, but do not lay hands on him." He says this so that he might rescue him later and restore him to his father. He is the oldest, the firstborn, and feels a responsibility to protect him.

When Yosef arrives they strip him of his beautiful tunic and throw him into the pit. Then, as they are eating their meal, they see a caravan of Yishma'ěli (Ishmaelites) on their way to Mitsrayim (Egypt) to sell their goods. Yahudah convinces his brothers to sell Yosef rather than to kill him, so they sell him for twenty pieces of silver, and the traders bring him into Mitsrayim. (In type, Messiah captive in the world.)

When Re'uven returns he is horrified that Yosef is gone. To cover up what they did, they kill a male goat, dip Yosef's beautiful tunic in the blood, and show it to their father for him to examine it. Yisra'ěl recognizes it, believes a wild beast has killed his son, and mourns for him. Meanwhile, the Midyani (Midianites) sell Yosef to Potifar, Par'oh's officer, the captain of the bodyguard (Gen 37:12-36).

Yisra'ěl's obvious preference for Yosef over the others is not good parenting. Also, it was not wise of Yosef to tell about his dreams, for this did not improve his relationship with his brothers. However, this is a type. Yisra'ěl is a type of the Father, our Strong One. Yosef is a type of Yahushua Messiah, the son of Elohim; and the others are a type of the lukewarm assembly, and also of the Jewish rulers at the time of Yahushua.

Elohim has obvious preference for Yahushua during his life on earth (Mk 9:7). The miracles he did are evidence of this. The dreams are prophetic of what would happen to him and his brothers in the future, and also, in type, of what would happen with Yahushua. The beautiful tunic is a type of the many varied spiritual gifts Elohim gave him—he has the spirit without limit (Jn 3:34-35). The jealousy of the brothers is the same as that of Qayin toward Hevel, of Leah toward Raḥel, and of Ěsaw toward Ya'aqov. So it will be of the lukewarm assembly toward the bride of Messiah when the last day bride, the male son, operates in the same and greater power than Yahushua did (Jn 14:12).

Yisra'ěl sending Yosef to his brothers is a type of Elohim sending his son into the world. His brothers refusing to receive him is a type of the world refusing to receive Yahushua. Selling him is a type of Judas selling Yahushua to be impaled.

Silver is a type of redemption. Twenty pieces of silver was the price which Mosheh afterwards fixed as the value of a boy between five and twenty (Lev 27:5), the average price of a slave being thirty (Ex 21:32). Judas sold Yahushua for thirty pieces of silver.

It should be noted in this story that the Yishma'ĕli and the Midyani are the same people. Avraham was the father of Yishma'ĕl by Hagar, and of Midyan by Qeturah. Their descendants lived in the same area and often traveled together in trading.

Yosef is a type of Messiah in the following ways: most loved by his father, hears from Yahuah, brothers jealous of him, sold for money, is in Mitsrayim/world, tempted to sin but doesn't yield, made perfect through suffering, saves Yisra'ĕl, and second in command under the king. There are many, many more.

Yahudah and Tamar, 38:1

AFTER THE BROTHERS show the bloody tunic to their father, Yahudah marries Shua's daughter, a Kena'ani woman, who bears him three sons, whom he names Ĕr, Onan and Shelah. When Ĕr is grown, Yahudah takes Tamar for him as wife. Because Ĕr is wicked, Yahuah takes his life.

Yahudah then tells Onan to marry Tamar and do the duty as a brother-in-law to her to raise up offspring for his brother. Onan marries her, but doesn't want to have a child by her, for it would be counted as Ĕr's child, so he spills his seed on the ground. For this wickedness, Yahuah also takes *his* life.

Yahudah then tells Tamar to wait in her father's house until Shelah is old enough to marry her. After some time Yahudah's wife dies. Shelah is now of marriage age, but his father has not given him to Tamar. He is afraid his third son might die like his brothers.

When the time of mourning for his wife ends, Yahudah goes up to his sheepshearers at Timnah. Tamar learns of it, removes her widow's garments, puts on a veil covering her face, wraps herself, and sits in the gateway of Enayim, which is on the road to Timnah. When Yahudah sees her, he doesn't recognize her but thinks she is a temple prostitute. He asks her if he may go into her. She asks what he is willing to pay. He promises a young goat. She asks what pledge he will give. He asks what pledge she would like. She says his seal, cord and the staff in his hand. He gives them to her and goes into her. She conceives, goes home, and changes back into her widow's garments.

Later, Yahudah sends a friend to the place with the young goat to receive back the pledge. His friend goes, and returns saying she wasn't there, and the people there said there is no temple prostitute. Yahudah, therefore, decides to let her keep the pledge so as not to become a laughingstock.

About three months later Yahudah is informed that his daughter-in-law Tamar is with child by harlotry. Yahudah says to bring her out to be burned. When she comes, she brings with her the signet ring, cord and staff and says that she is with child by the man who owns them. He recognizes that he is the owner, and says she is more righteous than he, for he had not given his son Shelah to her.

At the time of giving birth, Tamar has twins. One puts out a hand, and the midwife ties a scarlet thread on his hand to identify the firstborn. But the first draws his hand back and the other comes out first. The midwife says, "What a breach you have made for yourself!" and names him Parets (Perez, breach, breaker through). Then his brother comes out with the thread on his hand, and is named Zerah (exit, rising) (Gen 38:1-30).

Yahudah, the carrier of the Messianic seed, knew that he was supposed to marry in his own clan; instead, he married a pagan, a woman of the land. This is a type of the bride mixing with the world. We saw this at the time of Seth when the sons of Elohim married the daughters of men, and what resulted from that! Yahuah knows whom he wants to be in the line of Messiah. None of Yahudah's three sons qualified. Tamar, although a pagan, did qualify—*"the seed of the woman that will defeat the devil."* When Yahudah went into Tamar, he was a widower, and it was in the culture where he lived to go into temple prostitutes. To do so was to do homage to that strong one. Yahudah did it, however, because of sexual desire. He had just finished mourning the death of his wife.

Parets and Zerah, the twins that came from Tamar, are a type of the bride and the lukewarm. Zerah, a type of the lukewarm, started to come out first, but didn't make it to be first. Parets, a type of the bride, who was second in the womb, pushed past his brother and became first. This is another example, in type, of the flesh first and then the spirit. Four gentile women are noted in the line of Messiah: Tamar, Raḥav, Ruth and Bathsheba (Mt 1:3-6). This is a type of the bride of Messiah coming from both the Jews and gentiles.

Yosef Prospers, Imprisoned, 39:1

POTIFAR, a Mitsrayim officer of Par'oh, is in the slave market and sees Yosef being offered for sale. "I could use a young man like that," he thinks, so buys him, learns that his name is Yosef, that he is a Hebrew, and puts him to work doing household chores. While Yosef is learning the Mitsrayim language, Potifar sees that this slave is different from others, for he is honest and industrious, doing beyond what is asked of him. Not only that, but it seems that because of him his household is prospering. "Who are you and where are you from?" he asks.

"I am Yosef, a Hebrew, the eleventh of twelve sons. We are sheep-herders and sojourners living in the land of the Kena'ani. Our Strong One is Yahuah; he is the one to whom we bow. My brothers sold me to the Yishma'ĕli as a slave."

"I like you, Yosef. I like your attitude and how you work. It seems that because of you I am prospering. I am promoting you to be my personal servant."

In time, Potifar elevates Yosef even more, making him overseer over all his house and everything he owns, in house and field. He recognizes that he is prospering on account of Yosef and his Strong One.

In the background, unseen, the devil is at work. "What is your plan for Yosef?" asks one of his demons. "We failed in getting his brothers to kill him, but we did get him sold into slavery. But now he is prospering even in Mitsrayim. The Strong One is favoring him."

"The Strong One is not allowing us to kill him," Satan replies, "even as he didn't allow us to kill Iyov (Job) (Job 2:6). And he is not allowing us to put sickness on him. But he does allow us to tempt him, and Potifar's wife is our tool. She is already enjoying the feelings of lust for him that we are strengthening in her. Humans are such easy targets! So far he has rejected her advances. But we'll get the other servants out of the way and put him in a compromising position. She will accuse him to her husband, and we will give him rage so that he won't listen to what Yosef has to say. Indeed, how can a slave defend himself against his master's wife?! If we can't kill him, we can at least get him thrown into prison. That should be the end of him."

And so Yosef gets a new home—jail (Gen 39:1-20).

In the background, also unseen, Yahuah is at work. "What is your plan for Yosef?" asks one of his angels.

"I do not allow anyone to be tempted beyond what he is able to resist with my help (1Cor 10:13). I am humbling Yosef. I am bringing him to the bottom of his life so that he can be my instrument for salvation. He is gentle of spirit and not arrogant, which I love. He is learning to trust me, that his success is not because of his ability, but because of my favor. I am teaching him how to be a supervisor and administrator. I am training him for a much higher position. He is feeling that he is being treated unjustly and is yearning to be free and get back to his family. He will be free when he is ready, but it will be his family that will be coming to him.

"His brothers betrayed him and sold him. But the dreams I gave him will be fulfilled. I will bring them to the place that they will confess their sin and humble themselves before him, not because Yosef is great, but because I am great in him. I gave him favor under Potifar. I will also give him favor in prison."

And so Yosef, now under the chief jailer, prospers and is put in charge of all the prisoners in the jail (Gen 39:21-23).

Keep in mind that some of the narrative, although based on scripture, is "as it may have been."

Yosef Interprets Two Dreams in Prison, 40:1

YOSEF IS NOW twenty-eight years old. The chief jailor comes to him and says, "I have two new prisoners for you. They are the king's cupbearer and baker, high level officials. They offended Par'oh— something not wise to do—and he became furious with them and sent them here. I'm placing them under your charge. Take care of them. Maybe, when they get out, if they do, they will put a good word in for you. I know how badly you want to get back to your family in

Kena'an." By then, Yosef has been there several years.

Yosef does his best to tend to these two officials and regularly asks about their welfare and whether there is anything more he can do for them. One morning when he comes to them he sees that they are dejected. "Why are your faces so sad today?" he asks.

"We each have had a dream and there is no one to interpret it."

"Do not interpretations belong to Elohim? Tell me, please."

The chief cupbearer says, "In my dream I saw a vine with three branches in front of me. As it is budding, its blossoms come out and its clusters produce ripe grapes. Now Par'oh's cup is in my hand; so I take the grapes and squeeze them into his cup, and I put the cup into his hand."

"This is the interpretation," Yosef responds. "The three branches are three days; within three more days Par'oh will lift up your head and restore you to your office; and you will put Par'oh's cup into his hand according to your former custom when you were his cupbearer. Only, please, keep me in mind when it goes well with you, and please do me a kindness by mentioning me to Par'oh and get me out of this house. For I was in fact kidnapped from the land of the Hebrews, and even here I have done nothing that they should have put me into the dungeon."

The chief baker sees that Yosef interpreted favorably, so he says to him, "In my dream this is what I saw. Three baskets of white bread are on my head; and in the top basket are some of all sorts of baked food for Par'oh, and the birds are eating them out of the basket on my head."

"This is its interpretation," Yosef says. "The three baskets are three days; within three more days Par'oh will cut off your head and hang you on a tree, and the birds will eat your flesh off you."

And so it happens. The third day is Par'oh's birthday and he makes a feast for all his servants. He has the chief cupbearer and chief baker brought up from prison. Then he restores the chief cupbearer to his office, who, on being restored, puts the cup into Par'oh's hand; but he hangs the chief baker. The chief cupbearer, however, forgets Yosef. This forgetting, of course, is from Yahuah, for Yosef's time of release from prison is not yet (Gen 40:1-23).

Dear reader, are you in a trial that is pressing you down and it seems it will never end? You are in Elohim's plan. He is doing things in you for your benefit, that you be a vessel of honor in his house (Ro 9:21; 2Ti 2:21). Because you love Elohim and are called according to his purpose, all things are working for your good—ALL THINGS (Ro 8:28). Before the foundation of the world he has prepared works for you to do, works which only you can do (Eph 2:10). We are being built into a temple, each of us being one of many living stones (1Pe 2:5). Do not cry or blame him. Praise him. Trust him. Look to him. Don't listen to lying emotions. You are alive and experiencing your trials for a reason. In them, learn what Elohim wants from you. All trials should draw us deeper into him, to become the bride he is fashioning.

Yosef Interprets Par'oh's Dream, 41:1

TWO YEARS GO BY and Yosef, now thirty years old, is still in prison. But his release is about to happen. In the night Par'oh has a dream in which he sees himself standing by the Nile. He sees seven sleek and fat cows come up out of the water and graze on the marsh grass. Then he sees seven other cows come up, but these are ugly and gaunt, and they eat up the first seven. After this he has a second dream. He sees seven plump and good ears of grain come up on a single stalk. But after them, seven ears that are thin and scorched by the east wind sprout up and these ears swallow up the seven good ones. Then he wakes up and remembers the dream, and is troubled in his spirit.

His magicians and wise men are supposed to interpret such things, so he sends for them and relates the dreams to them, but they are unable to interpret. At this point the chief cupbearer speaks to Par'oh: "I would make mention today of my offenses. Par'oh was furious with his servants, and he put me in confinement in the house of the captain of the bodyguard, me and the chief baker. We had a dream on the same night, he and I. Now a Hebrew youth was with us there, a servant of the captain of the bodyguard. We related to him our dreams, and he interpreted them for us, that Par'oh would restore me to my office and hang the chief baker. And just as he interpreted, so it happened" (Gen 41:1-13).

"This is good news," says Par'oh. He has his servants make Yosef presentable and bring him. When Yosef arrives he says to him, "I had a dream, but no one can interpret it; and I have heard it said about you, that when you hear a dream you can interpret it."

Yosef answers, "It is not in me; the Strong One will give Par'oh a favorable answer."

Par'oh then relates the dreams, and Yosef gives the interpretation. "Both dreams are prophetic of what will happen," he says. "The seven good cows and ears of grain mean there will be seven years of great abundance in all the land of Mitsrayim; and the seven ugly cows and ears of grain mean there will be seven years of severe famine, famine so great that the abundance will be forgotten. Because the dream was given twice, it means that the matter is determined by the Strong One, and the Strong One will quickly bring it about."

After giving the interpretation, Yosef gives advice to Par'oh. He tells him to look for a man who is discerning and wise, and set him over the land of Mitsrayim, and then appoint overseers to be in charge of the land and take a fifth of the harvest in the seven years of abundance and store it for use during the seven years of famine.

Par'oh likes the idea and appoints Yosef to be that man. He places him over his house and over all the land of Mitsrayim and commands that all his people shall do homage to him; only in the throne will Par'oh be greater (see 1Cor 15:28). Then he removes his signet ring from his hand and puts it on Yosef's hand, clothes him in garments of fine linen, and puts the gold necklace around his neck. Then he has him ride in his second chariot, and the servants proclaim before him, "Bow the knee!"

Moreover, Par'oh says to Yosef, "I am Par'oh, yet without your permission no one shall raise his hand or foot in all the land of Mitsrayim." He then gives him the Mitsrayim name of Tsafenath-paneah and gives him Asenath, the daughter of Potipera priest of On (pronounced own), as his wife. And Yosef goes forth over the land of Mitsrayim, following the advice he gave to Par'oh. Even as the interpretation came from Elohim, so does the wisdom regarding what to do (Gen 41:14-49).

In this event, Par'oh is a type of the Father and Yosef is a type of Messiah. Even as Par'oh gave all authority over his kingdom to Yosef, except the throne itself, so our Father gave all authority over heaven and earth to his son Yahushua Messiah (Mt 28:18).

Yosef was thirty years old when he was released from prison and given all authority over the kingdom. This is the age in which a Lěwi could function in the office of priest (Num 4:3). This is also the age in which Yahushua began his ministry.

During the seven years of plenty Yosef's wife bears him two sons. The firstborn he names Manasseh (causing to forget), "Because Elohim has made me forget all my trouble and all my father's household." The second son he names Efrayim (Ephraim, double fruit), "Because Elohim has made me fruitful in the land of my affliction" (Gen 41:50-52).

When the seven years of plenty end, the famine begins and spreads throughout Mitsrayim and beyond, including Kena'an where Yosef's family are living. And when the peoples' own harvests are eaten up, they come to Yosef to buy grain from him, the grain which had been stored during the years of plenty. Thus all the earth came to Mitsrayim to buy grain from Yosef, because the famine was so severe (Gen 41:53-57).

The seven years of plenty is a type of spiritual completeness in which the bride of Messiah is completed. These believers are full of the spirit of Elohim and are manifesting Yahuah to the world with signs and wonders to confirm the message of repentance from sin, committing one's life wholeheartedly to serving Yahuah, and living in righteousness. The last day bride/man-child/male-son ministry lasts 3½ years, and then they are raptured from the earth to meet their bridegroom in the air, and so they shall ever be with the Master (1Th 4:17).

The seven years of drought is a type of the tribulation which follows the rapture. During this time the antichrist is ruling, requiring everyone to take the 666 "mark of the beast." There is a drought for the word of Elohim. In the first half of this seven years the believers who are left behind at the rapture, and any new believers, either take the mark and lose their salvation, or repent and be martyred. At the end of this period no believer is left alive on earth.

The second half of the seven years of tribulation experiences seven plagues from Yahuah as judgment for killing the believers and following the antichrist. The last plague is the return of Yahushua Messiah with his bride to end the "Battle of Armageddon" (in which the nations of the world are united in destroying Israel) and to begin his 1,000-year reign on earth, called the Millennium. By the end of these plagues only a remnant of humans, a few from each nation, remain alive on earth to enter the Millennium and fill the earth again with people. In the Millennium the nation of Yisra'ĕl is the top nation.

Yosef's Brothers Sent to Mitsrayim, 42:1

BECAUSE OF THE DROUGHT Ya'aqov sends ten of his sons to Mitsrayim to buy grain. He doesn't send Yosef's full brother Binyamin for fear harm might befall him.

Because Yosef is in charge of selling grain, his brothers bow down before him with faces to the ground. Yosef recognizes them, but they don't recognize him. They speak to each other through a translator, for Yosef is speaking the Mitsrayim language and they are speaking the Hebrew language (which is the same as the Kena'ani language), and he acts as though he needs someone to interpret.

Yosef's attitude toward his ten brothers is harsh. He asks why they have come, and they say they have come to buy grain. He remembers the dreams which he had about them and accuses them of being spies. They keep protesting they have only come for grain, and he keeps accusing them of being spies. In the process of questioning them he learns that his father is still alive, that originally they were twelve brothers, that the youngest, Binyamin, remained behind, and that the other, referring to Yosef whom they sold into slavery, is dead.

Yosef concludes by saying, "It is as I said to you, you are spies. To prove you are not spies, you will not go back to your place unless your youngest brother comes here. Send one of you that he may get your brother, while you remain confined, that your words may be tested, whether there is truth in you. But if not, by the life of Par'oh, surely you are spies." So he puts them all in prison for three days (Gen 42:1-17).

On the third day Yosef releases them and says they will not see him again until they bring their youngest brother with them. The brothers talk among themselves about what they had done to Yosef, and realize that this trouble has come upon them because of what they did to him. *"Be sure your sin will find you out"* (Num 32:23). Yosef understands what they were saying and leaves briefly to get his emotions under control. When he returns he binds Shim'on before their eyes to keep as a prisoner until they return. He then sells them the grain, filling their sacks. He also tells his servants to restore every man's money in his sack and give them provisions for the journey home.

When they stop at a lodging place on their way home, one of them opens his sack to give his donkey food. "What is this?!" he exclaims. "My money is in the mouth of my sack!" He tells his brothers about it and their hearts sink. Trembling, they say to one another, "What is this that Elohim has done to us?" They are not atheists as we have today in America and Europe—they recognize that when things happen it is because of Elohim (Gen 42:18-28).

When they arrive home they tell their father Ya'aqov all of what happened and why Shim'on isn't with them. They also tell him that they can't return to Mitsrayim for more grain unless they bring Binyamin with them. Then, when they empty their sacks, they discover that *every* man's bundle of money is in his sack. When they see this they are all dismayed.

In response to all these happenings their father Ya'aqov complains to them: "You have bereaved me of my children. Yosef is no more, and Shim'on is no more, and you would take Binyamin; all these things are against me."

Re'uven tries to soothe his father, saying, "You may put my two sons to death if I do not bring Binyamin to you; put him in my care, and I will return him to you."

"No!" exclaims Ya'aqov. "My son shall not go down with you; for his brother is dead, and he alone is left. If harm should happen to him on the journey you are taking, then you will bring my gray hair down to Sheol (the place of the dead) in sorrow" (Gen 42:29-38).

Yahuah is arranging all these events, including giving Yosef what to say (Ro 8:28). In all of this, Elohim is working to get the ten brothers to repent of what they did and to humble themselves before Yosef. Yosef is a type of Messiah, and the ten brothers are a type of the lukewarm assembly, Laodicea. Binyamin is a type of the bride assembly, Philadelphia (see Rev 3). We will see this develop more as we proceed with the story.

Binyamin Comes to Mitsrayim, 43:1

THE FAMINE CONTINUES and the grain they brought from Mitsrayim is finished. When Ya'aqov tells his sons to go back to Mitsrayim and buy more grain, Yahudah reminds him that the man from whom they must buy it had told them that they would not be permitted to see him unless they had Binyamin with them, so they won't go without him.

"Why did you do this to me," Yisra'ĕl complains, "telling the man that you had another brother?"

"The man questioned us harshly and very particularly. He wanted to know every detail about our family, while all the time accusing us of being spies. How could we know he would say to bring our brother?"

Yahudah then says, "Send the lad with me. If we don't go we will all starve to death, including our little ones. I myself will be guarantee for him. If I do not bring him back, then let me bear the blame before you forever. If we had not delayed, by now we could have returned twice."

"Okay. If it must be so, then do this: take some of the best products of the land in your bags, and take them to the man as a present. Take double the money in your hand, and take back in your hand the money that was returned in the mouth of your sacks; perhaps it was a mistake. Take your brother also. Go and return to the man. And may Ĕl the Almighty grant you compassion in the sight of the man, so that he will release to you your other brother and Binyamin. And as for me, if I am bereaved of my children, I am bereaved" (Gen 43:1-15).

They take Binyamin with them to Mitsrayim, and are standing before Yosef. When he sees Binyamin he orders his steward to bring the men to his house, and says, "Prepare a feast. I want them to eat with me at noon."

His brothers are very afraid when they are brought to Yosef's house. "It is because of the money that was returned to us the first time that we are being brought here. He seeks a reason to make us slaves and take our donkeys."

So they speak to the steward at the entrance of the house telling him what happened regarding the money and how they discovered it. The steward calms their fears saying, "Peace be to you. Do not be afraid. Your Strong One and the Strong One of your father has given you treasure in your sacks; I have your money." Then he brings

Shim'on out to them, brings the men in, gives them water for them to wash their feet, and gives their donkeys fodder. Then they prepare the present for Yosef's coming at noon; for they had heard that they were to eat a meal there.

When Yosef arrives home, they give him the present of produce they had brought with them and bow to the ground before him. He asks about their father, if he is well and still alive. They affirm that he is, and bow down again. Then he sees his brother Binyamin, his mother's son, and asks if he is their youngest brother about whom they had spoken, and says to him, "May Elohim give you favor, my son." Yosef's emotions start welling up in him, and he hurries to his room where he can weep privately. Then, after washing his face and controlling himself , he returns and orders the meal to be served.

Yosef sits at a table separate from them because it is loathsome for Mitsrayim to eat with Hebrews. The others sit according to their ages, the firstborn who has the birthright and the youngest according to his youth, and the men look at one another in astonishment: "How does he know the order of our births?"

Then Yosef gives them portions from his own table, but he gives Binyamin five times as much as the others. (In type, the bride gets the favor of Yahushua Messiah.) So they feast and drink freely with him (Gen 43:16-34).

Yosef is a type of Messiah. His house is a type of the assembly. Binyamin is a type of the last day bride/man-child/male-son that will do mighty works before the rapture. Five is the number of favor, and Messiah gives the bride favor to do these mighty works. Ten is the number of completion in this world, and the ten brothers are a type of the lukewarm church that miss the rapture. Their number is complete at the time of the rapture. They receive spiritual food from Messiah that they may endure during the tribulation that follows the rapture. Mitsrayim is a type of the world, and Yahuah accomplishes all this in the world.

In the letters to the seven assemblies in the book of Revelation, the Philadelphia assembly represents the bride, of which Binyamin is a type, and the Laodicea assembly represents the lukewarm assembly, of which the ten brothers are a type. Yahushua said to the Philadelphia assembly, *"I will make those who are of the synagogue of Satan* (the lukewarm), *who claim to be Jews* (that is, believers in Messiah) *though they are not, but are liars* (because they don't walk in righteousness)—*I will make them come and fall down at your feet and acknowledge that I have loved you"* (Rev 3:9).

The humbling of the ten brothers is not yet complete, and they are not yet ready for Yosef to reveal his identity to them. But Yosef has a plan.

Brothers Brought Back, 44:1

YOSEF HAS HIS STEWARD fill the men's sacks with food and put each man's money in the mouth of his sack. Further, he has him put his silver cup in the mouth of the youngest. In the morning, as soon as it is light, Yosef sends the men on their way with their donkeys. After they are out of the city he sends his steward after them and ask, "Why have you repaid evil for good? Is not this cup the one from which my master drinks and which he uses for divination? You have done wrong in doing this" (Gen 44:1-5).

The men proclaim their innocence, that they would never do such a thing. They then affirm, "With whomever of your servants it is found, let him die, and we also will be slaves of my master." The steward says that only the one with whom it is found will be his slave and the rest innocent.

Each man then hurries to lower his sack to the ground and opens it. The steward begins with the oldest, ending with the youngest, and there the cup is found in Binyamin's sack. The men are dismayed! They tear their clothes, reload their donkeys, and return to the city (Gen 44:6-13).

When they arrive at Yosef's house they fall to the ground before him. Yahudah speaks for the others: "What can we say to my master? What can we speak? And how can we justify ourselves? Elohim has found out the iniquity of your servants; behold, we are slaves of my master, both we and the one in whose possession the cup has been found." (In type, Messiah is interceding for the bride.) Yosef denies, saying only the one with whom the cup was found shall be his slave, and the others go in peace to their father.

Yahudah approaches him and begs, saying that if they don't bring back Binyamin to their father, their father will die. He has already lost one son and he alone is left of his mother, and his father loves him. (In type, the bride is all that is left of the assembly.) Then he relates how this all happened because of the close questioning about their family. He concludes by saying, "Now, therefore, please let your servant remain a slave to my master instead of the lad, and let the lad go up with his brothers. For how shall I go up to my father if the lad is not with me, for fear that I see the evil that would overtake my father?" (Gen 44:14-34).

Yosef Deals Kindly with his Brothers, 45:1

YOSEF CAN NO LONGER control himself and orders his servants to leave the room. When they are gone he makes himself known to his brothers, and weeps so loudly that the Mitsrayim and even Par'oh's household hear. He says, "I am Yosef! Is my father still alive?" But his brothers are too dismayed at his presence to answer him.

He calls them closer and tells them not to be grieved or angry that they sold him into Mitsrayim. Elohim knew there would be a famine and so had sent him ahead to preserve their lives. Then he told them to go back to his father and tell him that his son, Yosef, is still alive, and that Elohim has made him master of all Mitsrayim, and that they should come to him without delay and live in the land of Goshen. Yisra'ĕl should bring everyone and all that he has. There Yosef will provide for them, because there are five more years of famine to come. Then he falls on his brother Binyamin's neck and weeps, and Binyamin weeps on his neck. He kisses all his brothers and weeps on them, and afterward his brothers talk with him. Oh, what a reunion!

The news that Yosef's brothers have come pleases Par'oh and he tells him to send wagons to fetch his father's household. They are not to concern themselves with their goods, for they will have the best of the land of Mitsrayim (Gen 45:1-20).

Yosef gives his brothers wagons according to the command of Par'oh, and provisions for the journey. He also gives each of them changes of garments, but to Binyamin he gives three hundred pieces of silver and five changes of garments. To his father he sends ten donkeys loaded with the best things of Mitsrayim, and ten female donkeys loaded with things for his father on the journey. As he sends his brothers away he tells them, "Do not quarrel on the journey."

When they arrive home in Kena'an they tell their father, "Yosef is still alive, and indeed he is ruler over all the land of Mitsrayim." Ya'aqov is stunned and doesn't believe them. But when they tell him what Yosef had said to them, and when he sees the wagons that Yosef had sent to carry him, the spirit of Ya'aqov revives and he says, "It is enough; my son Yosef is still alive. I will go and see him before I die" (Gen 45:21-28).

Yosef giving his brothers wagons and provisions for the journey according to the command of Par'oh is a type of Messiah, at the command of Yahuah, giving the assembly strength for their spiritual journey to grow and become the bride of Messiah. Giving his brothers changes of garments is a type of believers being clothed with the righteousness of Messiah. Yosef's father in this situation is a type of pastors. Receiving ten donkeys loaded with the best things of Mitsrayim, and ten female donkeys loaded with provisions for the journey, is a type of pastors receiving double all they need to lead their assemblies in their spiritual walk in the world.

Binyamin being given five changes of garments is a type of receiving special favor in righteousness. The best is given to the bride. Silver is a type of redemption; ten is the number of completeness in this world, and one hundred, which is ten times ten, is completeness multiplied; and three is the number of resurrection. Thus, 300 pieces of silver is a type of the bride being fully completed and ready to be raptured.

Ya'aqov's Family Moves to Mitsrayim, 46:1

YISRA'ĔL SETS OUT for Mitsrayim with all that he has: his children and grandchildren, livestock and property—everything. When he comes to Be'ĕr-Sheva (Beersheba) he offers slaughterings to the Strong One of his father Yitshaq. That night Elohim speaks to him in visions: "I am the Strong One, Strong One of your father; do not be afraid to go down to Mitsrayim, for I will make you a great nation there. I will go down with you to Mitsrayim, and I will also surely bring you up again; and Yosef will close your eyes."

All the persons of the house of Ya'aqov who come to Mitsrayim are seventy in number (7x10, in type, spiritual completeness in the world). He sends Yahudah ahead to Yosef so they will know the way to Goshen.

When they arrive, Yosef is there to meet them, and when Yosef sees his father he falls on his neck and weeps a long time. Again, what a reunion! Yisra'ĕl says to Yosef, "Now let me die, since I have seen your face, that you are still alive" (Gen 46:1-30).

What a meeting it will be when we are with Yahuah forever on the other side! Every shepherd is an abomination to the Mitsrayim, so being settled in Goshen separates them from them. This is a type of Messiah arranging the assembly to be separate from the world. True believers in Yahushua are an abomination to the world.

Ya'aqov's Family Settles in Goshen, 47:1

YOSEF TELLS PAR'OH that his family has arrived in Goshen with their flocks and herds. He presents five of his brothers to him, and Par'oh asks their occupation. They say they are shepherds, both they and their fathers, and ask permission to sojourn in Goshen, because the famine is severe in Kena'an. Goshen is the best of the land of Mitsrayim, and Par'oh gives permission. He also says, "If you know any capable men among them, put them in charge of my livestock." Shepherding is an abomination to the Mitsrayim.

Yosef then presents his father Ya'aqov to Par'oh, and Par'oh asks how old he is. Ya'aqov replies, "The years of my sojourning are 130. Few and unpleasant have been the years of my life, nor have they attained the years that my fathers lived during the days of their sojourning." And Ya'aqov blesses Pharaoh and leaves.

So Yosef settles his father and his brothers and gives them a possession in the land of Mitsrayim, in the best of the land, in the land of Rameses, as Par'oh had ordered. And he provides his father and his brothers and all his father's household with food, according to their little ones (Gen 47:1-12).

Ya'aqov and his family are a type of the assembly (or church). Mitsrayim is a type of the world, and the assembly is in the world but not of it. Par'oh is a type of Yahuah in that he owns Mitsrayim. Yosef is a type of Messiah in that Par'oh has given him authority over all the land. Famine is a type of hardships in this life. Yahuah uses hardships to draw people to him. Even as Yahuah had sent Yosef ahead to prepare for deliverance from famine, so he sent Messiah ahead to prepare for our salvation from sin. Yosef providing food for Ya'aqov's family is a type of Messiah providing what is needed to believers. Binyamin is a type of the bride/man-child/male-son in that he is in the assembly, but specially favored.

Result of the Famine, 47:13

AS THE FAMINE CONTINUES, the people first use money to buy grain. Then they sell their houses and livestock. Finally they sell their land and their very lives to Par'oh, and thus Par'oh comes to own all the land and the people. The only land exempt from purchase is the priests', for Par'oh gives them an allotment and they live off that. As for the people, Yosef moved them to the cities of Mitsrayim so he can feed them.

When the famine is over Yosef gives seed to the people and they return to their lands and to farming. Par'oh, however, owns the land, and they are his slaves. They must give a fifth of the harvest to Par'oh; they will live off of the rest (Gen 47:13-26).

This is a type of giving everything to Yahuah, even our very lives and plans, and serving him. He bought us with a price. By his death, Messiah bought all the world for the Father.

You are not your own; you were bought at a price. Therefore honor Elohim with your body (1Cor 6:19b-20).

Yosef Swears Regarding Yisra'ĕl's Burial, 47:29

AFTER SEVENTEEN YEARS of living in Goshen, and now 147 years old, Yisra'ĕl is preparing to die. They have acquired property, been fruitful, and become very numerous. He calls for Yosef, and has him vow that he will not bury him in Mitsrayim, but in the burial place which Avraham bought to bury Sarah, and where Yitsḥaq, Rivqah and Leah are also buried. Yosef puts his hand under Yisra'ĕl's thigh and so swears to him. Yisra'ĕl, now contented, bows in homage to Elohim (Gen 47:29-31).

When Avraham bought the burial plot, it was like the down payment on all the land which Yahuah had promised to his seed. In type, it was believing the promise of heaven. Yisra'ĕl's desire to be buried there is a type of not wanting eternal life with the world, but with those who will inherit heaven.

Yisra'ĕl Blesses Yosef's Two Sons, 48:1

YOSEF IS TOLD that his father is sick, so he comes, bringing his two sons with him, Manasseh and Efrayim. On learning that his son has arrived, Yisra'ĕl gathers his strength and sits up in the bed and tells Yosef the vision he had in Kena'an in which Ĕl Shaddai (the Strong One Almighty) said to him: "Behold, I will make you fruitful and numerous, and I will make you a company of peoples, and will give this land to your seed after you for an everlasting possession." Yisra'ĕl then tells Yosef that his two sons, Manasseh and Efrayim, are his, just as Re'uven and Shim'on are, and thus receive the same inheritance rights. Any children Yosef might have later will be Yosef's.

Yisra'ĕl, eyes now dim with age, sees Yosef's sons and asks who they are. Yosef tells him, and Yisra'ĕl wants them brought to him so he may bless them. Yosef brings them close, and their grandfather kisses them and embraces them. He says to Yosef, "I never expected to see your face, and behold, Elohim has let me see your children as well." Then Yosef takes them from his father and places Manasseh at Yisra'ĕl's right side and Efrayim at his left. He does this so that the right hand blessing would be on the firstborn.

But Yisra'ĕl crosses his arms and places his right hand on the head of Efrayim, the younger, and his left hand on the head of Manasseh and says: "The Elohim before whom my fathers Avraham and Yitsḥaq walked, the Elohim who has been my shepherd all my life to this day, the angel who has redeemed me from all evil, bless the lads; and may my name live on in them, and the names of my fathers Avraham and Yitsḥaq; and may they grow into a multitude in the midst of the earth."

When Yosef sees what his father did with his hands, he tries to move his father's hands, saying Manasseh is the firstborn. But his father refuses and says, "I know, my son, I know; he also will become a people and he also will be great. However, his younger brother shall be greater than he, and his seed shall become a multitude of nations." So he blesses them that day, and future generations would say to their children, "May Elohim make you like Efrayim and Manasseh!" Then Ya'aqov tells Yosef that Elohim will bring him, Yosef, back to the land of his fathers. And he gives to him one portion more than his brothers, land which he bought at Shekem and had to leave because

188

of what his sons did there in revenge when Shekem raped Dinah (Gen 48:1-22).

There is no tribe called Yosef, but his two sons become two tribes of Yisra'ĕl. This makes thirteen tribes. However, the tribe of Lĕwi would not be counted in land distribution or in warfare, for they would be separated to the service of Yahuah as priests.

Yisra'ĕl Prophesies Concerning his Sons, 49:1

YISRA'EL CALLS FOR HIS SONS and prophesies over them regarding their futures. The words for Yosef are for his two sons.

Re'uven, the first born, will not be preeminent in power, because he went into his father's concubine.

Shim'on and Lĕwi will not receive esteem and will be scattered in Yisra'ĕl because of the slaughter they did at Shekem.

Yahudah (praise) will be the line through which the Messiah will come. Everything in the prophecy about Yahudah refers to Messiah. His brothers will praise him. He will rule forever. The peoples will obey him. He will judge the wicked, referring to "He washes his garments in wine and his robes in the blood of grapes."

Zevulun will be seafaring, having their land allotment at the seashore south of Lebanon.

Yissakar will be shepherds and will become slaves at forced labor.

Dan (dawn, judge) will judge his people.

Gad (gawd) will be raided, and will raid in turn.

Asher will have rich food.

Naftali will give beautiful words.

Yosef (fruitful) will be fruitful. He will be attacked and harassed, but will remain firm. He will be distinguished among his brothers.

Binyamin will be a ravenous wolf.

After finishing blessing them he tells them to bury him with his fathers in the field that Avraham bought in Kena'an. Then he draws up his feet into the bed, breathes his last, and is gathered to his people (Gen 49:1-33).

Much can be said about what happened to each of these tribes and how the prophecies fit, but that is not within the scope of this work. Yahuah knows everything, past, present and future. Here is a summary.

The Yisra'eli are in Mitsrayim for 430 years (Ex 12:41), during which time they become slaves, then Yahuah sends Mosheh to bring them to the Promised Land, then his servant Yahushua (Joshua) brings them across the Yardĕn and they take possession of the land. The tribes of Re'uven, Gad and half of Manasseh occupy the land east of the Yardĕn and the Dead Sea. They are the first to be taken captive by Ashur (Assyria). The tribes of Yahudah and Binyamin occupy the land west of the Dead Sea. The rest of the tribes occupy the land west of the Yardĕn and the Sea of Galilee.

The tribe of Lĕwi has no land allotment, for they serve as priests for all the tribes. Instead, they have forty-eight cities with surrounding lands, located throughout the tribes, six of them cities of refuge where the man-slayer can flee to be safe from "the avenger of blood," safe only, however, if the death was an accident.

When the tribes become a kingdom, Sha'ul (Saul) of Binyamin is the first king, succeeded by David and Shlomoh (Solomon) of Yahudah. The temple for all the slaughter offerings is located in Yerushalayim (Jerusalem) in Yahudah (Judea).

When Shlomoh dies and his son becomes king, the kingdom splits with a northern and southern kingdom. Yahudah and Binyamin make up the southern kingdom, plus Lĕwi, for the Lĕwiyim (Levites) are expelled from the northern kingdom when their king sets up his own worship system. Because of idolatry, the northern kingdom is taken into captivity by Ashur, leaving only the southern kingdom. Idolatry is also in the southern kingdom, and later they are taken into captivity by Bavel (Babylon), and Yerushalayim and the temple are destroyed.

After seventy years they are given permission to return to the land of Yahudah and rebuild Yerushalayim and the temple. After many more years Yahushua Messiah is born, and after his ministry he dies for our sins and is raised from the dead, taken to heaven, given all authority in heaven and on earth, pours out the set-apart spirit, and the gentile church age begins. That is where we are today.

Regarding the prophecies of Yisra'ĕl upon his sons, as it was with them, so it is with us. Yahuah knows you and your whole life before creation. Our job is to seek him and fulfill the plan he has for each of us.

Yisra'ĕl and Yosef Die, 50:1

YOSEF HAS HIS FATHER EMBALMED, a process that takes forty days, and the Mitsrayim mourn for him seventy days. When the mourning is over, by permission from Par'oh he takes his father to Kena'an to bury him. It is a very large group that goes, for all the servants of Par'oh, the elders of his household and all the elders of the land of Mitsrayim go with him with chariots and horsemen, as well as the household of Yosef and his brothers and his father's household. Only their little ones and their flocks and their herds are left behind in the land of Goshen (Gen 50:1-9).

When they come to the threshing floor of Atad, which is on the east side of the Yardĕn, they lament there with a very great and sorrowful lamentation; and Yosef observes seven days mourning for his father there. Then they come to the field which Avraham had bought and bury him in the cave. After burial, they all return to Mitsrayim (Gen 50:10-14).

Yosef's brothers are now worried. "What if Yosef bears a grudge against us and pays us back in full for all the wrong which we did to him?" they say. So they go to Yosef and beg forgiveness. They fall down before him and say, "Behold, we are your servants."

But Yosef says to them, "Do not be afraid, for am I in Elohim's place? As for you, you meant evil against me, but Elohim meant it for good (Ro 8:28) in order to bring about this present result, to preserve many people alive. So therefore, do not be afraid; I will provide for you and your little ones." So he comforts them and speaks kindly to them (Gen 50:15-21).

Yosef lives to be 110 years old, seeing many of his grandsons and great-grandsons. As he nears death he has his brothers swear, saying, "Elohim will surely take care of you, and you shall carry my bones up from here." Then he dies, is embalmed and placed in a coffin in Mitsrayim (Gen 50:22-26). When the Exodus takes place, they bring Yosef's body with them for burial in the Promised Land.

CONCLUSION

Among THE LIVES we looked at in Genesis, the ones most noted for their commitment and obedience to Yahuah are: Hevel (Abel), Seth, Ḥanoḥ (Enoch), Noaḥ, Avraham, Yitsḥaq (Isaac), Rivqah (Rebecca), Ya'aqov (Yisra'ĕl, Jacob), and Yosef. Each received his own set of circumstances, both good and bad, to bring them to repentance and commitment to live for Yahuah. Dear reader, how are you deciding to live your life?

Noaḥ was found righteous in his generation, and thus, by building an ark, he and the whole human race were saved. Righteousness and set-apartness are companions. When we are born again we set ourselves apart *from* the ways of the world and *to* the ways of Yahuah, that we may live a righteous life before him in loving obedience. Righteousness is doing what is right in his eyes.

And now, little children, live in him, so that when he shall appear we may have confidence and not be ashamed before him at his presence. If you know that he is righteous, you know also that everyone who does righteousness is born of him (1Jn 2:28-29). (See also 1Jn 3:4-10.)

Yahuah is righteous, he loves righteousness; the upright will see his face (Ps 11:7). (See also 1Th 3:12-13; Heb 12:14.)

"The time is near. ... Let the righteous still be righteous; and the one who is set-apart still be set-apart. Look, I am coming quickly, and my reward is with me, to render to every man according to what he has done" (Rev 22:10-12).

Amen and amen. Our goal is to become like Yahushua, who is the exact representation of Elohim in his character (Heb 1:3). May it be so in *your* life. I trust this study has been a help to you in understanding the book of Genesis, and in your walk with our Father Yahuah and his son Yahushua Messiah. Much, much more can be said about Genesis; the depths of scripture are endless.

EXPLANATION OF TERMS

OUR ENGLISH LANGUAGE is full of words that have their roots in paganism. And these words, therefore, are in the church. Why? Because we use language to convey or communicate ideas, and so we communicate in words people understand. But, in order to understand *our* subject, I use different words.

Those who wish to confirm the following usages are encouraged to do their own research. The internet has numerous articles on each of them. But don't settle for just one source. Look at many and dig deep. Often the surface definition is from tradition.

1. Elohim (eh-low-HEEM). Elohim is a Hebrew word that is most often translated as "God" or "gods." These English words have to do with supernatural beings, such as deity or godness. In fact, the English word God comes from the pre-Christian German sky-god Gott. But Elohim doesn't mean this. It means "Strong One" or "strong ones," depending on the context. Although it most often refers to our Father, the creator of all, it also refers to humans and angels. A judge in the Old Testament, for example, is sometimes referred to as *elohim* (Ex 22:8). In fact, Elohim himself refers to us humans as *elohim* (Ps 82:6). Other forms of Elohim are *Ĕl* and *Eloah*. Ĕl is often used as part of a person's name. For example, Nathaniel means "gift of Elohim," Ĕli means "my Elohim," Elijah (Ĕliyahu) means "my Elohim is Yahuah," and Elisha means "my Elohim is salvation."

2. Yahuah (yah-HOO-ah, or, yah-hoo-AH). Hebrew places the accent on the last or next to the last syllable. Yahuah is the personal name of Elohim. The Hebrew letters for this name in English are YHWH. You may be familiar with "Jehovah" and "Yahweh" as transliterations of these letters. Many believe, including this author, that "Yahuah" is the correct spelling.

The name Yahuah has a meaning, as do all Hebrew names. It means "He is." He is the self-existing one. In Exodus 3:15 Yahuah told Mosheh that this is his name forever and he is to be remembered by this name for all generations. And it was used for many centuries. The

Old Testament has it over 6000 times and his name was continually on the lips of the people. But when the Southern Kingdom of Yahudah (Judah) was taken into captivity by Bavel (Babylon), called the Babylonian Captivity, things changed. They stopped using his name. They even came to believe that it was blasphemy to *speak* his name. So they used a substitute title instead: they used "Adonai."

Adonai is a Hebrew word meaning Master or Lord. In fact, that is the practice of the Jews today when they read the Old Testament in Hebrew. Wherever *YHWH* appears, they say Adonai instead of Yahuah.

This practice has come into our English translations. So whenever you see LORD all in capital letters (and sometimes with only the first letter capitalized), it is not a translation (translating the meaning of a word into a different language), nor a transliteration (translating the letters of one language into another but not giving the meaning). Rather it is a substitution, a replacement. It is changing the word of Elohim into something different from what he inspired to be written. Proverbs 30:6 and Revelation 22:18-19 condemn this practice.

Yah is a shortened form of Yahuah, and is often used as part of a person's name. An example is Elijah. In Hebrew it is Ĕliyahu; it means "My Elohim is Yahuah," or "Elohim is Yahuah." Another example of "yah" is the much used word halleluyah. It means (you, plural) praise Yahuah.

3. Yahushua (yah-hoo-SHOO-ah, or yah-oo-SHOO-ah). Hebrew places the accent on the last or next to the last syllable, and the "h" is often silent. This is the Hebrew name of our Savior. It means Yahuah is salvation. The English name "Jesus" wasn't known until about 500 years ago when the letter "J" was invented. Before then it was Yesus. But even that is a migration from Hebrew into Greek (*Ieseus*), then into Latin (*Iesus*), and finally into English. By saying the name Yahushua we are saying the name of his Father, Yahuah, and that he is our savior. (See http://www.eliyah.com/yahushua.html)

4. Messiah. This is a Hebrew word meaning anointed one. Kings and priests were anointed when they came into office. The Greek equivalent is *christos*, or Christ, which also means anointed one, but the Greek word comes from paganism, the worship of *Chrestos* (tyndalearchive.com).

4. Master. This is a better translation than the word Lord. The source of the word Lord/lord is from paganism.

5. Assembly. This is a better translation than the word church. The Greek word *ekklesia* (ek-clay-SEE-ah), commonly translated as church, means assembly. The English word "church" comes from the name of the Greek goddess Kirke. She was a mythical goddess who turned people into pigs and other animals. Worshipers of Kirke met in circular buildings. Words beginning with cir-, such as circle, circus, circumcision, circumnavigate, etc., come from the name of this goddess.

6. Set-apart. This is a better translation than the word holy. Holy is a religious word from paganism. Both the Hebrew and Greek words translated as holy have as their root meaning separation. Something or a person can be set-apart (or consecrated), on the positive side to the true Elohim, or on the negative side to the false ones.

7. Favor. This is a better translation than the word grace. Grace is a religious word from paganism. Both the Hebrew and Greek words translated as grace mean favor, particularly undeserved favor.

8. Esteem. This is a better translation than the word glory. Again, glory is a religious word from paganism. The root meaning of the Hebrew and Greek words translated as glory is weight. Metaphorically, it means the weight of honor or esteem or splendor.

9. Slaughter-offering. This is a better translation than the word sacrifice. Again, sacrifice is a religions word from paganism. The root meaning of the Hebrew word *zevaḥ* means slaughter of an animal, whether for food or as an offering to a deity. Depending on the kind of offering, some of the flesh was eaten by the priests and the one doing the offering (Strong's # 2076, 2077, Word Study Dictionary of the Old Testament). (See also https://777denny.wordpress.com/2014/03/04/origins-and-definitions-of-words-holy-hallowed-sacred-sanctified-bible-grace-luck-lucifer-divine-divinity-deity-theos-god-christ-jesus-church-lord-gospel-amen-glory/.)

10. Bow down to. This is a better translation than the word worship, because it shows the action they are doing, such as what the Muslims do.

ADAM TO ABRAHAM CHART

Adam 4004 to 3074 = 930 years
Seth 3874 to 2962 = 912 years
Enosh 3769 to 2864 = 905 years
Kenan 3679 to 2769 = 910 years
Mahalalel 3609 to 2714 = 895 years
Jared 3544 to 2582 = 962 years
Enoch 3382 to 3017 = 365 years
Methuselah 3317 to 2348 = 969 years, year of the flood
Lamech 3130 to 2353 = 777 years
Noah 2948 to 1998 = 950 years
Shem 2445 to 1845 = 600 years
Flood 2348 lasted one year
Arphaxed 2345 to 1872 = 438 years
Shelah 2310 to 1877 = 433 years
Ebar 2280 to 1816 = 464 years
Peleg 2246 to 2007 = 239 years
Reu 2216 to 1977 = 239 years
Serug 2184 to 1954 = 230 years
Nahor 2154 to 2006 = 148 years
Terah 2125 to 1920 = 205 years
Abraham 2055 to 1880 = 175 years

According to this calculation:
Noaḥ was born 126 years after Adam died.
Noaḥ lived to see his descendants fall back into idolatry and the
   judgment of the languages being confused.
Avraham was 57 years old when Noah died.
Shĕm lived through the flood and outlived Avraham by 35 years.
Note the decline in how long they lived after the flood.

GLOSSARY OF NAMES

HEBREW NAMES in this commentary are transliterated more closely to the Hebrew spelling than in standard translations. Often there is no resemblance to the English spelling.

Some meanings of names are unknown, some uncertain, and some with different possible meanings. Regarding some of them, scholars differ.

Adah (aw-DAWH) = Adah (ornament, beauty)
Adam (ah-DAWM) = Adam (man, mankind, name of first *adam*)
Aharon (ah-har-OAN) = Aaron (a teacher, lofty, mountain of strength)
Ai (ah-EE) = Ai (ruins)
Ammoni (ahm-mow-NEE) = Ammonites (descendants of Bennami)
Amorah (ah-moh-RAW) = Gomorrah (a ruined heap)
Avi-meleḥ (aw-vee-MEH-lehkh) = Abimelech (my father is king)
Avram (awv-RAHM) = Abram (exalted father)
Avraham (awv-raw-HAWM) = Abraham (father of a multitude)
Bavel (bah-VEL) = Babel, Babylon (the gate of god)
Be'ĕr-Sheva (beh-AYR SHEH-vah) = Beersheba (well of an oath)
Ben-ammi (ben-ahm-MEE) = Benammi (son of my people)
Bethu'ĕl (beth-oo-AYL) = Bethuel (dwelling of Elohim)
Bil'am (bil-AWM) = Balaam (lord of the people, destroyer of the people)
Binyamin (bin-yah-MEEN) = Benjamin (son of the right hand)
Dammeseq (dawm-MEH-sek) = Damascus (meaning unknown)
Ĕlam (ay-LAWM) = Elam (hidden, distant)
Ĕli (AY-lee or ay-LEE) = Eli (high, exalted, or my Elohim)
Eli'ezer (el-ee-EHZ-er) = Eliezer (my Elohim is help)
Emori (ehm-or-EE) = Amorites (westerners, i.e. west of the Euphrates)
Enosh (eh-NOESH) = Enosh (mortal)
Ĕsaw (ay-SAW) = Esau (rough, hairy)
Ĕval (ay-VALL) = Ebal (bald) (Mount Ebal)
Gerar (ger-AR) = Gerar (a rolling country; a lodging place)
Gerizim (geh-rih-ZEEM) = Gerizim (rocky) (Mount Gerizim)
Gilgal (gil-GAWL) = Gilgal (rolling)

Hagar (ha-GAR) = Hagar (flight)

Hevel (HEH-vel) = Abel (breath)

Ḥam (khawm) = Ham (hot)

Ḥannah (khaw-NAW) = Hannah (favored)

Ḥanoḥ (khaw-NOEKH) = Enoch (initiated, consecrated)

Haran (haw-RAWN) = Haran (mountaineer)

Ḥaran (khaw-RAWN) = the city of Haran

Ḥawwah (khaw-WAH) = Eve (life-giver)

Ḥermon (kher-MOAN) = Hermon (mountain nose, peak) (Mount Hermon)

Ḥevron (khehv-ROAN) = Hebron (a community, alliance, seat of association)

Ḥorĕv (khoe-RAYV) = Horeb (desolate) (Mt Horeb, mountain of Elohim)

Ḥitti (khit-TEE) = Hittite (dread, a descendent of Ḥam)

Ḥovah (khoe-VAH) = Hobah (hiding place)

Ivri (ih-VREE) = Hebrew (the land beyond [the Euphrates])

Kena'an (keh-NAH-ahn) = Canaan (humiliated)

Kasdim (kaws-DEEM) = Chaldeans

Kush (koosh) = Cush (black, the region of Ethiopia)

Lavan (law-VAWN) = Laban (white)

Lemeḥ (LEH-mehkh) = Lamech (powerful, wild man)

Lĕwi, Lewiyim (lay-WEE, lay-wee-YEEM) = Levi, Levites (joined)

Lot (LOET) = Lot (pebble, small stone used for casting lots)

Malki-tsedeq (mall-kee-TSEH-dehk) = Melchizedek (king of righteousness.)

Milkah (mill-KAW) = Milcah (queen)

Mamrĕ (mawm-RAY) = Mamre (manliness, vigor)

Medan (meh-DAWN) = Midian (strife)

Mitsrayim (mits-RAW-yeem) – Egypt

Mitsri, Mitsrim (mits-REE, mits-REEM) = Egyptian, Egyptians

Mo'av (mow-AHV) = Moab (from father)

Mo'avi (mow-ah-VEE)= Moabites (descendents of Mo'av)

Moleḥ (MOW-lekh) = Molech (king, chief god of the Ammoni)

Moreh (mow-REH) = Moreh (archer, teacher, fruitful)

Moriyah (mow-ree-YAH) = Moriah (seen of Yahuah)

Mosheh (mow-SHEH) = Moses (drawn out)

Na'amah (naw-ah-MAW) = Naamah (beautiful)

Naftali (nawf-tah-LEE) = Naphtali (my wrestling)

Naḥor (nah-KHOR) = Nahor (snorting)

Negev (NEH-gev) = Negev (south, dry)

Nimrod (nim-ROAD) = Nimrod (rebellion)

Noaḥ (noe-AWKH) = Noah (consolation, or peace)

Ovadyahu (oh-vawd-YAH-hoo) = Obadiah (servant of Yahuah)

Pa'ran (paw-RAWN) = Paran, (ornamental, a wilderness area)

Par'oh (par-OH) = Pharoah (the sun-god, or the great house)

Peleg (PEH-leg) = Peleg (division, earthquake)

Plishtim (plish-TEEM) = Philistines (meaning unknown)

Qayin (KAH-yin) = Cain (a possession, a spear)

Qeturah (keh-too-RAH) = Keturah (incense)

Rivqah (riv-KAW) = Rebeka, Rebecca (a noose, one who ensnares)

Raḥel (raw-KHAYL) = Rachel (a ewe, female sheep)

Shalĕm (shaw-LAIM) = Salem (peace)

Shĕm (shaym) = Shem (name)

Sedom (seh-DOEM) = Sodom (burning)

Shavĕh (shaw-VAY) = Shaveh (plain)

Shekem (sheh-KEM)= Shechem (shoulder, ridge)

Shlomoh (shloeh-MOEH) = Solomon (peaceful)

Shemu'ĕl (sheh-moo-AYL) = Samuel (heard of Elohim)

Shur (shoor) = Shur (enclosure)

Sinai (see-NAHee) = Sinai (Mount Sinai, Horeb, meaning unknown)

Teraḥ (teh-RAKH) = Terah (the wanderer)

Torah (toe-RAW) = Torah (instructions, teachings, 1st 5 books of the OT)

Tsillah (tsil-LAW) = Zilla (shadow)

Tso'ar (tsoe-AR) = Zoar (little)

Tuval-Qayin (tu-VALL KAH-yin) = Tubal-Cain (smith, a possession)

Ya'aqov (yah-ah-KOAV) = Jacob (holding the heel, supplanter)

Yahuah-yir'eh (Yah-hoo-AH yir-EH) (Jehovah Jireh, Yahuah will see [to it])

Yardĕn (yar-DAYN) = Jordan (descending)

Yaval (yah-VAHL) = Jabal (stream)

Yefeth (YEH-fehth) = Japheth (expansion)

Yerushalayim (yeh-rue-shaw-LAW-yeem) = Jerusalem (foundation of peace)

Yishma'ĕl (yish-mah-AYL) = Ishmael (Elohim hears)

Yitsḥaq (yits-KHAWK) = Isaac (laughter)

Yo'av (yoe-AWV) = Joab (Yahuah is father)

Yo'el (yoe-EL) = Joel (Yahuah is Elohim)

Yosef (yoe-SEHF) = Joseph (increaser)

Yuval (yoo-VALL) = Jubal (music)

Books by Dr Gilbert Olson

BRIDE OF MESSIAH SERIES

GOD IN MAN
God's Plan of Incarnation

YAHUSHUA MESSIAH, THE LAST ADAM
His Humanity According to Scripture

THE BRIDE AND THE RAPTURE
From Born Again to a Mature Bride

GENESIS
In the Beginning
A Typological Commentary

www.ingramcontent.com/pod-product-compliance
Lightning Source LLC
LaVergne TN
LVHW051511080426
835509LV00017B/2030